Software Reliability and Testing

Software Reliability and Testing

Hoang Pham

Published by John Wiley & Sons, Inc., Hoboken, New Jersey
Published simultaneously in Canada

For general information on our other products and services, or technical support, please contact our Customer Care Department within the United States at 800-762-2974, outside the United States at 317-572-3993 or fax 317-572-4002.

Wiley also publishes its books in a variety of electronic formats. Some content that appears in print may not be available in electronic books.

For more information about Wiley products, visit our web site at www.wiley.com.

Library of Congress Cataloging-in-Publication Data:

10 9 8 7 6 5 4 3 2 1

CONTENTS

PREFACE

Software reliability is the probability that a given software will be functioning without failure in a given environment during a specified period of time. Although extensive research has been done in the area of hardware reliability, the growing importance of software dictates that the focus shift to software reliability. As computers are used increasingly to monitor and control critical systems, software reliability becomes ever more essential; failures in air traffic control systems, nuclear reactors, or hospital patient monitoring systems can bring catastrophic consequences.

The cost of developing software and the costs resulting from software failures are the major expenses in current computer systems. This book includes 14 recent papers from the rapidly growing literature on this topic. The book's purpose is to review the latest software reliability models, testing techniques, and applications, providing an overview of recent directions in research and stimulating further research in the field.

Hoang Pham
April 1995

INTRODUCTION

Computers are being used increasingly to monitor and control critical systems, for example, in air traffic control, nuclear reactors, aircraft, real-time military applications, industrial process control, automotive mechanical and safety control, and hospital patient monitoring systems. As the functionality of computer operations becomes more essential and complicated in our modern society and critical software applications increase in complexity, the reliability of computer software not only becomes more important, but errors in software design become more subtle. A computer system comprises two major components—hardware and software. Although extensive research has been done in the area of hardware reliability, the growing importance of software dictates that the focus shift to software reliability. In recent years, the costs of developing software and the penalty costs of software failures have become the major expenses in a system. Neglecting the importance of software reliability would be a grave mistake.

Software errors have caused spectacular failures. For example, on September 17, 1991, a power outage at the AT&T switching facility in New York City interrupted service to 10 million telephone customers for several hours. The problem was the deletion of three bits of code in a software upgrade and failure to test the software before its installation in the public network. From March through June of 1986, radiation therapy machines in Marietta, Georgia; Boston, Massachusetts; and Tyler, Texas, overdosed cancer patients, apparently because the computer program controlling the highly automated devices was flawed. During the 1991 Gulf War, a software problem may have prevented the Patriot missile system from tracking the Iraqi Scud missile that killed 28 US soldiers.

In theory, software can be made to be error-free, and unlike hardware components, software does not wear out. All design faults are present from the time the software is installed into the computer. In principle, these faults could be removed completely. Yet the aim of perfect software remains elusive [Littlewood and Strigini 1992]. Computer programs can make the wrong decision because the particular inputs that triggered the problem had not been tested during the phase when faults could be corrected. Such inputs may even have been misunderstood or unanticipated by the designer, who either correctly programmed the wrong interpretation or failed to take the problem into account altogether. These situations and other such events have made it apparent that we must determine the reliability of our systems prior to putting them into operation. Yet development of effective software is improving slowly.

Classification of software reliability models

Research activities in software reliability engineering have been conducted over the past 20 years, and more than 50 statistical models have been proposed for the estimation of software reliability. Nevertheless, not many practitioners, developers, or software users use these models to evaluate the reliability of computer software because they do not know how to select and apply them. A survey conducted by the American Society for Quality Control reported that only 4 percent of the survey participants responded positively when asked if they used a software reliability model. Indeed, there is a great need to develop a technique acceptable for determining and predicting the reliability level of software systems.

General description of software and software reliability

Software is a collection of instructions or statements in a computer language. It is also called a computer program, or simply a program. Upon execution of a program, an input state is translated into an output state. Hence, a program can be regarded as a function f mapping the input space to the output space (f: input → output), where the input space is the set of all input states, and the output space is the set of all output states. An input state can be defined as a combination of input variables or a typical transaction to the program. A software program is designed to perform specified functions. When the actual output deviates from the expected output, a failure occurs. It is worth noting that the definition of failure differs from application to application and should be clearly defined in specifications. For instance, a response time of 30 seconds could be a serious failure for an air traffic control system, but acceptable for an airline reservation system. A fault is incorrect logic, an incorrect instruction, or an inadequate instruction that, by execution, will cause a failure. In other words, faults are the sources of failures, and failures are the realizations of faults. When a failure occurs, there must be a corresponding fault in the program, but the existence of faults may not cause the program to fail, and a program will never fail as long as the faulty statements are not executed.

The existing software reliability models can be classified into different groups:

- error seeding
- failure rate
- curve fitting
- reliability growth
- program structure
- input domain
- execution path
- nonhomogeneous Poisson process
- Markov
- Bayesian and unified

Error seeding

The error seeding group of models estimates the number of errors in a program by using the capture-recapture sampling technique. Errors are divided into indigenous errors and induced errors (seeded errors). The unknown number of indigenous errors is estimated from the number of induced errors and the ratio of the two types of errors obtained from the debugging data.

Failure rate

The failure rate group of models is used to study the functional forms of the per-fault failure rate and program failure rate at the failure intervals. Since mean time between failure is the reciprocal of failure rate in the exponential distribution random variable, models based on time between failure also belong to this category.

Models included in this group are the following:

- Jelinski and Moranda de-eutrophication [Jelinski and Moranda 1972]
- Schick and Wolverton [Schick and Wolverton 1978]
- Jelinski-Moranda geometric de-eutrophication [Moranda 1979]
- Moranda geometric Poisson [Littlewood 1979]

2

- modified Schick and Wolverton [Sukert 1977]
- Goel and Okumoto imperfect debugging [Goel and Okumoto 1978]

Curve fitting

The curve fitting group of models uses regression analysis to study the relationship between software complexity and the number of errors in a program, the number of changes, failure rate, or time between failures. Both parametric and nonparametric methods have been attempted in this field.

This group consists of four models:

- estimation of errors
- estimation of change
- estimation of time between failures
- estimation of failure rate

Reliability growth

The reliability growth group of models measures and predicts the improvement of reliability through the debugging process. A growth function is used to represent the progress. The independent variables of the growth function can be time, number of test cases, or testing stages, and the dependent variables can be reliability, failure rate, or cumulative number of errors detected.

This group comprises the following models:

- Duane growth [Dhillon 1983]
- Weibull growth [Wall and Ferguson 1977]
- Wagoner's Weibull [Wagoner 1973]
- logistic growth curve [Yamada and Osaki 1985]
- Gompertz growth curve [Nathan 1979]

Program structure

The program structure group of models views a program as a reliability network. A node represents a module or a subroutine, and the directed arc represents the program execution sequence among modules. By estimating the reliability of each node, the reliability of transition between nodes, and the transition probability of the network, and by assuming independence of failure at each node, we can solve the reliability of the program as a reliability network problem.

There are two models in this group:

- Littlewood Markov structure [Littlewood 1979]
- Cheung's user-oriented Markov [Cheung 1980]

Input domain

The input-domain group of models uses *run* (the execution of an input state) as the index of function reliability. Reliability is defined as the number of successful runs over the total number of runs. Emphasis is placed on the probability distribution of input states or the operational profile.

Two models are included in this group:

- Nelson [Nelson 1978]
- input-domain-based stochastic [Bastani and Ramamoorthy 1986, Weiss and Weyuker 1988]

Execution path

The execution path group of models estimates software reliability based on the probability of executing a logic path of the program and the probability of an incorrect path. This model is similar to the input-domain model because each input state corresponds to an execution path.

The group consists of one model:

- Shooman decomposition [Shooman 1984]

Nonhomogeneous Poisson process

The nonhomogeneous Poisson process (NHPP) group of models provides an analytical framework for describing the software failure phenomenon during testing. The main issue in the NHPP model is to estimate the mean value function of the cumulative number of failures experienced up to a certain time point.

Models included in this group are the following:

- Musa exponential [Musa 1975]
- Goel and Okumoto NHPP [Goel and Okumoto 1979]
- S-shaped growth [Ohba 1984, Yamada et al. 1984]
- hyperexponential growth [Huang 1984, Ohba 1984]
- modified NHPP with imperfect debugging [Pham 1993]

Markov

The Markov group of models is a general way of representing the software failure process. The number of remaining faults is modeled as a stochastic counting process. When a continuous-time discrete-state Markov chain is adapted, the state of the process is the number of remaining faults, and time between failures is the sojourning time from one state to another. If we assume that the failure rate of the program is proportional to the number of remaining faults, linear death process and linear birth-and-death process are two models readily available. The former assumes that the remaining errors are monotonically nonincreasing, whereas the latter allows faults to be introduced during debugging.

When a nonstationary Markov model is considered, the model becomes very rich and unifies many of the proposed models. The nonstationary failure rate property can also simulate the assumption of nonidentical failure rates of each fault.

Three models make up this group:

- linear death with perfect debugging [Shooman 1972]
- linear death with imperfect debugging [Ohba and Chou 1989]
- nonstationary linear death with perfect debugging [Kock and Spreij 1983]

Bayesian and unified

The Bayesian and unified groups of models assume a prior distribution of the failure rate. These models are used when the software reliability engineer has a good feeling about the failure process and the failure data are rare.

These groups consist of the following:

- continuous-time discrete-state Markov chain
- exponential order statistics [Littlewood 1975, 1976; Ohba and Yamada 1984]
- shock model [Kareer et al. 1990, Musa and Okumoto 1984]

Definitions of terms

This section contains definitions of terms and brief discussions of concepts:

- *Availability.* The probability that the system will be available for use.
- *Correctness.* Whether or not the software satisfies its specification.
- *Error incidence.* The number of errors in the software, normalized to some measure of size.
- *Error.* An incorrect response from a software system. The occurrence of an error indicates that a fault is present in the software—that the system has been given an incorrect input. An error will lead to the failure of a system unless tolerance of the underlying fault has been provided.
- *Fault tolerance.* The use of protective redundancy to permit continued correct operation of a software system after the occurrence of specified faults.
- *Safety.* The preservation of human life and property under specified operating conditions.
- *Security.* The resistance of the software to unauthorized use, theft of data, and modification of programs.
- *Software redundancy.* Extra software can be used to provide fault detection, fault diagnosis, or fault tolerance of software faults.
- *Trustworthiness.* The probability that there are no errors in the software that will cause the system to fail catastrophically.

Trustworthiness [US Congress 1988] and correctness are important indicators of performability for critical software applications. Security is important when valuable data or services may be damaged or used in unauthorized ways. Safety is important in applications involving risk to human life. With life-critical systems, every precaution is needed.

Software reliability and testing

Software reliability is the probability that a given software system will function without failure in a given environmental condition during a specified period of time. A software failure here means the inability to perform an intended task specified by a requirement.

In software reliability, one emphasis is the analysis of failure mechanisms. Most software reliability models are analytical models derived from assumptions of how failures occur. To develop a useful software reliability model and to make sound judgments when using the models, we need an in-depth understanding of how software is produced, how errors are introduced, how software is tested, how errors occur, the types of errors, the environmental factors that justify the reasonableness of assumptions, the usefulness of a model, and the applicability of a model in a given user environment.

Software testing is the process of executing a program with the intent of finding an error [Myers 1979]. A good test case is one that has a high probability of finding undiscovered error(s).

In software testing, it is not possible to continue testing the software until all faults are detected and removed, because, for most computer programs, testing of all possible inputs would require millions of years! Therefore, failure probabilities must be inferred from testing a sample of all the possible inputs, called the input space. As we know, different inputs will have different chances of being selected, and we can never be sure which inputs will be selected in the operational phase of real-world applications. Two interesting questions arise here:

1. Is it possible to determine the sizes and locations of the fault regions in the input space?
2. How do we determine the reliability that a program will execute correctly for a particular length of time?

To select a good software model to make an accurate reliability prediction, we should, as far as possible, incorporate the testing strategy into the software reliability model. And we must recognize that the best models may vary from time to time and differ from software to software.

The evaluation of software reliability cannot be done without software failure data. Therefore, the establishment of a software failure database will be useful to both practitioners and researchers for predicting and estimating software reliability, and for determining the total testing time needed to reach a prescribed reliability or a prescribed acceptable risk. Collected data are usefully grouped into four categories: component data, management data, dynamic failure data, and fault removal data. Each category is characterized by a unique set of information:

- *component data.* The number of executable source lines of code, the total number of comments and the total number of instructions, and the source language used for each system component.
- *management data.* The starting and ending date for each life-cycle phase (design, code, test, and operation), the definitions and requirements of each life-cycle phase, and the models used for estimating software reliability.
- *dynamic failure data.* The number of CPU hours since the last failure, the number of test cases executed since the last failure, the severity of the failure, the method of failure detection, and the unit complexity and size where the fault was detected.
- *fault removal data.* The date and time of fixing an error, the CPU hours required to fix an error, and the labor hours required to fix an error for each failure corrected.

The data collection will also help address these questions of interest:

- Are any defects discovered as a result of simply testing artifacts of prior modifications or are they previously undetected defects?
- What taxonomic categories are required for defense, aerospace, military, and commercial systems, and what defect percentages reside in each category?

Selected papers

I have selected 14 recent papers from the rapidly growing literature on this topic with the purpose to overview the latest software reliability models, testing techniques, and applications to indicate recent directions of research and to stimulate further research in the field.

Software reliability

Recent research has shown that in some applications the existing software reliability growth models provide reasonable estimates of the test effort needed. The characteristics for using the existing models vary, but generally include independence in the interarrival times of failures, uniform system load during test and operation, and uniform magnitude of impact of failures.

The first paper, by Zeitler, describes necessary realistic assumptions for applications of software reliability growth modeling to software systems in general and to real-time software systems and real-time avionic software, in particular. The author has shown that software reliability must be modeled as an autoregressive integrated moving average time series. The next paper, by Khoshgoftaar and Munson, investigates aspects of the relationship between program complexity measures and program errors. The authors develop predictive models that incorporate such aspects based on factor analysis of empirical data. The paper by Butler and Finelli explores the inherent difficulty of accurately modeling software reliability and examines the possibility of quantifying experimentally the reliability of real-time software. The authors demonstrate that the conventional techniques for evaluating reliability and reliability growth models would require exorbitant amounts of testing when applied to life-critical software.

The remaining papers in the section present new models useful in estimating the reliability of software systems and also deal with the cost-reliability-optimal software release policies in software systems. The paper by Levendel presents a birth-death model considering defect detection, defect removal, and the factor of introducing new faults resulting from the imperfect removal of defects. Shooman presents a new micro software reliability model by considering the module testing phase, integration testing phase, and field operation in order to improve the prediction.

Large software packages that comprise several programs, each of which performs a different function as required by the user, are common in practice. Ashrafi and Berman present two optimization models for selecting available programs on the market, based on reliability and cost. These models apply to large software packages that consist of several programs and can be used as decision tools for choosing the most reliable programs on the market within budget.

Most software reliability models developed are based on the assumption that errors are completely removed from the software when they are detected. However, in practice, such an assumption is unrealistic, and debugging actions in testing environments are not always performed perfectly. Yamada, Tokuno, and Osaki develop a software reliability growth model assuming that not all software faults detected are corrected and removed. The model is formulated based on a semi-Markov process. They further discuss optimal software release problems that evaluate both software reliability and cost criteria, simultaneously.

Software testing

The first paper in this group, by Hamlet, presents an excellent investigation of the relationship between reliability and testing. It explains the applicability of reliability models, discusses how testing can and cannot improve reliability, and discusses how trustworthy the results are from such an analysis. The next paper, by McDermid, discusses the nature of safety arguments and the role of software and system reliability, and briefly outlines an approach to support the development of safety arguments. The author also demonstrates what role in a general set of safety arguments might be played by software reliability arguments and shows how such arguments might be managed in practice.

It is a challenge to conduct testing that produces a level of quality satisfactory to the customer within acceptable cost. Ehrlich, Stampfel, and Wu describe the importance of an operational profile in testing a large-scale industrial software system for the purpose of estimating the software quality from the customer's perspective.

They indicate that use of an operational profile must be taken into account when predicting field reliability from reliability measured during testing.

The remaining papers present new models useful in testing software systems. Downs and Garrone present new models of software testing by extending the two previous testing models based on the path-testing strategy developed by Downs. The two models were developed under these assumptions:

1. A software system can be partitioned into two sections, one of which is heavily tested, the other lightly tested.
2. Each fault in a given section of code affects the same number of paths.

These assumptions are relaxed in the new models. The authors' studies show that one of the new models outperforms the existing models under all three measures.

To obtain better estimates, we need better measures of how a program has been tested and how it will be used in operation. Lennselius and Rydström study problems of estimating the software fault content and reliability, based on several industrial projects. They present a model determining the initial number of software faults, which takes into account both the development process and the developed software product. They also present a method to predict when these faults occur during the testing phase.

The failure to initially estimate cost and schedule for the software project can lead to project inefficiencies. Abdel-Hamid discusses such issues. He then develops a hybrid estimation model to support adaptive, corrective, and perfective estimation activities. This model can also be used to demonstrate the feasibility and utility of a continuous estimation process.

For a transaction-oriented software system, tests and verifications are commonly applied at regular intervals concerning the system data and the transactions it has executed in order to eliminate errors during normal system operation. Gelenbe and Hernández present a new technique called *failure tests* for enhancing the reliability and availability of a transaction-oriented software system. They also propose an algorithm to determine the best possible choice of intervals between dumps and failure test intervals so as to maximize system availability.

Future trends

Currently, the computer software areas of most concern to such US government agencies as the Department of Defense, Department of Energy, Nuclear Regulatory Commission, and Federal Aviation Administration are the following:

1. Verification and validation of software in the process control of nuclear power plants.
2. Development of highly reliable software.

There exists a need to identify or develop techniques, tools, and methods to minimize the effects of ambiguous errors in software applications for control of defense systems, hospital patient monitoring, and nuclear power plants. The reliability of software used in both operator and safety systems must obviously be high.

Today, most existing models for predicting software reliability are based purely upon observation of failures of the product. These models also require considerable numbers of failure data to obtain an accurate reliability prediction. Other information concerning the development of the software product, the method of failure detection, and so on, are ignored.

Many researchers are pursuing the development of statistical models to assess the reliability of practical software systems. Indeed, these models would be valuable to software developers, users, and practitioners if they are capable of using information about the software development process and can give greater confidence in estimates based on small numbers of failure data.

A reading list of software reliability and testing

There are many survey papers on software reliability and testing that can be read at an introductory stage. Interested readers are referred to the review papers by Ramamoorthy and Bastani (1982), Shooman (1984), Musa and Okumoto (1984), Goel (1985), and Yamada and Osaki (1985).

The book *Software Reliability: Measurement, Prediction, Application*, by J. Musa, A. Iannino, and K. Okumoto (McGraw-Hill, 1987), and the book *Software Testing Techniques*, by B. Beizer (2nd edition, Van Nostrand Reinhold, New York, 1990), are good textbooks for students and practitioners. *The State of the Art Report: Software Reliability*, edited by T. Bendell and P. Mellor (1986), *Software Reliability: Achievement and Assessment*, edited by B. Littlewood (1987), and *Software Reliability Handbook*, edited by P. Rook (1990), are good reference books containing many interesting results. In addition, the books *Software Reliability Models: Theoretical Developments, Evaluation, and Application*, edited by Y. Malaiya and P. Srimani (IEEE Computer Society Press, 1991), and *Software Reliability and Safety*, edited by B. Littlewood and D. Miller (Elsevier Applied Science, 1991), recently reprinted many classic and quality papers on the subject.

Many research and tutorial papers on software reliability and testing have been published in *IEEE Transactions on Software Engineering*, *IEEE Transactions on Reliability*, and *IEEE Softwxare*. Several special issues on software reliability are of practical interest:

> Special issue of *J. Systems and Software* on "Software Reliability," Vol. 1, No. 1, 1980.
>
> Special issue of *IEEE Trans. Software Eng.* on "Software Reliability," Part I, Vol. SE-11, No. 12, Dec. 1985; Part II, Vol. SE-12, No. 1, Jan. 1986.
>
> Special issue of *Information and Software Technology* on "Software Quality Assurance," Vol. 32, No. 1, 1990.
>
> Special issue of *Reliability Eng. and System Safety J.* on "Software Reliability and Safety," Vol. 32, Nos. 1 & 2, 1991.
>
> Special issue of *IEEE Trans. Computers* on "Fault-Tolerant Computing," Vol. 41, No. 5, May 1992.
>
> Special issue of *IEEE Software* on "Reliability Measurement," Vol. 9, No. 4, July 1992.
>
> Special issue of *IEEE Trans. Reliability* on "Fault-Tolerant Software," Vol. 42, No. 2, Feb. 1993.
>
> Special issue of *IEEE Trans. Software Eng.* on "Software Reliability," Vol. 19, No. 11, Nov. 1993.

Several other journals occasionally publish papers on the subject:

> *Journal of Systems and Software*
>
> *International Journal of Reliability, Quality and Safety Engineering*
>
> *Reliability Engineering and System Safety Journal*
>
> *Microelectronics and Reliability—An International Journal*

There are a great number of proceedings of international conferences where many interesting papers on software reliability and testing can be found, for example:

> *IEEE Annual Reliability and Maintainability Symposium*;
>
> *ISSAT International Conference on Reliability and Quality in Design*;
>
> *IEEE International Computer Software and Applications Conference*;

IEEE International Conference on Fault-Tolerant Computing;
IEEE International Conference on Software Engineering;
IEEE International Symposium on Software Reliability Engineering;
IASTED International Conference on Reliability, Quality, and Risk Assessment.

A subcommittee of the IEEE Computer Society's Technical Committee on Software Engineering is devoted to software reliability engineering. This subcommittee publishes a newsletter about practical applications of software reliability. Contact Dr. Lyu at (201) 829-3999 to get on the mailing list. The US Air Force's Rome Laboratory publishes a technical report "Reliability Techniques for Combined Hardware and Software," Tech. Report RL-TR-92-15. Contact Frank Born, (315) 330-4726.

This list is by no means exhaustive, but I believe it will help readers get started learning about software reliability and testing.

This book *Software Reliability and Testing* targets design engineers, software engineers, researchers, computer scientists, technical managers, and professors and students wishing to conduct research or update themselves in the field of software reliability engineering and software testing.

References

Bastani, F.B., and C.V. Ramamoorthy, "Input-Domain-Based Models for Estimating the Correctness of Process Control Programs," in *Reliability Theory*, A. Serra and R.E. Barlow, eds., North-Holland, Amsterdam, The Netherlands, 1986, pp. 321–378.

Cheung, R.C., "A User-Oriented Software Reliability Model," *IEEE Trans. Software Eng.*, Vol. SE-6, No. 2, March 1980, pp. 118–125.

Dhillon, B.S., *Reliability Engineering in Systems Design and Operation*, Van Nostrand Reinhold Co., New York, N.Y., 1983.

Goel, A.L., and K. Okumoto, "An Analysis of Recurrent Software Errors in a Real-Time Control System," *Proc. ACM Conf.*, 1978.

Goel, A.L., and K. Okumoto, "Time-Dependent Error-Detection Rate Model for Software and Other Performance Measures," *IEEE Trans. Reliability*, Vol. R-28, No. 3, Aug. 1979, pp. 206–211.

Goel, A.L., "Software Reliability Models: Assumptions, Limitations, and Applicability," *IEEE Trans. Software Eng.*, Vol. SE-11, No. 12, Dec. 1985, pp. 1411–1423.

Huang, X.Z., "The Hypergeometric Distribution Model for Predicting the Reliability of Software," *Microelectronics and Reliability*, Vol. 24, No. 1, 1984.

Jelinski, Z., and P.B. Moranda, "Software Reliability Research," in *Statistical Computer Performance Evaluation*, W. Freiberger, ed., Academic Press, New York, N.Y., 1972, pp. 465–484.

Kareer, N., P.K. Kapur, and P.S. Grover, "An S-Shaped Software Reliability Growth Model with Two Types of Errors," *Microelectronics and Reliability*, Vol. 30, No. 6, 1990.

Kock, H.S., and P.J.C. Spreij, "Software Reliability as an Application of Martingale and Filtering Theory," *IEEE Trans. Reliability*, Vol. R-32, No. 4, Oct. 1983, pp. 342–345.

Littlewood, B., "Software Reliability Model for Modular Program Structure," *IEEE Trans. Reliability*, Vol. R-28, No. 3, Aug. 1979, pp. 241–246.

Littlewood, B., "A Semi-Markov Model for Software Reliability with Failure Cost," *Proc. Symp. Computer Software Eng.*, 1976, pp. 55–63.

Littlewood, B., "A Reliable Model for Systems with Markov Structure," *Applied Statistics*, Vol. 24, No. 2, 1975, 172–177.

Moranda, P.B., "An Error Detection Model for Application During Software Development," *IEEE Trans. Reliability*, Vol. R-28, No. 5, 1979, pp. 325–329.

Musa, J.D., and K. Okumoto, "A Logarithmic Poisson Execution Time Model for Software Reliability Measurement," *Proc. 7th Int'l Conf. Software Eng.*, IEEE CS Press, Los Alamitos, Calif., 1984, pp. 230–238.

Musa, J.D., "A Theory of Software Reliability and Its Applications," *IEEE Trans. Software Eng.*, Vol. SE-1, No. 3, Sept. 1975, pp. 312–327.

Myers, G., *The Art of Software Testing*, Wiley, New York, N.Y., 1979.

Nathan, I., "A Deterministic Model to Predict Error-Free Status of Complex Software Development," *Workshop on Quantitative Software Models*, 1979, pp. 28–34.

Nelson, E., "Estimating Software Reliability from Test Data," *Microelectronics and Reliability*, Vol. 17, 1978.

Ohba, M., "Software Reliability Analysis Models," *IBM J. Research and Development*, Vol. 28, No. 4, July 1984, pp. 428–443.

Ohba, M., and S. Yamada, "S-Shaped Software Reliability Growth Models," *Proc. 4th Int'l Conf. Reliability and Maintainability*, Perros Guirec, France, 1984, pp. 430–436.

Ohba, M., and X.M. Chou, "Does Imperfect Debugging Affect Software Reliability Growth?" *Proc. 11th Int'l Conf. Software Eng.*, IEEE CS Press, Los Alamitos, Calif., 1989, pp. 237–244.

Pham, H., "Software Reliability Assessment: Imperfect Debugging and Multiple Failure Types in Software Development," EGG-RAAM-10737, Idaho National Eng. Laboratory, Idaho Falls, Idaho, 1993.

Ramamoorthy, C.V., and F.B. Bastani, "Software Reliability Status and Perspective," *IEEE Trans. Software Eng.*, Vol. SE-8, No. 4, July 1982, pp. 354–371.

Schick, G.J., and R.W. Wolverton, "An Analysis of Competing Software Reliability Models," *IEEE Trans. Software Eng.*, Vol. SE-4, No. 2, Mar. 1978, pp. 104–120.

Shooman, M.L., "Probabilistic Models for Software Reliability Prediction," in *Statistical Computer Performance Evaluation*, W. Freiberger, ed., Academic Press, New York, N.Y., 1972.

Shooman, M.L., "Structure Models for Software Reliability Prediction," *Proc. Int'l Conf. Software Eng.*, IEEE CS Press, Los Alamitos, Calif., 1984, pp. 135–141.

Sukert, A.N., "An Investigation of Software Reliability Models," *Proc. Ann. Reliability and Maintainability Symp.*, 1977, pp. 212–216.

US Congress, Office of Technology Assessment, "SDI: Technology, Survivability, and Software," OTA-ISC-353, US Govt. Printing Office, Washington, D.C., 1988.

Wagoner, W.L., "The Final Report on a Software Reliability Measurement Study," TOR-0074(41221)-1, Aerospace Corp., El Segundo, Calif., 1973.

Wall, J.K., and P.A. Ferguson, "Pragmatic Software Reliability Prediction," *Proc. Ann. Reliability and Maintainability Symp.*, 1977, pp. 112–117.

Weiss, S.N., and E.J. Weyuker, "An Extended Domain-Based Model of Software Reliability, *IEEE Trans. Software Eng.*, Vol. SE-14, No. 10, Oct. 1988, pp. 1512–1524.

Yamada, S., M. Ohba, and S. Osaki, "S-Shaped Software Reliability Growth Models and Their Applications," *IEEE Trans. Reliability*, Vol. R-33, No. 4, Oct. 1984, pp. 289–292.

Yamada, S., and S. Osaki, "Software Reliability Growth Modeling: Models and Applications," *IEEE Trans. Software Eng.*, Vol. SE-11, No. 12, Dec. 1985, pp. 1431–1437.

Realistic Assumptions For Software Reliability Models

David Zeitler

Smith's Industries Aerospace & Defense Systems, Inc.
4141 Eastern Avenue, S.E., Grand Rapids, MI 49518-8727
PHONE: (616)241-8168 / EMAIL: zeitler@si.com

Abstract

A definition of reliability appropriate for systems containing significant software that includes trustworthiness and is independent of requirements will be stated and argued for. The systems addressed will encompass the entire product development process as well as both product and its documentation. Cost incurred as a result of faults will be shown to be appropriate as a performance measurement for this definition. This and more realistic assumptions will then be shown to lead to the use of auto-regressive integrated moving average (ARIMA) mathematical models for the modeling of reliability growth.

Key Words: Reliability definition, trustworthiness, growth models, software system reliability, model assumptions.

1 GROUNDWORK

Most authors find the assumptions made in modeling reliability questionable for application to the real world of software development. To more firmly anchor theoretical development to the real world, I will start by reviewing the reasons for reliability models in general and specifically how considerations for the reliability of software based systems dictate that we both change the measurement of reliability considered and the assumptions upon which the model must be based.

1.1 Reliability Enhancement Framework

A good framework from which to start considering software reliability is presented in RADC-TR-87-171 [6]. It does a good job of identifying the tasks involved in statistical reliability improvement and relating them to the DOD-STD-2167A terminology. Too often, reliability discussion begins at the mathematical models for reliability growth and ignore the larger picture of the full reliability program. The RADC document is also the first attempt I've seen to pull together a specification for implementation of a software reliability program. I have added relationships to the framework to show explicitly the presence of the three major types of reliability models.

As shown in figure 1. There are four tasks in this framework with associated outputs: Goal Specification, Prediction, Estimation and Assessment. Goal Specification is a nearly independent process that provides targets for the development process based on an application level model. Predictions take a second model based on development metrics and provide feedback into the design process. Estimations take test measurements and a third model to provide feedback into the test and burn in processes. Finally the assessments take operational data and feed it back into all the models to help tune their predictive and estimation capabilities. The three models identified roughly correspond to component count predictions, stress analysis predictions and growth estimation models currently in use in hardware reliability work.

So we have three separate models, each with a different goal. The first two models are predictive in nature, while the third is estimating the reliability of an existing product. Most current work is aimed at the development of this third type of reliability model. Since the strongest inferences will be possible at this later stage of a program, this is also the most productive area to be addressing.

1.2 Software, Hardware & Systems Reliability

It is often stated that software reliability is very different from hardware reliability, but what exactly is this difference? Usually the statement is made in relation to the idea that software doesn't wear out, but the differences are more fundamental. Software is a set of instructions, like a blueprint or schematic, *it* cannot fail. It can however be wrong in a multitude of ways.

Analogous component levels for software and hardware are illustrated in table 1. The basis of this analogy is comparative equality in the level of functionality provided by the components on each side of the table. For example, both resistors and processor instructions provide a fundamental functionality for their respective disciplines. Note that on either side of this table the levels shown are hazy. The table's primary purpose is to illustrate relationships between software terminology and roughly equivalent hardware structures for comparison purposes.

Hardware reliability analysis almost exclusively addresses the first two levels of the hierarchy (discrete components), with more recent work attempting to extend the models to the higher levels. Since usage of parallel paths through the system is not uniform, this type of analysis quickly becomes extremely complex and highly dependent on the end users input distribution.

From this relationship between hardware and software we can see first that there are equivalent ways of thinking of the two seemingly very different disciplines. Software is most comparable to the blueprints, schematics and production process specifications of hardware. At best, if we compare software programs with hardware components, we then must think of development methods, standards, etc. as the blueprints or production specifications. Thus each program developed is analogous to an individual hardware unit from production. We can now see from this analogy that statistical analysis of software must be carried out across many software units to achieve the same effects as applying statistical analysis of hardware components to many parts.

Carrying this analogy just a bit farther, to parallel hardware reliability we should be looking at the reliability of individual CPU instructions much as hardware has determined the reliability of individual components. This is quite different from the current work in software reliability, which jumps in at the higher levels, treating the software as a black box, without attempting to address the low levels which hardware has built upon. Hardware has discrete components at these levels that can be analyzed independent of the particular use of the component. This examination of fundamental software components independent of their use will yield only that the components do not fail. Therefore, something different must be going on when

we discuss reliability for software systems.

In hardware we are looking at reliability hazard functions as the probability that an individual component will fail. In software, we are looking at the probability that a given component will be used in an inappropriate manner. This implies that we are looking not at the probability of failure of a concrete replicate of a design, as in hardware, but rather at the probability that the designer incorrectly uses a component in the design. For example, choosing the correct packaging of a resistance component for the target environmental conditions and reliability requirements, but using the wrong resistance value in the circuit for the full range of the circuits intended function (i.e., incorrect functional design as opposed to incorrect environmental design).

Reliability analysis now recommends reduced part counts and greater operational margins to improve reliability. In the context of the software system reliability improvement process I'm suggesting, reliability might also be suggesting that the use of complex components, which have a high probability of misuse, be minimized. This would reduce the probability of design errors.

An example of the kind of design criteria that might come out of this type of analysis would be 'Reduce use of complex non-programmable components'. Or perhaps, the development of software modules unique to the system should be minimized, since they probably would not have the maturity and/or level of testing of common software. As a confirmation that we're on the right track, note that this agrees with common practice for quality software development today. So we can see from this analogy that software reliability *is* significantly different from hardware reliability.

1.3 Separation of Software from System Reliability

We are at the point where the functionality of systems are primarily resident in the software. Special purpose or single purpose hardware is nearly a thing of the past. Since we have shown above that software reliability is more related to functionality than to physical components, addressing software reliability is equivalent to addressing system reliability. It is also equivalent to addressing the reliability of the software/system development process, since the reliability of the end product is as much a result of the process that developed it as of the product itself.

This then suggests that a system level approach to the overall reliability problem will be more effective than attempting to isolate either hardware or software.

Figure 1: Software Reliability Framework

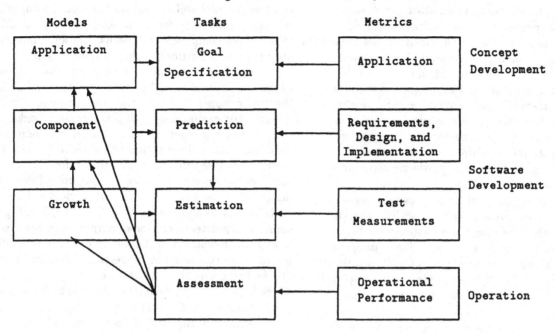

Table 1: analogous Hardware/Software Structures

Hardware	Software
Primitive Components Resistors,Capacitors, etc.	Primitive Instructions move, shift, add, etc.
Integrated Chips CPU, UART, MMU, etc.	Units Procedures, Modules, etc.
Sub-circuits RS422, ARINC, etc.	CPC's Packages, Objects, etc.
Boards Serial I/O, Memory, etc.	TLCSC's Exec, I/O, etc.
Sub-systems (HWCI's) Display, Keyboard, etc.	Programs (CSCI's) Operational Flight Program
Systems Navigation System, Weapon System, Fuel Savings System, etc.	

What's more, if we solve the reliability problem as discussed here, the solution will be equally applicable to areas that hardware reliability has traditionally considered out of scope. A solution to software reliability then should cover not only the software aspects of the reliability question, but the wider system aspects simultaneously.

In [7] Fabio Schreiber concludes that the time is ripe for the unification of several research areas into a unified investigation of system reliability. I am taking his suggestion a step further here in including not only the system performance, but also in effect the performance of the development process as well. This is not only desirable from the relationship of reliability to functionality, but is necessitated by the inadequacy of requirement specification techniques for complex systems.

1.4   Definition of Software Reliability

Most authors that address the definition of systems reliability, address it in terms of adherence to requirements. With the present state of the art in requirements specification for complex systems, this hardly seems reasonable. We cannot yet determine if a system adheres to requirements when these requirements are incomplete and/or ambiguous as they invariably are.

According to Webster's New Collegiate Dictionary, two possible meanings of reliability seem to apply. The first is consistency in response, in which case software (or any other deterministic process) cannot be unreliable. Another definition has reliability meaning 'to be dependable, or trustworthy'. The first definition doesn't seem to fit at all. We can be sure that software does not have perfect reliability. So it appears reliability means to perform with little probability of unexpected behavior, (i.e., we can depend on or trust it). This is beyond just repeatable behavior and does seem to get at the issue here. So if the system always does what is expected of it, it is perfectly reliable. Thus we see that trustworthiness is a major component of reliability.

Reliability is then more closely associated with meeting user expectations, regardless of stated requirements. (Note: this is not in addition to meeting requirements. Any given requirement, regardless of source, may not meet user expectations and meeting them will still be considered a failure!) Reliability is then related to perceived failures as opposed to what may be considered actual failures. It is well known that, although we're making progress, the precise specification of a complex system is not at this time possible.

The result is that there is room for user interpretation, which can lead to perceived failures. These failures are as expensive (or more expensive) than 'actual' failures. In either case, the user is not satisfied with the operation of the system and it is considered unreliable.

So I am defining reliability as that which minimizes the users perceived failures.

1.5   Measurement of Reliability

Perceived failures can be measured in terms of cost due to user complaints, so I'm suggesting we use cost as a measure of reliability. These costs consist of the lost productivity or production due to down time, management costs for handling the return of faulty product, costs associated with negotiation of variances against requirements, etc. The cost does not however stop at the customer. We also will need to consider the cost to the developer. This cost is in terms of the lost prestige (and therefore presumably potential market share in the future) as well as the immediate cost to analyze and fix the product returned. This can be modeled as a constant times the cumulative cost incurred by the customer.

Measurement of perceived failures at the user is too late to help us estimate the growth curve of the system reliability during development. It will provide adequate feedback into future reliability analyses, but a measure of perceived failures during the development process is needed. This can be obtained through the early application of operational testing using actual users. Early testing can be focused on the user interface, with gradual incorporation of functionality as the integration of the system progresses.

In [5] Ragnar Huslende lays out an extension of standard reliability concepts for degradable systems or any partially operable system. As Huslende states, any system can be viewed as degradable. Using cost as a measure of the system performance we can see that zero cost is equivalent to the no-fault state of Huslende's $H(t)$. So I will be looking at cost as a measure of system performance.

$$c(t) = c_u(t) + c_p \cdot c_u(t) + c_f(t)$$

where:

c_u =   cost to the user with respect to time

c_p =   impact of customers costs on developers

c_f =   developers cost to fix the product

This gives us a value that can be measured tangibly (although not necessarily precisely) regardless of the specifications, development process, or other variables (controllable or not). Using the cost as our performance measure also gives us a handle on the varying degree of severity that failures tend to cause.

Measuring reliability performance as cost also allows us to focus on those problems that are important to us and the customer. We all know of little problems that are annoyances in software based systems, but are certainly not worth spending massive effort to correct. Likewise, we all would consider any effort expended to eliminate risk of life to be spent well. With cost as our measure of reliability, little problems that are soon worked around have a negligible impact on reliability, while loss of life has a correspondingly large impact.

These costs can be measured through existing or augmentation of existing accounting systems for tracking product that has been fielded. For systems under development, we, will need to make use of the user interaction with early prototypes to measure relation to expectations. This also implies that we need to make the actual users an integral part of the standard testing process in order to improve reliability of systems.

2 MODELING

Essentially all proposed reliability models are growth models, an exception being the linear univariate predictive model(s) attempted by SAIC for RADC-TR-87-171. The intent of the reliability growth modeling process is to be able to predict, from actual failure data collected during early development or testing, both the expected end product reliability and the magnitude of effort necessary to achieve the target reliability, and hence the date when a system release can be achieved. Reliability growth models have been applied to several programs for these purposes. These applications have shown considerable promise. Many programs now also use an intuitive form of this by monitoring a problem reporting system during the late stages of a program with an eye toward determining when the software is ready for release.

Martin Trachtenberg in [8] provides a general formulation of software reliability with the relationship of his general model to major existing models. This work is a good foundation upon which to base further modeling work. In particular, my measure of reliability performance as cost can be easily incorporated into the model. Modification of the general model to incorporate dynamics is somewhat more complex however.

In Trachtenberg's model, failure rate is a function of

software errors encountered. He considers f=f(e) and e=e(x) where f is the number of failures, e is the number of errors encountered and x is the number of executed instructions. To determine a failure rate, he differentiates f(e(x(t)) with respect to time to obtain a form in terms of current number of failures per encountered error (s), apparent error density or number of encountered errors per executed instruction (d), and software workload in terms of instructions per time unit (w). Thus arriving at failure rate $\lambda(t)$ as below:

$$\lambda(t) = \frac{df}{dt} = \frac{df}{de} \cdot \frac{de}{dx} \cdot \frac{dx}{dt} = s \cdot d \cdot w$$

This model is intuitively attractive and does provide a general structure from which other models can be viewed. In the following paragraphs I will consider each basic assumption and show the modification necessary for a realistic model. When possible, I will be using the notation from Trachtenburg's paper.

2.1 A Semi-structural Approach

As Schreiber stated in [7], cost based modeling can be extremely complex. This due to the complexities of incorporating variable failure impact into structural equations for the process. In addition, adding the development process into the reliability equations adds human systems into the equations. I am suggesting that an intermediate approach be taken. From a few basic assumptions about the relationships expected, I will be proposing a high level empirical model capable of capturing the necessary characteristics of the process, thereby avoiding the complexities of attempting to specify the micro level structural model under which the system actually operates.

2.2 Assumptions

Recent work (one specifically is Ehrlich, et al [3]) has shown that in some applications the current growth models proposed for software reliability provide reasonable estimates of test effort needed. The work discussed was specifically designed to meet the given assumptions of the models. Necessary characteristics for using the current available models vary, but generally include independence in the interarrival times of failures, uniform magnitude of impact of failures (making failure rate a reasonable measure of reliability), and uniform system load during test and/or operation (i.e., random test execution). None of these assumptions hold for many real-time systems and avionic systems in particular.

A clear indication that we have autocorrelation even in systems with uniformity in testing can be seen in the telephony system test data analyzed by Ehrlich et.al. The plots show a good match between the homogeneous Poisson model being fitted and the actual data, but there is visual evidence of positive autocorrelation in the data sets. This suggests the presence of auto regressive factors needed in the model even for a process which fits the assumptions well.

In systems that cannot be easily tested in a random fashion, these auto regressive factors are likely to be sufficiently significant to trigger an early release of software or an over intensification of test effort by excursions from the too simplistic model that are merely based on random variation. At the very least, they will reinforce the positive feedback reactive effect seen where increased failures during test causes increased test effort (lagged by management response time constants of course).

2.2.1 Time base for real time systems

Real time systems have a more-or-less uniform instructions (or cycles) per unit time pattern. This makes measurement of instructions executed per unit time a poor measure for system load. Instead, we need to be measuring the number of instructions outside the operating system per time unit. This number will increase proportionally with system load.

No changes in the equations are necessary here, since we're just modifying the interpretation. This modification transfers us from the time domain to the computation domain, as discussed in [1]. More specifically, we are working in the application computation domain.

2.2.2 Cost of Failures

Including a non-constant cost for failures will remove the uniform failure impact assumptions made in the standard models, this puts our emphasis on cost per unit time. The cost of a failure is both a function of the fault that causes it and of the situation in which the failure occurs.

$$c(f) \quad = \quad c(f, b) \cdot p_b(t)$$
where:
$$c_f(a, b) \quad = \quad \text{cost of failure } a \text{ occurring in situation } b$$
$$p_b(t) \quad = \quad \text{probability of situation } b \text{ at time } t$$

Since situations (or test cases) cannot occur randomly in the types of systems we're looking at, but occur in the context of an operational profile, cost due to the occurrence of any particular failure is a time based function related to the operational profiles. These operational profiles will produce a 'fine grain' correlation structure in the occurrences of failures.

Our early measurements for growth estimation are taken during the integration of the system. This integration process limits the nature of the profiles to functions currently integrated and operational. Thus we will also see a 'coarse grain' correlation structure to the occurrences of failures.

For our cost based reliability measurement we replace failure rate, with cost rate ($\gamma(t)$) based measures. These cost based measures will be more directly usable by management and give planners a better handle on appropriate test effort feedback into the development process. We can also see that this process level feedback into the product will impact failure occurrences.

$$\gamma(t) \quad = \quad \frac{dc}{dt}$$
$$= \quad \frac{dc}{df} \cdot \frac{df}{de} \cdot \frac{de}{dr} \cdot \frac{dr}{dt}$$
$$= \quad c \cdot s \cdot d \cdot w$$

2.2.3 Failure inter-arrival time

Software can be viewed as a transfer function. Its input must be taken as the combination of the values present at its inputs and the state of its memory at the beginning of execution. Output is the combination of values presented to its outputs and its internal state upon completion of execution. In many software systems, this transfer function is applied to essentially independent inputs and the system state is reset before each execution. In real-time avionic software, and most other real-time software systems, the inputs are sequences of highly correlated values applied to a system that retains its internal state from the previous input set.

Clearly then, the assumption of random distribution of inputs is not feasible here. Therefore a primary assumption of our growth models cannot be applied. We must then prepare our models for the likely autocorrelation of failure occurrence. This will imply some form of time-series model for the occurrence of software failures.

It also can be argued that a piece of code with many faults being found is likely to have more faults remaining in it, since the same factors that produced the faulty code affect the remainder of the code as well. Combined with this is the operational profile nature necessary for most real time systems testing. The operational profile ensures that the conditions that caused a failure must persist for some period of time, thus increasing the probability of recurrence or related failure detection.

So we see that software systems failure occurrences are not independent, and in fact, will exhibit correlation structure that is dependent on the correlation structure of the inputs coming from an operational profile as well as on the system itself. This is not easily modelable in general.

2.2.4 Fault correction process

When a fault is corrected, the same process as that which created the fault is used to fix it. The fix then has a probability of introducing new faults (or not correcting the original fault) that is clearly not zero. If we look at the magnitude of the change in changed or added instructions, schematic symbols, drawing symbols, etc., (M_e) and the probability of introducing faults as the proportion of faults (e_0) to instructions at the beginning of the program (I), $p_0 = \left(\frac{e_0}{I}\right)$ and let $p_e(t) =$ the probability of fixing a fault at time t, we can view the remaining faults in the code at time t as

$$e(t) = e(t-1) + p_e(t) \cdot (M_e \cdot p_0 - 1)$$

rather than

$$e(t) = e(t-1) - p_e(t)$$

Using B as the linear lag operator, we have

$$(1 - B)e(t) = p_e(t) \cdot (M_e \cdot p_0 - 1)$$

The right hand side of the previous equation represents the random process of finding and fixing faults in the system. This random process is the combination of the above processes of failure inter-arrivals, fault recurrence and fault removal. Since together these represent a dynamic process driven by random noise, we can let the rhs $= \theta_0 + \theta(B)\epsilon_t$, $\epsilon(t)$ is a white noise driver for the process. We can see then that the fault content of the system is modelable as a standard autoregressive integrated moving average (ARIMA) [2] time-series model.

Note that this relationship implies that the fault content of the system is not strictly decreasing and in fact may exceed the initial fault content.

2.2.5 Recurrent faults & fault removal

Faults are not removed immediately in the real world. Often minor faults are determined to be not worth the effort to fix at all. Thus a realistic model of software maintenance must be a cost prioritized queue. The result is a clear dependence of the number of failures per

fault on the cost of removing the fault when compared with the cost of encountering the fault and the expected number of occurrences of the fault if its not fixed.

For our context, the queueing process can be expressed as a finite difference equation using the sum of the expected cost of not fixing the faults as the state variable. State changes occur whenever there is a fault with an expected cost for not fixing greater than the cost of repairing. The fault fixed will be the one with the highest return (not necessarily the first or last).

Thus we can see that known faults may never reach zero (as one would expect) and that the expected number of recurrences of a failure due to a given fault is a function of both the cost to fix it and its expected impact on lifetime cost of the system. Since the cost to fix is known to be increasing with time during development and the expected impact is dependent on the operational use of the system, we will have the number of failures occurring for each fault being dynamic also.

3 Summary

I have shown here that we can expect the occurrences of failures and the magnitude of their impact to vary dynamically in time and that they are all interdependent. Thus our model is clearly dynamic and an a priori determination of its order (let alone the exact structure) will be difficult. This is identically the case for work in social, economic and other human systems. Not really a surprise since we can see from the necessary definition of reliability in terms of customer expectations that products containing significant software components are deeply embedded in human systems. The approach taken to modeling and forecasting in human based systems is fitting autoregressive integrated moving average models to the real world data. I'm suggesting here that we need to do the same for estimating reliability growth.

In the September '90 QualityTIME section of IEEE Software [4], Richard Hamlet has an excellent discussion of quality and reliability. He clearly delineates for us the distinction between failures and faults. I suspect that Mr. Hamlet will disagree with my definition of reliability, as will Parnas. If however, we separate trustworthiness from reliability as suggested, we end up with the conclusion that software systems are perfectly reliable. If this is the case, we then should drop this thrashing over software reliability, and attack the problem of software trustworthiness. Webster however includes trustworthiness as a part of reliability. I will then stand by my arguments. Reliability of software systems is a measure of how much trust the user can put in the software performing as expected.

More realistic assumptions are necessary for application of reliability growth modeling to software systems. The assumptions are:

- Failures do not have equal impact.

- Failure rates have dynamic structure.

- The fault removal process is a cost prioritized queue depending on the ratio of expected cost to cost to fix.

- Fault content has a dynamic structure and is not strictly decreasing.

I have shown that, because of my definition and these less restrictive assumptions on our model, software reliability must be modeled as an ARIMA time series. The intent here is not to replace existing models. They have already shown their value in some real world situations. My intent is to provide an avenue for further application of reliability analysis in software system development applications where the restrictive assumptions of current models will make them of little use.

3.1 Further research.

Considerable empirical work is needed to validate my claims. Costs need to be collected to perform this empirical work. Initial efforts could however make use of estimates from existing information and/or apply simulation techniques to initially validate the approach by showing that ARIMA models could produce the kinds of behavior known to be present in the software system development process. Eventually, it is hoped that information gained from this more empirical approach will lead to greater understanding of the process and structural models.

4   Acknowledgements

Thanks to Gerry Vossler and Derek Hatley for their review of this work and to Smiths Industries for their support. I would also like to thank the reviewers who pointed me toward related work in systems reliability which was quite helpful.

References

[1] Beaudry, M. Danielle, *Performance-Related Reliability Measures for Computing Systems*, IEEE Transaction on Computers, Vol c-27. No. 6, June 1978, pp 540-547.

[2] Box, George E. P. & Gwilym M. Jenkins, *Time Series Forecasting and Control*, Holden-Day 1976.

[3] Ehrlich, Willa K., S. Keith Lee, and Rex H. Molisani. *Applying Reliability Measurement: A Case Study*, IEEE Software, March 1990.

[4] Hamlet, Richard *New answers to old questions*, IEEE Software, September 1990.

[5] Huslende, Ragnar, *A Combined Evaluation of Performance and Reliability for Degradable Systems*, ACM-SIGMETRICS Conf. on Measurement and Modeling of Comput. Syst., 1981, pp. 157-163.

[6] *Methodology for Software Reliability Prediction*, RADC-TR-87-181, Science Applications International Corporation for Rome Air Development Center 1987.

[7] Schreiber, Fabio A., *Information Systems: A Challenge for Computers and Communications Reliability*, IEEE Journal on Selected Areas in Communications, Vol. SAC-4, No. 6, October 1986, pp 157-164.

[8] Trachtenberg, Martin, *A General Theory of Software Reliability Modeling*. IEEE Transactions on Reliability, Vol. 39, No. 1, 1990 April, pp 92-96.

Predicting Software Development Errors Using Software Complexity Metrics

TAGHI M. KHOSHGOFTAAR, MEMBER, IEEE, AND JOHN C. MUNSON, MEMBER, IEEE

Abstract—Various software metrics have been developed for the purpose of evaluating certain characteristics of the computer programming process. Attempts to use these software metric data have met with questionable success in program development scenarios. Similarly, there are many different models of software reliability. Each of these models fundamentally studies the computer program as a black box. The intrinsic assumption underlying each of the models is that the black box has one or more parameters that are uniquely determined for that particular box. Complexity metrics do provide substantial information on the distinguishing differences among the software systems whose reliability is being modeled and may be used in the determination of initial parameter estimates. Many of the existing complexity metrics measure common aspects of program complexity and thus have shared variance. In this paper, we develop predictive models that incorporate a functional relationship of program error measures with software complexity metrics and metrics based on factor analysis of empirical data. Specific techniques for assessing regression models are presented for analyzing these models.

I. INTRODUCTION

RECENT research in the area of computer program reliability has focused on the identification of program modules that are most likely to contain errors. It has been found that a relatively few number of modules in a set of modules constituting a program will contain a disproportionate number of errors. A major research effort is underway to try to determine, *a priori*, which modules might contain a significant number of errors so that the program test and validation process might be focused in the most productive direction.

Software complexity metrics have been shown to be closely related to the distribution of errors in program modules. That is, there is a direct relationship between some complexity metrics and the number of errors later found in test and validation [15]. Many different research programs have sought to develop a predictive relationship between complexity metrics and errors. In particular, a close relationship has been found between the software measures of lines of code and errors. Previous studies [2], [16], [17] have developed estimates of fault rates ranging from 0.3 to 0.5 faults per 100 lines of code. Lipow [10]

Manuscript received May 10, 1989; revised September 28, 1989. This work was presented at the ASA 1989 Symposium, Orlando, FL, April 9–12, 1989.

T. M. Khoshgoftaar is with the Department of Computer Science, Florida Atlanta University, Boca Raton, FL 33431.

J. C. Munson is with the Division of Computer Science, University of West Florida, Pensacola, FL 32514.

IEEE Log Number 8932737.

developed a model which predicts the number of faults per line of code based on Halstead's [5] software science metrics. Gaffney [3] proposed formulas relating the number of faults to the number of lines of code and to the number of conditional jumps.

This paper will identify some of the basic problems associated with the prediction of errors using complexity metrics and suggest solutions to these problems. A basic statistical tool which will be used to determine the relationship between errors is that of regression analysis. As will be shown, there are many methods of developing a regression model for the same data. The choice of a particular model should be viewed as the selection of a *best* model from a pool of candidate models.

A major problem in the development of regression model centers around the problem of multicollinearity. The basic regression model is based on the assumption that the independent variables of the analysis are not linear compounds of each other nor do they share an element of common variance. Two variables sharing a common element of variance are said to be collinear. To meet this assumption of nonmulticollinearity, another statistical procedure called factor analysis may be used. The specific value of factor analysis is that the technique will reduce a data matrix to a set of orthogonal variables or factors that are, in fact, noncollinear.

This technique of factor analysis is also useful in the reduction of the complexity metric space to a set of orthogonal complexity dimensions. A distinct relationship between individual program complexity measures and reliability has been found, although it has not been modeled [12]. The specific contribution of the variance of each of these complexity dimensions to the number of errors in a program may then be studied with regression analysis. Sections II and III of this paper will, then, summarize the basic statistical issues of factor analysis and regression analysis. Subsequently, we will then show the appropriate application of these techniques to the problem of predicting software development errors using software complexity metrics.

II. FACTOR ANALYSIS

The essential purpose of factor analysis is to describe, if possible, the covariance relationships among variables in terms of a few underlying, but understandable, random quantities called factors. Basically, the factor model is motivated by the following argument. Suppose variables can be grouped by their correlations. That is, all variables within a particular group are highly correlated among themselves but have relatively small correlations with variables in a different group. It is conceivable that each group of variables represents a single underlying construct, or factor, that is responsible for the observed correlations.

Factor analysis can be considered as an extension of principal component analysis [6]. Both can be viewed as attempts to approximate the covariance matrix Σ. However, the approximation based on the factor analysis model is more elaborate. The primary question in factor analysis is whether the data are consistent with a prescribed structure. For our investigative purposes, this matrix Σ can be reconstructed from a correlation matrix.

Assume that we are given p random variables $X = (X_1, \cdots, X_p)$ having a multivariate distribution with mean $\mu = (\mu_1, \cdots, \mu_p)$ and a covariance matrix Σ. The factor model postulates that X is linearly dependent on a few unobservable random variables $F_1, \cdots, F_m$, called common factors, and p additional sources of variation, $\epsilon_1, \cdots, \epsilon_p$, called errors or, sometimes, specific factors. In particular, the factor analytic model is

$$ X_i = \sum_{j=1}^{m} \alpha_{ij} F_j + \epsilon_i, \qquad i = 1, 2, \cdots, p. $$

The coefficient α_{ij} is called the loading of the ith variable on the jth factor. The variables $F_1, \cdots, F_m$ are assumed to be uncorrelated with unit variances.

The technique of factor analysis concerns itself with estimating the factor loadings α_{ij}. Once the factor loadings have been obtained, the major task is to make the best interpretation of the common factors. It is important to note that the burden of interpretation lies on the observer and is not intrinsic in the factor analysis. Usually, it is relatively simple to observe the relationships of variables grouped by their association with a common factor and attach a name to this set.

To aid in the interpretation of the extracted factor loadings, we exploit the indeterminancy of the factor solution whereby we can find new common factors, $F_1^{(R)}, \cdots, F_m^{(R)}$, that are linear combinations of the old factors and which are uncorrelated with unit variances. Thus, the new set of factors also satisfies the factor model. Furthermore, there are an infinite number of such sets. The process of obtaining a set of new factors is called an orthogonal factor rotation. The objective of the rotation is to obtain some theoretically meaningful factors and to simplify the factor structure.

An example of the application of factor analysis to the field of software complexity metrics may be seen in the authors' recent study [13]. The most important conclusion that can be drawn from this investigation is that the domain of complexity measures does not appear to be unrestricted. There are many software complexity metrics in the literature, but there are relatively few dimensions in the complexity measure space. It would appear perfectly

reasonable to characterize the complexity of a program with a simple function of a small number of variables that convey all or most of the information in the original set. The principal components are constructed so that they represent transformed scores on dimensions that are mutually orthogonal.

Associated with each principle component is an eigenvalue λ. These eigenvalues are the solutions to the determinental equation $|\Sigma - \lambda I| = 0$ where Σ is the covariance matrix. The eigenvalues are merely the variance of a principal component in the factor analysis. If any one of the λ's is exactly equal to zero, there is a perfect linear relationship among the original variables which is the extreme case of multicollinearity. If one of the λ's is much smaller than the others (and near zero), multicollinearity is present.

Through the use of factor analysis, it is possible to have a set of highly related variables, such as complexity metrics, be reduced to a relative small number of complexity dimensions. When this mapping is accomplished by factor analysis, the transformed and reduced complexity dimensions are in fact orthogonal. This definitively solves the problem of multicollinearity in subsequent regression analysis.

III. REGRESSION ANALYSIS

The general notion of linear regression is to select from a set of independent variables a subset of these variables which will explain the most amount of variance in a dependent variable. Coefficients for the independent variables are produced by a least squares fit of these variables to sample data. The key to model development is to choose the subset of independent variables in such a manner as to not introduce more variance (or noise) in the model than might be contributed by the independent variable itself. The selection of the appropriate subset of independent variables may be accomplished in one of several ways. We will now introduce several methodologies for this subset selection together with the evaluation criteria for model selection.

A. The Detection and Analysis of Collinear Data

When there is a complete absence of linear relationship among the independent variables, they are said to be orthogonal. In most regression applications, the independent variables are not orthogonal. Usually the lack of orthogonality is not serious enough to affect the analysis. However, in software development, the independent variables, software complexity metrics, are so strongly interrelated that the regression results are ambiguous. Typically, it is impossible to estimate the unique effects of individual software complexity metric in the regression equation. The estimated values of the coefficients are very sensitive to slight changes in the data and to the addition or deletion of variables in the regression equation. The regression coefficients have large sampling errors which affect both inference and forecasting that is based on regression model. The condition of severe nonorthogonality is also referred to as the problem of collinear data, or multicollinearity. It is important to know when multicollinearity is present and to be aware of its possible consequences.

Principal component analysis may be used to detect and analyze collinearity in the explanatory variables which are, in this case, software complexity metrics. When confronted with a large number of variables measuring a single construct, it may be desirable to represent the set by some small number of variables that convey all or most of the information in the original set. The principal components are constructed so that they represent transformed scores on dimensions that are mutually orthogonal.

B. The Selection of an Appropriate Regression Model

The most intuitively obvious technique to use in the identification of the appropriate subset of independent variables is to perform all possible regressions (the combinatorial solution). For example, consider the case where we might want to relate four possible independent variables to a dependent variable, such as program errors. First, there would be four regression models developed, each with one independent variable. Next, there would be six models with two of the four possible variables, and then four models with three of the four possible independent variables. Finally, there would be a regression model with all independent variables. Thus, there would be 15 regression models to choose from. Notwithstanding the fact that this can be a very labor-intensive process for a regression model with a large number of independent variables, there still remains the problem of the selection of the *best* of the models so produced. Clearly, some evaluation standard must be applied. Also, this particular technique lends itself well to the selection of an inappropriate model due to spurious random variation of independent variables not related in any way to the systematic variation of the dependent variable.

The next alternative for the development of a regression model is to use a stepwise regression procedure which involves the systematic incorporation of variables in the regression model in an iterative manner. Within this class there are essentially three methods. First, there is the stepwise regression analysis. In this procedure, an initial model is formed by selecting the independent variable with the highest simple correlation with the dependent variable. In subsequent iterations, new variables are selected for inclusion based on their partial correlation with variables already in the regression equation. Variables in this model may be removed from the regression equation when they no longer contribute significantly to the explained variance. There must be an *a priori* level of significance (p) chosen for the inclusion or deletion of variables from the model. The second stepwise procedure is forward inclusion. In the case of this procedure, a variable once entered in the regression equation may not be removed. The third technique, backward elimination, forms a regression equation with all variables and then systematically eliminates variables, one by one, which do not contribute significantly to the model. Stepwise procedures for the selection of variables in a regression problem should be used with caution. These are useful tools for variable selection only in the circumstances of noncollinearity. We recommend a different set of procedures in the presence of collinearity. Once the collinearity are identified, a set of new variables, common factors, can then be formed by using factor analysis. These new variables will not, then, be collinear. Then stepwise procedures are used to select the factors which are important for predicting dependent variable, which in our case will be an enumeration of programming errors.

A third technique, which shows the most promise to the study of the prediction of errors in software is the reduced model. With this procedure, the set of independent variables are mapped onto a smaller number of orthogonal dimensions through the use of factor analysis. A significant value in this process is the fact that multicollinearity among the variables is first eliminated by the factor analysis. Also, the factor analysis serves to reduce the apparent dimensionality of the set of independent variables. From a regression analysis of variance perspective, this also will have the net effect of reducing the degrees of freedom due to regression in that fewer total variables are presented as independent variables to the regression model.

C. The Evaluation of Regression Models

The net result of the previous discussion is that most regression studies will produce more than one possible model. An excellent discussion of the model evaluation process is available from Myers [14]. The objective, now, is to be able to evaluate the several models in terms of their predictive value. In our particular case, we are interested in predicting the number of potential errors in a program module based on its relative complexity. There are several statistical measures of the performance of a regression model. In general, there are two distinct classes of these evaluation criteria. The first of these classes contains statistics developed from the regression analysis of variance. Two of these, which will be employed in this study, are the coefficient of determination R_p^2 and the C_p statistic [14]. Another approach, the PRESS statistic, is based on residual analysis [14].

Traditionally, the R_p^2 statistic is used almost exclusively in empirical studies in software engineering. There are some distinct problems associated with the use of R_p^2, which is defined as follows: $R_p^2 = SSR_p/SST$, where p represents the number of parameters in the regression equation, SSR is the regression sum of squares, and SST is the total sum of squares. In that SST is constant for all regression models, R_p^2 can only increase as independent variables are added to a regression equation, whether or not they will account for a significant amount of variance in the dependent variable. A variation on the R^2 statistics is the adjusted R^2 (or $AdjR^2$) which does attempt to correct for the number of variables in the regression equation (regression degrees of freedom, d.f.). The R_p^2 statistic does not assess the quality of future prediction, only the quality of fit on the sample data.

The case for the C_p statistic is very different. C_p may be defined in terms of R_p^2 as follows: $C_p = (1 - R_p^2)(n - T)/(1 - R_T^2) - (n - 2p)$, where n represents the number of observations and T represents the total number of parameters in the complete model. The statistic, C_p, is a measure of the total squared error in a regression. Thus, a researcher should choose a model with the smallest value of C_p. This statistic is to be preferred to R_p^2 because a penalty is introduced for overfitting the model with excess independent variables which bring with them an additional noise component.

The PRESS statistic is based on a systematic examination of the residuals. A residual is the difference between an observed value of the dependent variable y and the value $\hat{y}$ predicted by the model. A major problem with regression modeling and the prediction of errors in a program relates to the fact that some programs have disproportionately few or many errors in them. These outliers have a tendency to overbias a least square model. The PRESS statistic provides the opportunity to investigate models controlling for the effects of these outliers. This statistic is developed from PRESS residuals, $y_i - \hat{y}_i$, where y_i is the value of the ith dependent variable and $\hat{y}_i$ is the predictive value from a regression equation formed with all observations, *except* the ith. Thus, if there are n sample points, n separate regression equations will be formed, each with $n - 1$ observations. The PRESS statistic is computed as follows: $PRESS = \Sigma_{i=1}^{n} (y_i - \hat{y}_i)^2$. The choice of a regression model is determined by selecting the one with the lowest value of PRESS.

An alternate method of validating regression models is a technique known as data splitting. In this methodology, a model is formed with a subset of data and validated on the excluded data subset. However, in software engineering modeling, the data cost is far too high for this technique to be practical. Thus, the PRESS statistic is eminently suited to replace the data splitting methodology as a validation technique.

IV. THE PREDICTION OF ERRORS FROM COMPLEXITY DATA

The problem of the multicollinearity among the software complexity metrics which are used to develop estimates of errors in telecommunication software are quite evident in the literature. An example of this problem may be found in a study by Lennselius [9]. In this study, ten software metrics, together with error measures, were collected for a software development project in a telecommunication system. Correlation coefficients were then computed for these data. The results of this analysis are presented in Table I. From a statistical perspective, the disturbing fact here is that the correlation coefficients between all of the software metrics studied were greater than 0.82. This reflects a high degree of multicollinearity among these metrics.

TABLE I
CORRELATION COEFFICIENTS FOR LENNSELIUS DATA

METRIC	INP	SDL	C(G)	NC	B	MSDL	MC(G)	V	EXE	LOC
SDL	.90									
C(G)	.91	.99								
NC	.83	.89	.92							
B	.89	.98	.99	.95						
MSDL	.93	.94	.95	.92	.96					
MC(G)	.93	.93	.96	.93	.97	.99				
V	.94	.91	.92	.89	.92	.94	.94			
EXE	.91	.90	.91	.88	.91	.94	.93	.99		
LOC	.87	.93	.94	.93	.94	.93	.96	.96	.97	
ERRORS	.95	.88	.90	.85	.89	.93	.92	.94	.91	.87

The particular metrics used in this study and shown in Table I are as follows. The SDL label represents the number of symbols in an SDL language description, C(G) is a modified cyclomatic complexity metric, B represents a count of the total program branches, NC represents the maximum nesting level, V is Halstead's volume, LOC represents lines of code, EXE is the number of executable lines of code. The metrics MSDL and MC(G) represent weighted sums of the metrics SDL and C(G), respectively.

When these data are factor analyzed, only one factor emerges. The resultant factor structure is shown in Table II. In this case, then, any one of the metrics might be used equally well in a regression model for the prediction of errors. Intuitively, we believe there are other complexity dimensions which also relate to the determination of errors. There is some indication that the single factor which emerged in this analysis is closely related to the LOC (Volume) metric. A relationship was developed by Lennselius on the SDL descriptions in a nonlinear regression model which showed some promise. Further analysis of the Lennselius data was not possible due to the lack of availability of the original data on which the correlations were developed. However, data were available from two other sources which did permit further analysis. We will now examine these data using our correction for problems of multicollinearity.

A. The Harrison Data

The use of complexity metrics as predictors of software errors is particularly subject to difficulties from a statistical point of view. This is so because of the high degree of multicollinearity among the various complexity metrics. One such study, which will be used as an example, was done by Harrison [7]. Herein, several selected complexity metrics were determined for 20 logical modules of C code from a project consisting of 30 000 lines of code. Error logs were maintained during the program development phase for each of the program modules. These errors were then correlated with a set of complexity metrics. The results of this analysis are presented in Table III.

The specific software metrics employed in this study (from Table III) are representatives from three groups identified by Harrison as microlevel, macrolevel, and

23

TABLE II
Factor Pattern for Lennselius Data

METRIC	FACTOR 1
MC(G)	.98
MSDL	.98
B	.98
C(G)	.98
V	.97
LOC	.97
SDL	.97
EXE	.96
INP	.95
ERROR	.94
NC	.94

TABLE III
Correlation Coefficients for Harrison Data

	Error	LOC	V(G)	E	MMC	HNK	HNP	PRC
Error	1.0000							
LOC	0.7600	1.0000						
V(G)	0.7390	0.7719	1.0000					
E	0.6919	0.8179	0.9329	1.0000				
MMC	0.8228	0.6703	0.9107	0.8072	1.0000			
HNK	0.6231	0.7747	0.8998	0.9807	0.7795	1.0000		
HNP	0.7652	0.7515	0.9810	0.8653	0.9933	0.8275	1.0000	
PRC	0.6493	0.7055	0.9244	0.9370	0.7981	0.9175	0.8442	1.0000

micro/macrolevel complexity metrics—from the class of microlevel metrics, lines of code (LOC), McCabe's [11] Cyclomatic Complexity (V(G)), Halstead's software science Effort (E), and a numerical count of the number of procedures (PRC). Representative of the class of macrolevel complexity were Henry and Kafura's [8] Information Flow Complexity (HNK) and Hall and Preiser's [4] Combined Network Complexity metric (HNP).

One representative member of the macro/microlevel complexity category is Harrison's MMC metric. The MMC of a system of program modules was calculated as follows:

$$MMC = \sum_{i=1}^{n} \left(SC(i) * MC(i) \right),$$

where $SC(i)$ is the system level complexity contributed by subprogram i, and $MC(i)$ is the microlevel complexity contributed by subprogram i from a set of n subprograms. The metric $SC(i)$ is calculated as

$$SC(i) = \left(Glob(i) * (n - 1) + Param(i) \right) * \left(1 - DI(i) \right),$$

where

Glob(i) is the number of times global variables are used in subprogram i,

Param(i) is the number of formal parameters used in subprogram i, and

DI(i) is the *Documentation Index* for subprogram i, where $0 \leq DI(i) \leq 1$ based on the relative proportion of comments present in the subprogram.

In this particular study, the microlevel complexity measure $MC(i)$ for the ith subprogram was derived from McCabe's V(G).

An inspection of Table III shows that there is a high correlation among all of the selected complexity metrics. Hence, it may be assumed that there is a high degree of multicollinearity among these measures. There is also a relatively high correlation between the individual metrics and the measure of errors (Error). If a regression model were to be formed that incorporated the software metrics as independent variables and error as a dependent variable, it is clear that there might be several ambiguous but plausible models which might result. To show the underlying structure of the variation in these data, they were factor analyzed with error as a variable in the analysis. The results of the analysis are shown in Table IV.

In this analysis, three factors clearly emerge. After factor rotation, the resulting factor pattern is as shown in Table IV. In keeping with our earlier work in this area, we are able to identify these factors. Factor 1 from this table has associated with it those metrics from a **Modularity** or **Control** dimension. Factor 2 consist of metrics apparently from a **System** or **Structure** dimension. This dimension also includes the Error variable. Finally, there is a **Volume** dimension which is represented here by the LOC metric. From this preliminary analysis, we would conclude that the variability in the Error measure is closely related to the variability in the MMC metric and the HNP metric. The relatively large factor loading (0.57) of Error on the **Volume** dimension would also indicate some relationship to that dimension as well.

To return to the problem of the multicollinearity among the complexity metrics, these metrics were subsequently factor analyzed without the Error variable. These results are presented in Table V. The intent of this analysis is to reduce the dimensionality of the metrics space represented by the set of complexity metrics studied to a small number of orthogonal dimensions. In Table V, the same factor structure emerges as was shown in Table IV. With the error variance component now not present, there is some realignment which has occurred in Table V. That is, the McCabe metric, V(G), has now realigned with the **Structure** dimension. This, again, is not surprising due to the relatively high factor loading this metric had in Table IV (0.57). From the factor structure presented in Table V, factor scores were computed for each observation vector which represent the individual mappings of each of the metrics values for each of the subprograms onto this new orthogonal set of three new metric dimensions, thus eliminating subsequent problems of multicollinearity in subsequent regression modeling.

B. The Regression Models for Harrison Data

Our objective, now, is to explore the potential use of the new factor dimensions for their predictive value in terms of errors. To this end, a stepwise regression was run with these new factors as independent variables and error as a dependent variable. For the sake of comparison,

TABLE IV
Rotated Factor Pattern with Error Component

	FACTOR1 MOD/ CONTROL	FACTOR2 SYS/ STRUCTURE	FACTOR3 VOLUME
HNK	**0.8649**	0.2757	0.3752
PRC	**0.8517**	0.3758	0.2575
E	**0.8299**	0.3396	0.4223
V(G)	**0.7585**	0.5725	0.2777
MMC	0.5453	**0.7947**	0.1985
Error	0.2146	**0.7636**	0.5673
HNP	0.6504	**0.6781**	0.2573
LOC	0.4646	0.3124	**0.8097**

TABLE V
Rotated Factor Pattern

	FACTOR1 MOD/ CONTROL	FACTOR2 SYS/ STRUCTURE	FACTOR3 VOLUME
PRC	**0.8036**	0.4901	0.2645
HNK	**0.8020**	0.4057	0.4005
E	**0.7643**	0.4509	0.4463
MMC	0.3849	**0.8610**	0.2692
HNP	0.4469	**0.8012**	0.3679
V(G)	0.5971	**0.7051**	0.3612
LOC	0.3726	0.3397	**0.8616**

TABLE VI
Model Anova

Model	Source	D.F.	SS	M.S.	F
1	Regression	2	1884.8257	942.4129	19.1890
	Error	17	834.9243	49.1132	
	Corrected Total	19	2719.7500		
2	Regression	2	2055.9061	1027.9531	26.3240
	Error	17	663.8439	39.0496	
	Corrected Total	19	2719.7500		
3	Regression	1	5273.8033	5273.8033	81.651
	Error	19	1227.1967	64.5893	
	Uncorrected Total	20	6501.0000		
4	Regression	1	5335.2065	5335.2065	86.953
	Error	19	1165.7935	61.3576	
	Uncorrected Total	20	6501.0000		

three other regression models were developed for these same data. The regression analysis of variance for the four models is presented in Table VI.

The first regression model, labeled Model 1 in Table VI, involved the stepwise regression of the three factors produced by the factor analysis of the complexity metrics against the error variable. The second regression study involved the exhaustive use of the complexity metrics, first in all possible regressions, next in stepwise regression, and finally in backward elimination. In all cases, the selection criterion employed throughout this study was that the incoming (or outgoing) variable must contribute significantly ($p < 0.05$) to the regression analysis of variance F statistics. This statistic is, of course, the ratio of the regression mean square ($MS = SS/\text{d.f.}$) to the mean square error term. The best model from this analysis is labeled Model 2 in Table VI. The regression model labeled Model 3 in Table VI is based on Gaffney's model as follows: $y = a + b * (LOC)^{4/3}$, where the coefficients a and b represent the slope and intercept, respectively, and y is the dependent variable (Error).

The close relationship between LOC and errors has been studied for some time. The exponential form by Gaffney did seem to suggest that a nonlinear regression model might also hold some promise. Hence, a nonlinear model also based on LOC was studied. This nonlinear model is presented as Model 4 in Table VI. This model may be summarized as follows: $y = b_0 + b_1(LOC)^{b_2}$, where b_0, b_1 and b_2 are determined empirically.

There are now four basic models which all are seen to predict errors in programs. The problem now is to identify which of the four models is best. To this end, we will look at the predictive quality of each model. The associated statistics for this model predictive quality are presented in Table VII. Here it can be seen that based on the usual statistic of R^2 (or Adj R^2 for that matter) that Table VII is, in fact, already ordered by the quality of the fit of the models for Models 1 (which is the smallest value of R^2) to 4 (which has the largest value of R^2). If, on the other hand, we examine the predictive quality based on the PRESS statistic, the two models which emerge as clearly superior in regards to residual variation are Models 1 and 2. For the values present here, these models are essentially identical in that aspect.

The use of the C_p statistic permits further resolution into the model selection process. A reasonable value for C_p to take would be p, where p represents the number of parameters to be estimated by the model. Without further knowledge of the underlying regression model, the values of C_p for Models 1 and 2 may not be interpreted directly. These final models are shown in Table VIII. Here we see that these models have the same number of independent variables, in which case the values of C_p are directly comparable. In which case, the factor regression model (Model 1) is in fact the best regression model overall. Because there is only one independent variable in the regression models which employed only LOC as a predictor, computation of C_p for these models was not possible. For Table VIII, the term "estimate" is the regression coefficient, and the standard error is a measure of the variance of this estimate.

In all fairness, it must be stated that there was a regression model in the set of all possible regressions that did seem to have better overall predictive quality with the metrics LOC, MMC, and HNK in the regression equation ($R^2 = 0.80$, $C_p = 3.85$). However, in the stepwise regression procedure, it was clearly established that HNK would not contribute significantly to a model already containing LOC and MMC (Model 2). We may assume, then, that it was a spurious attribute of the sample data which made this model seem attractive: a latent danger always inherent in the use of all possible regressions.

TABLE VII
MODEL PREDICTIVE QUALITY

Model	PRESS	R^2	Adj R^2	C_p
1	1084.99	0.6930	0.6569	4.6277
2	1073.71	0.7559	0.7272	5.6028
3	1489.42	0.8112	0.8013	--
4	1362.04	0.8207	0.8112	--

TABLE VIII
MODEL DESCRIPTION

Model	Parameter	Estimate	Std Error
1	Intercept	13.7500	1.5671
	F2	7.7282	1.6078
	F3	6.2831	1.6078
2	Intercept	13.7500	1.3973
	LOC	4.5297	1.9319
	MMC	6.8078	1.9319
3	LOC1	0.0005	0.0001
4	LOC2	0.0165	0.0018

The direct interpretation of the results in Table VIII will now be pursued. The final regression model for Model 1 consists of Factors 2 and 3. From Table V, it can be seen that Factor 2 is a complexity dimension closely associated with the MMC, HNP, and $V(G)$ metrics. Factor 3 is directly related to LOC. The ultimate importance of Model 1 is that it incorporates those metrics associated with structure and also LOC. Also, LOC, in and of itself, is not necessarily a sufficient metric for the prediction of errors. Model 2 incorporates LOC and MCC. From a factor analytic standpoint, there is a component of variance also shared by MMC and HNP not represented adequately in this model.

For Model 3, the intercept term was not significant. The basic regression model consisted only of the slope for the term $(LOC)^{4/3}$. In Model 4, also, the intercept was not significant. What is important about Model 4 is the empirically derived value for the exponent b_2 in the model. The value of b_2, as derived from the nonlinear regression model, was 0.8969, a value less than 1 as opposed to Gaffney's value of 1.333. Furthermore, on comparison of the two Models 3 and 4 using the chosen measures of predictive quality, Model 4 performs rather better than Model 3.

C. The Akiyama Data

Akiyama's classic study [1], often referred to in the literature, will provide the basis for further analysis of our regression procedure. In this study, Akiyama sought to relate program errors (B, for bugs) to the decisions (D) and calls or jumps (J) as opposed to number of program statements (PS) in an assembly language programming environment. A matrix of correlation coefficients was prepared and is shown in Table IX. As is typical of complexity data, there is a high degree of correlation between

TABLE IX
CORRELATION COEFFICIENTS FOR AKIYAMA DATA

	PS	D	J	B
PS	1.0000			
D	0.8540	1.0000		
J	0.8530	0.8856	1.0000	
B	0.8961	0.9594	0.9445	1.0000

all of the variables which, in turn, is an indication of a high degree of multicollinearity.

When the data of Table IX were factor analyzed, only one factor dimension emerged. Necessarily, the underlying principal components analysis will produce a mapping of the four variable dimensions onto a new orthogonal space also with four dimensions. However, the relevant first dimension also accounts for over 95% of the total variance, the rest being distributed rather evenly over the remaining three dimensions. These three remaining dimensions may be regarded as systematic error or noise components. The results of the factor analysis are presented in Table X. The tally errors (B) have been included to show their relationship with the other three variables.

D. The Akiyama Regression Analysis

As was done with the Harrison data, the Akiyama complexity data were factor analyzed in an analysis containing just the complexity data, sans error variable. Factor scores were then produced which represented a mapping of all three complexity metrics onto a common dimension with the individual error components removed. Our hypothesis was that this new complexity measure by itself would serve as a better predictor than a linear compound of the original three variables, or perhaps a nonlinear measure of any of the single variables.

In a very similar fashion to the first study, four regression models were now developed and evaluated. The first regression model, Model 1, consisted of our single independent variable of the factor scores from the factor analysis. For comparison purposes, Model 2 consisted of a single variable $(C = D + J)$ which represented a linear combination of decision and calls, which Akiyama used in his regression model. Model 3 was Gaffney's model where the independent variable was $(PS)^{4/3}$. Model 4 of this analysis was selected as the best regression model of all possible regression models, stepwise selection, and backward elimination ($p < 0.05$). The regression analysis of variance for each of these models is presented in Table XI.

As before, several statistics representing predictive quality were computed for each model. These are given in Table XII. The results of these models are essentially indistinguishable on the basis of R^2 and the Adj R^2. The PRESS statistic, however, does show some rather dramatic differences in the performance of the various models. In this case, Model 1 is apparently the best overall model. This is not surprising in that the single inde-

TABLE X
FACTOR PATTERN WITH ERROR COMPONENT

	FACTOR1
B	0.9867
D	0.9603
J	0.9588
PS	0.9367

TABLE XII
MODEL PREDICTIVE QUALITY

Model	PRESS	R^2	Adj R^2
1	1280.37	0.9512	0.9442
2	1295.56	0.9505	0.9434
3	3539.10	0.9428	0.9357
4	1663.40	0.9512	0.9349

TABLE XI
MODEL ANOVA

Model	Source	D.F.	SS	M.S.	F
1	Regression	1	14421.5401	14421.5401	136.3350
	Error	7	740.4599	105.7800	
	Corrected Total	8	15162.0000		
2	Regression	1	14411.5585	14411.5585	134.429
	Error	7	750.4415	107.2059	
	Corrected Total	8	15162.0000		
3	Regression	1	45525.9778	45525.9778	131.958
	Error	8	2760.0222	345.0028	
	Uncorrected Total	9	48286.0000		
4	Regression	2	14421.8069	7210.9035	58.452
	Error	6	740.1931	123.3655	
	Corrected Total	8	15162.0000		

TABLE XIII
MODEL DESCRIPTION

Model	Parameter	Estimate	Std Error
1	Intercept	60.6666	3.4283
	F1	42.4578	3.6363
2	Intercept	-17.5031	7.5741
	C	0.1712	0.0148
3	PS1	0.0014	0.0001
4	Intercept	-16.8505	8.4345
	D	0.1552	0.05764
	J	0.1932	0.0779

pendent variable represented in Model 1 consists of a mapping of PS, D, and J onto a single dimension with an error component removed. It was not possible for this analysis to compute values of C_p for Models 1, 2, and 3 in that only a single independent variable was used in each case.

The final regression models are presented in Table XIII. Models 1, 2, and 3 consisted only of a single variable. For Model 1, the variable F1 in Table XIII represents the factor score for that regression model. Variable C for Model 2 is the sum of D and J. In Model 3, the variable labeled PS1 represents the term $(PS)^{4/3}$. From the set of all possible regressions, a model was chosen that had a linear compound of D and J in it. This, of course, is consistent with the earlier observations of Akiyama and his choice of C as a predictor.

V. SUMMARY

Fault introduction and error detection are stochastic processes which are dependent on different activities during the life cycle of telecommunication system software products. Furthermore, both environment characteristics and the characteristics of the construction, testing, and maintenance routines are company dependent. In software reliability studies, it is not sufficient to consider only the stages after the testing phase. The faults revealed during the field operation are very much related to software specification, development strategy, planning, design, manufacturing, and testing. The influence of human factors and complexity during these stages also contributes to the mean time to failure after testing has been completed. The major factor emerging from the above considerations is the overall complexity of the software.

The specific focus of this study has been to investigate some aspects of the relationship between program complexity measures and program errors which occur during development. The specific statistical vehicle chosen to measure this relationship was regression analysis. Within the framework of regression analysis, we have examined two separate means of exploring the connection between complexity and errors. First, the regression models were formed from the raw complexity metrics. Essentially, these models confirmed a known relationship between program lines of code and program errors. The second methodology involved the regression of complexity factor measures and measures of errors. These complexity factors were orthogonal measures of complexity from an underlying complexity domain model. From this more global perspective, we believe there is a relationship between program errors and complexity domains of program structure and size (volume). Further, the strength of this relationship suggests that predictive models are indeed possible for the determination of program errors from these orthogonal complexity domains.

The basic technique we have developed in this study relates to some major problems we have observed in the effort to develop reliable and meaningful predictors for program modules in terms of the number of errors that these modules might contain. Software complexity metrics certainly would be useful in this regard in that they are numerical measures which may be obtained prior to the test and validation of a program. As has been shown, these metrics are quite interrelated. They are also, for the most part, highly correlated with measures of program errors. This high correlation by itself is an unreliable indicator of the predictive quality of models used in the study of software development errors. In fact, the large correlations are certainly indicators of multicollinearity which can only confound attempts at developing predictive models.

27

Through the judicious use of factor analysis, predictors may be mapped onto orthogonal dimensions. Our experience in this area indicates that there are relatively few such complexity dimensions in the existing set of complexity metrics. Measures developed from the reduced complexity metric space may then be used to develop predictive models of error of relatively great predictive quality.

The subject of predictive quality and appropriateness of the models has also failed to receive the attention that it deserves in many reliability models we have studied. In general, there are many statistics which aid in the determination of the predictive quality of regression models. We have examined several in this paper. Typically, research in this area is driven only based on the R^2 measure of predictive quality. As we have seen, this statistic can only increase as new predictors are incorporated in a regression model whether or not they contribute to the overall predictive capability of the model. The PRESS statistic, on the other hand, does provide a good measure of predictive quality.

ACKNOWLEDGMENT

The authors would like to express their sincere thanks to W. Harrison for providing the data set which was used in this study, and to the referees whose comments have helped greatly in improving the presentation and clarity of the paper.

REFERENCES

[1] F. Akiyama, "An example of software system debugging," in *Inform. Processing, Proc. IFIP Congr.*, Aug. 1972, pp. 353-359.
[2] A. Endres, "An analysis of errors and their causes in system programs," in *Proc. 1975 Int. Conf. Rel. Software*, Apr. 1975, pp. 327-336.
[3] J. E. Gaffney, Jr., "Estimating the number of faults in code," *IEEE Trans. Software Eng.*, vol. SE-10, pp. 459-464, July 1984.
[4] N. Hall and S. Preiser, "Combined network complexity measures," *IBM J. Res. Develop.*, pp. 15-27, Jan. 1984.
[5] M. H. Halstead, *Elements of Software Science*. New York: Elsevier, 1977.
[6] H. H. Harman, *Modern Factor Analysis*, 2nd ed. Chicago, IL: University of Chicago Press, 1967.
[7] W. Harrison, "A micro/macro measure of software complexity," *J. Syst. Software*, vol. 7, pp. 216-219, 1987.
[8] S. Henry and D. Kafura, "Software structure metrics based on information flow," *IEEE Trans. Software Eng.*, vol. SE-7, pp. 510-518, Sept. 1981.
[9] B. Lennselius, "Software complexity and its impact on software handling processes," in *Proc. 6th Int. Conf. Software Eng. Telecommun. Switching Syst.*, Apr. 1986, pp. 148-153.
[10] M. Lipow, "Number of faults per line of code," *IEEE Trans. Software Eng.*, vol. SE-8, pp. 437-439, July 1982.
[11] T. McCabe, "A complexity measure," *IEEE Trans. Software Eng.*, vol. SE-2, pp. 308-320, Dec. 1976.
[12] J. McCall, W. Randall, S. Fenwick, C. Bowen, P. Yates, and N. McKelvey, "Methodology for software prediction and assessment," vol. 1 (of two), RACD-TR-87-171, Rome Air Development Center, Griffiss Air Force Base, NY, 1987.
[13] J. C. Munson and T. M. Khoshgoftaar, "The dimensionality of program complexity," in *Proc. 11th Annu. Int. Conf. Software Eng.*, May 1989, pp. 245-253.
[14] R. H. Myers, *Classical and Modern Regression with Applications*. Boston, MA: Duxbury, 1986.
[15] V. Y. Shen, T. Yu, S. M. Thebaut, and L. R. Paulsen, "Identifying error-prone software—An empirical study," *IEEE Trans. Software Eng.*, vol. SE-11, pp. 317-323, Apr. 1985.
[16] M. L. Shooman and M. I. Bolsky, "Types, distribution, and test and correction times for programming errors," in *Proc. 1975 Int. Conf. Rel. Software*, Apr. 1975, pp. 347-362.
[17] W. L. Wagoner, "The final report on a software reliability measurement study," Aerospace Corp., Rep. TOR-0074(4112)-1, Aug. 1973.

The Infeasibility of Quantifying the Reliability of Life-Critical Real-Time Software

Ricky W. Butler and George B. Finelli

Abstract— This paper affirms that the quantification of life-critical software reliability is infeasible using statistical methods, whether these methods are applied to standard software or fault-tolerant software. The classical methods of estimating reliability are shown to lead to exorbitant amounts of testing when applied to life-critical software. Reliability growth models are examined and also shown to be incapable of overcoming the need for excessive amounts of testing. The key assumption of software fault tolerance—separately programmed versions fail independently—is shown to be problematic. This assumption cannot be justified by experimentation in the ultrareliability region, and subjective arguments in its favor are not sufficiently strong to justify it as an axiom. Also, the implications of the recent multiversion software experiments support this affirmation.

Index Terms— Design error, life-critical, software fault tolerance, software reliability, ultrareliability, validation.

I. INTRODUCTION

THE potential of enhanced flexibility and functionality has led to an ever-increasing use of digital computer systems in control applications. At first, the digital systems were designed to perform the same functions as their analog counterparts. However, the availability of enormous computing power at a low cost has led to expanded use of digital computers in current applications and their introduction into many new applications. Thus, larger and more complex systems are being designed. The result has been, as promised, increased performance at a minimal hardware cost; however, it has also resulted in software systems which contain more errors. Sometimes, the impact of a software bug is nothing more than an inconvenience. At other times a software bug leads to costly downtime. But what will be the impact of design flaws in software systems used in life-critical applications such as industrial-plant control, aircraft control, nuclear-reactor control, or nuclear-warhead arming? What will be the price of software failure as digital computers are applied more and more frequently to these and other life-critical functions? Already, the symptoms of using insufficiently reliable software for life-critical applications are appearing [1]–[3].

For many years, much research has focused on the quantification of software reliability. Research efforts started with reliability growth models in the early 1970's. In recent years, an emphasis on developing methods that enable reliability quantification of software used for life-critical functions has emerged. The common approach offered is the combination of software fault-tolerance and statistical models.

In this paper, we investigate the software reliability problem from two perspectives. We first explore the problems that arise when you test software as a black box, i.e., subject it to inputs and check the outputs without examining the internal structure. Then, we examine the problems that arise when software is not treated as a black box, i.e., some internal structure is modeled. In either case, we argue that the associated problems are intractable—i.e., they inevitably lead to a need for testing beyond what is practical.

II. SOFTWARE RELIABILITY

For life-critical applications, the validation process must establish that system reliability is extremely high. Historically, this ultrahigh reliability requirement has been translated into a probability of failure on the order of 10^{-7} to 10^{-9} for 1- to 10-h missions. Unfortunately, such probabilities create enormous problems for validation. For convenience, we will use the following terminology:

name	failure rate (per hour)
ultrareliability	$< 10^{-7}$
moderate reliability	10^{-3} to 10^{-7}
low reliability	$> 10^{-3}$

Software does not physically fail as hardware does. Physical failures (as opposed to hardware design flaws) occur when hardware wears out, breaks, or is adversely affected by environmental phenomena such as electromagnetic fields or alpha particles. Software is not subject to these problems. Software faults are present at the beginning of and throughout a system's lifetime. To such an extent, software reliability is meaningless—software is either correct or incorrect with respect to its specification. Nevertheless, software systems are embedded in stochastic environments. These environments subject the software program to a sequence of inputs over time. For each input, the program produces either a correct or an incorrect answer. Thus, in a systems context, the software system produces errors in a stochastic manner; the sequence of errors behaves like a stochastic point process.

In this paper, the inherent difficulty of accurately modeling software reliability is explored. To facilitate the discussion, we will construct a simple model of the software failure process. The driver of the failure process is the external system that supplies inputs to the program. As a function of its inputs and

Manuscript received August 1, 1992. Recommended by N. Leveson and P. G. Neumann.

The authors are with NASA Langley Research Center, Hampton, VA 23665-5225.

IEEE Log Number 9205023.

Reprinted from *IEEE Trans. Software Eng.*, Vol. 19, No. 1, Jan. 1993, pp. 3–12.

internal state, the program produces an output. If the software were perfect, the internal state would be correct and the outputs produced would be correct. However, if there is a design flaw in the program, it can manifest itself either by production of an erroneous output or by corruption of the internal state (which may affect subsequent outputs).

In a real-time system, the software is periodically scheduled, i.e., the same program is repeatedly executed in response to inputs. It is not unusual to find "iteration rates" of 10–100 cycles per second. If the probability of software failure per input is constant, say p, we have a binomial process. The number of failures S_n after n inputs is given by the binomial distribution:

$$P(S_n = k) = \binom{n}{k} p^k (1-p)^{n-k}.$$

We wish to compute the probability of system failure for n inputs. System failure occurs for all $S_n > 0$. Thus,

$$P_{sys}(n) = P(S_n > 0) = 1 - P(S_n = 0) = 1 - (1-p)^n.$$

This can be converted to a function of time with the transformation $n = Kt$ where K is the number of inputs per unit time. The system failure probability at time t, $P_{sys}(t)$, is thus:

$$P_{sys}(t) = 1 - (1-p)^{Kt}. \qquad (1)$$

Of course, this calculation assumes that the probability of failure per input is constant over time.[1]

This binomial process can be accurately approximated by an exponential distribution since p is small and n is large:

$$P_{sys}(t) = 1 - e^{-Ktp}. \qquad (2)$$

This is easily derived using the Poisson approximation to the binomial. The discrete binomial process can thus be accurately modeled by a continuous exponential process. In the following discussion, we will frequently use the exponential process rather than the binomial process to simplify the discussion.

III. ANALYZING SOFTWARE AS A BLACK BOX

The traditional method of validating reliability is life testing. In life testing, a set of test specimens are operated under actual operating conditions for a predetermined amount of time. Over this period, failure times are recorded and subsequently used in reliability computation. The internal structure of the test specimens is not examined. The only observable is whether a specimen has failed or not.

For systems that are designed to attain a probability of failure on the order of 10^{-7} to 10^{-9} for 1-h missions or longer, life testing is prohibitively impractical. This can be shown by an illustrative example. For simplicity, we assume that the time

---

[1] If the probability of failure per input were not constant, then the reliability analysis problem is even harder. One would have to estimate $p(t)$ rather than just p. A time-variant system would require even more testing than a time-invariant one, since the rate must be determined as a function of mission time. The system would have to be placed in a random state corresponding to a specific mission time and subjected to random inputs. This would have to be done for each time point of interest within the mission time. Thus, if the reliability analysis is intractable for systems with constant p, it is unrealistic to expect it to be tractable for systems with nonconstant $p(t)$.

TABLE I
EXPECTED TEST DURATION FOR $r = 1$

No. of Replicates (n)	Expected Test Duration D_t
1	10^{10} h = 1 141 550 yr
10	10^9 h = 114 155 yr
100	10^8 h = 11 415 yr
10 000	10^6 h = 114 yr

to failure distribution is exponential.[2] Using standard statistical methods [4], the time on test can be estimated for a specified system reliability. There are two basic approaches: 1) testing with replacement and 2) testing without replacement. In either case, one places n items on test. The test is finished when r failures have been observed. In the first case, when a device fails a new device is put on test in its place. In the second case, a failed device is not replaced. The tester chooses values of n and r to obtain the desired levels of the α and β errors (i.e., the probability of rejecting a good system and the probability of accepting a bad system respectively). In general, the larger r and n are, the smaller the statistical estimation errors are. The expected time on test can be calculated as a function of r and n. The expected time on test, D_t, for the replacement case is

$$D_t = \mu_o \frac{r}{n} \qquad (3)$$

where μ_o is the mean failure time of the test specimen [4]. The expected time on test for the nonreplacement case is:

$$D_t = \mu_o \sum_{j=1}^{r} \frac{1}{n-j+1}. \qquad (4)$$

Even without specifying an α or β error, a good indication of the testing time can be determined. Clearly, the number of observed failures r must be greater than 0 and the total number of test specimens n must be greater than or equal to r. For example, suppose the system has a probability of failure of 10^{-9} for a 10-h mission. Then the mean time to failure of the system (assuming exponentially distributed) μ_o is:

$$\mu_o = \frac{10}{-ln[1 - 10^{-9}]} \approx 10^{10}.$$

Table I shows the expected test duration for this system as a function of the number of test replicates n for $r = 1$.[3]

Note that a value of r equal to 1 produces the shortest test time possible, but at the price of extremely large α and β errors. To get satisfactory statistical significance, larger values of r are needed and, consequently, even more testing. Therefore, given that the economics of testing fault-tolerant systems (which are very expensive) rarely allow n to be greater than 10, life testing is clearly out of the question for ultrareliable systems. The technique of statistical life testing is discussed in more detail in the Appendix.

---

[2] In Section II, the exponential process was shown to be an accurate approximation to the discrete binomial software failure process.

[3] The expected time with or without replacement is almost the same in this case.

IV. RELIABILITY GROWTH MODELS

The software design process involves a repetitive cycle of testing and repairing a program. A program is subjected to inputs until it fails. The cause of failure is determined; the program is repaired and is then subjected to a new sequence of inputs. The result is a sequence of programs $p_1, p_2, \ldots, p_n$ and a sequence of interfailure times $T_1, T_2, \ldots, T_n$ (usually measured in number of inputs). The goal is to construct a mathematical technique (i.e., model) to predict the reliability of the final program p_n based on the observed interfailure data. Such a model enables one to estimate the probability of failure of the final "corrected" program without subjecting it to a sequence of inputs. This process is a form of prediction or extrapolation and has been studied in detail [5]–[7]. These models are called "reliability growth models." If one resists the temptation to correct the program based on the last failure, the method is equivalent to black-box testing the final version. If one corrects the final version and estimates the reliability of the corrected version based on a reliability growth model, one hopefully has increased the efficiency of the testing process in doing so. How much efficiency is gained by use of a reliability growth model and is it enough to get us into the ultrareliable region? Unfortunately, the answer is that the gain in efficiency is not anywhere near enough to get us into the ultrareliable region. This has been pointed out by several authors. Keiller and Miller [8] write:

> The reliability growth scenario would start with faulty software. Through execution of the software, bugs are discovered. The software is then modified to correct for the design flaws represented by the bugs. Gradually the software evolves into a state of higher reliability. There are at least two general reasons why this is an unreasonable approach to highly-reliable safety-critical software. The time required for reliability to grow to acceptable levels will tend to be extremely long. Extremely high levels of reliability cannot be guaranteed a priori.

Littlewood [9] writes:

> Clearly, the reliability growth techniques of §2 [a survey of the leading reliability growth models] are useless in the face of such ultrahigh reliability requirements. It is easy to see that, even in the unlikely event that the system had achieved such a reliability, we could not assure ourselves of that achievement in an acceptable time.

The problem alluded to by these authors can be seen clearly by applying a reliability growth model to experimental data. The data of Table II were taken from an experiment performed by Nagel and Skrivan [10]. The data were obtained for program A1, one of six programs investigated. The versions represent the successive stages of the program as bugs were removed. A log-linear growth model was postulated and found to fit all six programs analyzed in the report. A simple regression on the data of Table II yields a slope and y intercept of -1.415 and 0.2358, respectively. The line is fitted to the log of the raw data as shown in Fig. 1. The correlation coefficient is -0.913.

It is important to note that, in the context of reliability growth models, the failure rates are usually reported as failure rates per *input*, whereas the system requirements are given as failure rates per hour or as a probability of failure for a specified mission duration (e.g., 10). However, (2) can be

TABLE II
NAGEL DATA FROM PROGRAM A1

Number of Bugs Removed	Failure Probability per Input
1	0.9803
2	0.1068
3	0.002602
4	0.002104
5	0.001176
6	0.0007659

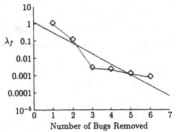

Fig. 1. Loglinear fit to program A1 failure data.

rearranged into a form that can be used to convert the system requirements into a required failure rate per input.

$$p = \frac{-\ln(1 - P_{sys})}{Kt} \quad (5)$$

If the system requirement is a probability of failure of 10^{-9} for a 10-h mission and the sample rate of the system (i.e., K) is $10/s$, then the required failure rate per input p can be calculated as follows:

$$p = \frac{-\ln(1 - P_{sys})}{Kt}$$

$$= \frac{-\ln(1 - 10^{-9})}{(10/s)(3600 \text{ s/h})(10 \text{ h})}$$

$$= 2.78 \times 10^{-15}.$$

The purpose of a reliability growth model is to estimate the failure rate of a program after the removal of the last discovered bug. The loglinear growth model plotted in Fig. 1 can be used to predict that the arrival rate of the next bug will be 6.34×10^{-5}. The key question, of course, is how long will it take before enough bugs are removed so that the reliability growth model will predict a failure rate per input of 2.78×10^{-15} or less. Using the loglinear model we can find the place where the probability drops below 2.78×10^{-15} as illustrated in Fig. 2.

Based on the model, the twenty-fourth bug will arrive at a rate of 2.28×10^{-15}, which is less than the goal. Thus, according to the loglinear growth model, 23 bugs will have to removed before the model will yield an acceptable failure rate. But how long will it take to remove these 23 bugs? The growth model predicts that bug 23 will have a failure rate of about 9.38×10^{-15}. The expected number of test cases

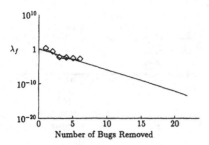

Fig. 2 Extrapolation to predict when ultrareliability will be reached.

TABLE III
TEST TIME TO REMOVE THE LAST BUG TO OBTAIN ULTRARELIABILITY

Program	Slope	y Intercept	Last Bug	Test Time (yr)
A1	−1.415	0.2358	23	3.4×10^5
B1	−1.3358	1.1049	25	3.3×10^5
A2	−1.998	2.4572	17	1.5×10^5
B2	−3.623	2.3296	9	4.5×10^4
A3	−0.54526	−1.3735	58	6.8×10^5
B3	−1.3138	0.0912	25	5.3×10^5

until observing a binomial event of probability 9.38×10^{-15} is 1.07×10^{14}. If the test time is the same as the real time execution time, then each test case would require 0.10 s. Thus, the expected time to discover bug 23 alone would be 1.07×10^{13} s or 3.4×10^5 yr. In Table III, the above calculations are given for all of the programs in [10].[4]

These examples illustrate why the use of a reliability growth model does not alleviate the testing problem even if one assumes that the model applies universally to the ultrareliable region.

A. Low Sample Rate Systems and Accelerated Testing

In this section, the feasibility of quantifying low-sample rate systems (i.e., systems where the time between inputs is long) in the ultrareliable region will be briefly explored. Also, the potential of accelerated testing will be discussed.

Suppose that the testing rate is faster than real time and let R is the test time per input. Since each test is an independent trial, the time to the appearance of the next bug is given by the geometric distribution. Thus, the expected number of inputs until the next bug appears is $1/p$ and the expected test time, D_t, is given by:

$$D_t = R/p.$$

Using (5), D_t becomes:

$$D_t = \frac{RKt}{-\ln(1 - P_{sys})} \approx \frac{RKt}{P_{sys}}. \qquad (6)$$

From (6) it can be seen that a low sample rate system (i.e., a system with small K) requires less test time than a high sample rate system (assuming that R remains constant). Suppose that

[4] Table V assumes a perfect fit with the log-linear model in the ultrareliable region.

TABLE IV
EXPECTED TEST TIME AS A FUNCTION OF K FOR $R = 0.1$ s

K	Expected Test Time, D_t
10/s	$1/14 \times 10^6$ yr
1/s	1.14×10^5 yr
1/min	1.9×10^3 yr
1/h	31.7 yr
1/day	1.32 yr
1/month	16 days

the system requirement is a probability of failure of 10^{-9} for a 10-h mission (i.e., $P_{sys} = 10^{-9}, t = 10$). If the system has a fast sample rate (e.g., $K = 10$ inputs/s) and the time required to test an input is the same as the real-time execution time (i.e., $R = 0.10$ s), then the expected test time is 10^{10} h $= 1.14 \times 10^6$ yr. Now suppose that R remains constant but K is reduced. (Note that this usually implies an accelerated testing process. The execution time per input is usually greater for slow systems than fast systems. Since R is not increased as K is decreased, the net result is equivalent to an accelerated test process.) The impact of decreasing K while holding R constant can be seen in Table IV, which reports the expected test time as a function of K.

Thus, theoretically, a very slow system that can be tested very quickly (i.e., much faster than real time) can be quantified in the ultrareliable region. However, this is not as promising as it may look at first. The value of K is fixed for a given system and the experimenter has no control over it. For example, the sample rate for a digital flight control system is on the order of 10 inputs per second or faster and little can be done to slow it down. Thus, the above theoretical result does nothing to alleviate the testing problem here. Furthermore, real-time systems typically are developed to exploit the full capability of a computing system. Consequently, although a slower system's sample rate is less, its execution time per input is usually higher and so R is much greater than the 0.10 s used in Table IV. In fact, one would expect to see R grow in proportion to $1/K$. Thus, the results in Table IV are optimistic. Also, it should be noted that during the testing process, one must also determine whether the program's answer is correct or incorrect. Consequently, the test time per input is often much greater than the real-time execution time rather than being shorter. In conclusion, if one is fortunate enough to have a very slow system that can exploit an accelerated testing process, one can obtain ultrareliable estimates of reliability with feasible amounts of test times. However, such systems are usually not classified as real-time systems and thus, are out of the scope of this paper.

B. Reliability Growth Models and Accelerated Testing

Now let us revisit the reliability growth model in the context of a slow system that can be quickly tested. Suppose the system under test is a slow real-time system with a sample rate of 1 input per minute. Then, the failure rate per input must be less than $10^{-9}/60 = 1.67 \times 10^{-11}$ in order for the program to have

TABLE V
TEST TIME TO REMOVE THE LAST BUG TO OBTAIN ULTRARELIABILITY

Program	Slope	y Intercept	Last Bug	Test Time (yr)
A1	-1.415	0.2358	17	42
B1	-1.3358	1.1049	19	66
A2	-1.998	2.4572	13	31
B2	-3.623	2.3296	7	19
A3	-0.5452	-1.3735	42	66
B3	-1.3138	0.0912	19	32

a failure rate of 10^{-9}/h. Using the regression results, it can be seen that approximately 17 bugs must be removed:

Bug	Failure Rate per Input
16	1.87332×10^{-10}
17	4.55249×10^{-11}
18	1.10633×10^{-11}

Thus one could test until 17 bugs have been removed, remove the last bug and use the reliability growth model to predict a failure rate per input of 1.106×10^{-11}. But, how long would it take to remove the 17 bugs? Well, the removal of the last bug alone would, on average, require approximately 2.2×10^{10} test cases. Even if the testing process were 1000 times faster than the operational time per input (i.e., $R = 60/1000$ s), this would require 42 years of testing. Thus, we see why Littlewood and Keiller and Miller see little hope of using reliability growth models for ultrareliable software. This problem is not restricted to the program above but is universal. Table V repeats the above calculations for the rest of the programs in [10].

At even the most optimistic improvement rates, it is obvious that reliability growth models are impractical for ultrareliable software.

V. SOFTWARE FAULT TOLERANCE

Since fault tolerance has been successfully used to protect against hardware physical failures, it seems natural to apply the same strategy against software bugs. It is easy to construct a reliability model of a system designed to mask physical failures using redundant hardware and voting. The key assumption that enables both the design of ultrareliable systems from less reliable components and the estimation of 10^{-9} probabilities of failure is that the separate redundant components fail independently or nearly so. The independence assumption has been used in hardware fault tolerance modeling for many years. If the redundant components are located in separate chassis, powered by separate power supplies, electrically isolated from each other and sufficiently shielded from the environment it is not unreasonable to assume failure independence of physical hardware faults.

The basic strategy of the software fault-tolerance approach is to design several versions of a program from the same specification and to employ a voter of some kind to pro-

tect the system from bugs. The voter can be an acceptance test (i.e., recovery blocks) or a comparator (i.e., N-version programming). Each version is programmed by a separate programming team.[5] Since the versions are developed by separate programming teams, it is hoped that the redundant programs will fail independently or nearly so [11], [12]. From the version reliability estimates and the independence assumption, system reliability estimates could be calculated. However, unlike hardware physical failures which are governed by the laws of physics, programming errors are the products of human reasoning (i.e., actually improper reasoning). The question thus becomes one of the reasonableness of assuming independence based on little or no practical or theoretical foundations. Subjective arguments have been offered on both sides of this question. Unfortunately, the subjective arguments for multiple versions being independent are not compelling enough to qualify it as an axiom. The reasons why experimental justification of independence is infeasible and why ultrareliable quantification is infeasible despite software fault tolerance are discussed in the next section.

A. Models of Software Fault Tolerance

Many reliability models of fault-tolerant software have been developed based on the independence assumption. To accept such a model, this assumption must be accepted. In this section, it will be shown how the independence assumption enables quantification in the ultrareliable region, why quantification of fault-tolerant software reliability is unlikely without the independence assumption, and why this assumption cannot be experimentally justified for the ultrareliable region.

1) Independence Enables Quantification of Ultrareliability: The following example shows how independence enables ultrareliability quantification. Suppose three different versions of a program control a life-critical system using some software fault tolerance scheme. Let $E_{i,k}$ be the event that the ith version fails on its kth execution. Suppose the probability that version i fails during the kth execution is $p_{i,k}$. As discussed in Section II, we assume that the failure rate is constant. Since the versions are voted, the system does not fail unless there is a coincident error, i.e., two or more versions produce erroneous outputs in response to the same input. The probability that two or more versions fail on the kth execution causing system failure is:

$$P_{sys,k} = P((E_{1,k} \wedge E_{2,k}) \text{ or } (E_{1,k} \wedge E_{3,k}) \\ \text{or } (E_{2,k} \wedge E_{3,k}) \text{ or } (E_{1,k} \wedge E_{2,k} \wedge E_{3,k})). \quad (7)$$

Using the additive law of probability, this can be written as:

$$P_{sys,k} = P(E_{1,k} \wedge E_{2,k}) + P(E_{1,k} \wedge E_{3,k}) \\ + P(E_{2,k} \wedge E_{3,k}) - 2P(E_{1,k} \wedge E_{2,k} \wedge E_{3,k}). \quad (8)$$

If independence of the versions is assumed, this can be rewritten as:

$$P_{sys,k} = P(E_{1,k})P(E_{2,k}) + P(E_{1,k})P(E_{3,k}) \\ + P(E_{2,k})P(E_{3,k}) - 2P(E_{1,k})P(E_{2,k})P(E_{3,k}). \quad (9)$$

---

[5] Often these separate programming teams are called "independent programming" teams. The phrase "independent programming" does not mean the same thing as "independent manifestation of errors."

The reason why independence is usually assumed is obvious from the above formula—if each $P(E_{i,k})$ can be estimated to be approximately 10^{-6}, then the probability of system failure due to two or more coincident failures is approximately 3×10^{-12}.

Equation (9) can be used to calculate the probability of failure for a T hour mission. Suppose that $P(E_{i,k}) = p$ for all i and k. Then

$$P_{sys,k} = 3p^2 - 2p^3 \approx 3p^2$$

and the probability that the system fails during a mission of T h can be calculated using (1):

$$P_{sys}(T) = 1 - (1 - P_{sys,k})^{KT} \approx 1 - (1 - 3p^2)^{KT}$$

where K is the number of executions of the program in an hour. For small p_i the following approximation is accurate:

$$P_{sys}(T) \approx 1 - e^{(-3p^2 KT)} \approx 3p^2 KT.$$

For the following typical values of $T = 1$ and $K = 3600$ (i.e., 1 execution per second), we have

$$P_{sys}(T) \approx 3p^2 KT = 3(10^{-6})(10^{-6})(3600) = 1.08 \times 10^{-8}.$$

Thus, an ultrareliability quantification has been made. But, this depended critically on the independence assumption. If the different versions do not fail independently, then (7) must be used to compute failure probabilities and the above calculation is meaningless. In fact, the probability of failure could be anywhere from 0 to about 10^{-2} (i.e., 0 to $3pKT$[6]).

2) Ultrareliable Quantification Is Infeasible without Independence: Now consider the impact of not being able to assume independence. The following argument was adapted from Miller [13]. To simplify the notation, the last subscript will be dropped when referring to the kth execution only. Thus,

$$\begin{aligned} P_{sys} = {} & P(E_1 \wedge E_2) + P(E_1 \wedge E_3) + P(E_2 \wedge E_3) \\ & - 2P(E_1 \wedge E_2 \wedge E_3). \quad (10) \end{aligned}$$

Using the identity $P(A \wedge B) = P(A)P(B) + [P(A \wedge B) - P(A)P(B)]$, this can be rewritten as:

$$\begin{aligned} P_{sys} = {} & P(E_1)P(E_2) + P(E_1)P(E_3) + P(E_2)P(E_3) \\ & - 2P(E_1)P(E_2)P(E_3) \\ & + [P(E_2 \wedge E_1) - P(E_1)P(E_2)] \\ & + [P(E_3 \wedge E_1) - P(E_3)P(E_1)] \\ & + [P(E_3 \wedge E_2) - P(E_3)P(E_2)] \\ & - 2[P(E_1 \wedge E_2 \wedge E_3) - P(E_1)P(E_2)P(E_3)]. \end{aligned}$$
$$(11)$$

This rewrite of the formula reveals two components of the system failure probability: 1) the first line of (11) and 2) the last four lines of (11). If the multiple versions manifest errors independently, then the last four lines (i.e., the second component) will be equal to zero. Consequently, to establish independence experimentally, these terms must be shown

---

[6] $3pKT$ is a first-order approximation to the probability that the system fails whenever any one of the three versions fail.

to be 0. Realistically, to establish "adequate" independence, these terms must be shown to have negligible effect on the probability of system failure. Thus, the first component represents the "noncorrelated" contribution to P_{sys} and the second component represents the "correlated" contribution to P_{sys}. Note that the terms in the first component of P_{sys} are all products of the individual version probabilities.

If we cannot assume independence, we are back to the original equation (10). Since $P(E_1 \wedge E_2 \wedge E_3) \leq P(E_i \wedge E_j)$ for all i and j, we have

$$P(E_i \wedge Ej) \leq P_{sys} \quad \text{for all} \quad i, j.$$

Clearly, if $P_{sys} < 10^{-9}$ then $P(E_i \wedge E_j) < 10^{-9}$. In other words, in order for P_{sys} to be in the ultrareliable region, the interaction terms (i.e., $P(E_i \wedge E_j)$) must also be in the ultrareliable region. To establish that the system is ultrareliable, the validation must either demonstrate that these terms are very small or establish that P_{sys} is small by some other means (from which we could indirectly deduce that these terms are small.) Thus, we are back to the original life-testing problem again.

From the foregoing discussion, it is tempting to conclude that it is necessary to demonstrate that each of the interaction terms is very small in order to establish that P_{sys} is very small. However, this is not a legitimate argument. Although the interaction terms will always be small when P_{sys} is small, one cannot argue that the *only* way of establishing that P_{sys} is small is by showing that the interaction terms are small. However, the likelihood of establishing that P_{sys} is very small without directly establishing that all of the interaction terms are small appears to be extremely remote. This follows from the observation that without further assumptions, there is little more that can be done with (10). It seems inescapable that no matter how (10) is manipulated, the terms $P(E_i \wedge E_j)$ will enter in linearly. Unless a form can be found where these terms are eliminated altogether or appear in a nonlinear form where they become negligible (e.g., all multiplied by other parameters), the need to estimate them directly will remain. Furthermore, the information contained in these terms must appear somewhere. The dependency of P_{sys} on some formulation of interaction cannot be eliminated.

Although the possibility that a method may be discovered for the validation of software fault-tolerance remains, it is prudent to recognize where this opportunity lies. It does not lie in the realm of controlled experimentation. The only hope is that a reformulation of (10) can be discovered that enables the estimation of P_{sys} from a set of parameters that can be estimated using moderate amounts of testing. The efficacy of such a reformulation could be assessed analytically before any experimentation.

3) Danger of Extrapolation to the Ultrareliability Region: To see the danger in extrapolating from a feasible amount of testing that the different versions are independent, we consider some possible scenarios for coincident failure processes. Suppose that the probability of failure of a single version during a 1-h interval is 10^{-5}. If the versions fail independently, then the probability of a coincident error is on the order of 10^{-10}. However, suppose in actuality the arrival rate of a coincident error is 10^{-7}/h. One could test for 100 years and most likely not see a coincident error. From such experiments it would be tempting to conclude that the different versions are independent. After all, we have tested the system for 100 years and not seen even one coincident error! If we make the independence assumption, the system reliability is $(1 - 3 \times 10^{-10})$. But actually the system reliability is approximately $(1 - 10^{-7})$. Likewise, if the failure rate for a single version were 10^{-4}/h and the arrival rate of coincident errors were 10^{-5}/h, testing for 1 yr would most likely result in no coincident errors. The erroneous assumption of independence would allow the assignment of a 3×10^{-8} probability of failure to the system when in reality the system is no better than 10^{-5}.

In conclusion, if independence cannot be assumed, it seems inescapable that the intersection of the events E_1, E_2, and E_3 (i.e., $P(E_i \wedge E_j)$) must be directly measured. As shown above, these occur in the system failure formula not as products, but alone, and thus must be less than 10^{-12} per input in order for the system probability of failure to be less than 10^{-9} at 1 h. Unfortunately, testing to this level is infeasible and extrapolation from feasible amounts of testing is dangerous.

Since ultrareliability has been established as a requirement for many systems, there is great incentive to create models that enable an estimate in the ultrareliable region. Thus, there are many examples of software reliability models for operational ultrareliable systems. Given the ramifications of independence on fault-tolerant software reliability quantification, unjustifiable assumptions must not be overlooked.

B. Feasibility of a General Model for Coincident Errors

Given the limitations imposed by nonindependence, one possible approach to the ultrareliability quantification problem is to develop a general fault-tolerant software reliability model that accounts for coincident errors. Two possibilities exist:

1) The model includes terms which cannot be measured within feasible amounts of time.
2) The model includes only parameters which can be measured within feasible amounts of time.

It is possible to construct elaborate probability models that fall into the first class. Unfortunately since they depend upon unmeasurable parameters, they are useless for the quantification of ultrareliability. The second case is the only realistic approach.[7] The independence model is an example of the second case. Models belonging to the second case must explicitly or implicitly express the interaction terms in (10) as "known" functions of parameters that can be measured in feasible amounts of time:

$$P_I = f(p_1, p_2, p_3, \ldots, p_n).$$

The known function f in the independence model is the zero function, i.e., the interaction terms P_I are zero identically irrespective of any other measurable parameters.

A more general model must provide a mechanism that makes these interaction terms negligibly small in order to

produce a number in the ultrareliable region. These known functions must be applicable to all cases of multiversion software for which the model is intended. Clearly, any estimation based on such a model would be strongly dependent upon correct knowledge of these functions. But how can these functions be determined? There is little hope of deriving them from fundamental laws, since the error process occurs in the human mind. The only possibility is to derive them from experimentation, but experimentation can only derive functions appropriate for low or moderate reliability software. Therefore, the correctness of these functions in the ultrareliable region can not be established experimentally. Justifying the correctness of the known functions requires far more testing than quantifying the reliability of a single ultrareliable system. The model must be shown to be applicable to a specified sample space of multiversion programs. Thus, there must be extensive sampling from the space of multiversion programs, each of which must undergo life-testing for over 100 000 years in order to demonstrate the universal applicability of the functions. Thus, in either case, the situation appears to be hopeless—the development of a credible coincident error model which can be used to estimate system reliability within feasible amounts of time is not possible.

C. The Coincident-Error Experiments

Experiments have been performed by several researchers to investigate the coincident error process. The first and perhaps most famous experiment was performed by Knight and Leveson [14]. In this experiment, 27 versions of a program were produced and subjected to 1 000 000 input cases. The observed average failure rate per input was 0.0007. The major conclusion of the experiment was that the independence model was rejected at the 99% confidence level. The quantity of coincident errors was much greater than that predicted by the independence model. Experiments produced by other researchers have confirmed the Knight–Leveson conclusion [12], [15]. A excellent discussion of the experimental results is given in [16].

Some debate [16] has occurred over the credibility of these experiments. Rather than describe the details of this debate, we would prefer to make a few general observations about the scope and limitations of such experiments. First, the N-version *systems* used in these experiments must have reliabilities in the low to moderate reliability region. Otherwise, no data would be obtained that would be relevant to the independence question.[8] It is not sufficient (to get data) that the individual versions are in this reliability region. The coincident error rate must be observable, so the reliability of "voted" outputs must be in the low to moderate reliability region. To see this consider the following. Suppose that we have a three-version system where each replicate's failure rate is 10^{-4}/h. If they fail independently, the coincident error rate should be 3×10^{-8}/h. The versions are in the moderate reliability region, but the system is potentially (i.e., if independent) in the ultrareliable region. In order to test for independence, "coincident" errors

---

[7] The first case is included for completeness and because such models have been proposed in the past.

[8] That is, unless one was willing to carry out a "Smithsonian" experiment, i.e., one which requires centuries to complete.

must be observed. If the experiment is performed for one year and no coincident errors are observed, then one can be confident that the coincident error rate (and consequently the system failure rate) is less than 1.14×10^{-4}. If coincident errors are observed then the coincident error rate is probably even higher. If the coincident error rate is actually 10^{-7}/h, then the independence assumption is invalid, but one would have to test for over 1000 years in order to have a reasonable chance to observe them! Thus, future experiments will have one of the following results, depending on the actual reliability of the test specimens.

1) Demonstration that the independence assumption does *not* hold for the low reliability system.
2) Demonstration that the independence assumption does hold for systems for the low reliability system.
3) No coincident errors were seen, but test time was insufficient to demonstrate independence for the potentially ultrareliable system.

If the system under test is a low-reliability system, the independence assumption may be contradicted or vindicated. Either way, the results will not apply to ultrareliable systems except by way of extrapolation. If the system under test were actually ultrareliable, the third conclusion would result. Thus, experiments can reveal problems with a model such as the independence model when the inaccuracies are so severe that they manifest themselves in the low or moderate reliability region. However, software reliability experiments can only demonstrate that an interaction model is inaccurate, never that a model is accurate for ultrareliable software. Thus, negative results are possible, but never positive results.

The experiments performed by Knight and Leveson and others have been useful to alerting the world to a formerly unnoticed critical assumption. However, it is important to realize that these experiments cannot accomplish what is really needed—that is, to establish with scientific rigor that a particular design is ultrareliable or that a particular design methodology produces ultrareliable systems. This leaves us in a terrible bind. We want to use digital processors in life-critical applications, but we have no feasible way of establishing that they meet their ultrareliability requirements. We must either change the reliability requirements to a level that is in the low to moderate reliability region or give up the notion of experimental quantification. Neither option is very appealing.

VI. Conclusions

In recent years, computer systems have been introduced into life-critical situations where previously caution had precluded their use. Despite alarming incidents of disaster already occurring with increasing frequency, industry in the United States and abroad continues to expand the use of digital computers to monitor and control complex real-time physical processes and mechanical devices. The potential performance advantages of using computers over their analog predecessors have created an atmosphere where serious safety concerns about digital hardware and software are not adequately addressed. Although fault-tolerance research has discovered effective techniques to protect systems from physical component failure, practical methods to prevent design errors have not been found. Without a major change in the design and verification methods used for life-critical systems, major disasters are almost certain to occur with increasing frequency.

Since life-testing of ultrareliable software is infeasible (i.e., to quantify 10^{-8}/h failure rate requires more than 10^8 h of testing), reliability models of fault-tolerant software have been developed from which ultrareliable-system estimates can be obtained. The key assumption that enables an ultrareliability prediction for hardware failures is that the electrically isolated processors fail independently. This assumption is reasonable for hardware component failures, but not provable or testable. This assumption is not reasonable for software or hardware design flaws. Furthermore, any model that tries to include some level of nonindependent interaction between the multiple versions cannot be justified experimentally. It would take more than 10^8 h of testing to make sure there are no coincident errors in two or more versions that appear rarely but frequently enough to degrade the system reliability below $(1 - 10^{-8})$.

Some significant conclusions can be drawn from the observations of this paper. Since digital computers will inevitably be used in life-critical applications, it is necessary that "credible" methods be developed for generating reliable software. Nevertheless, what constitutes a "credible" method must be carefully reconsidered. A pervasive view is that software validation must be accomplished by probabilistic and statistical methods. The shortcomings and pitfalls of this view have been expounded in this paper. Based on intuitive merits, it is likely that software fault tolerance will be used in life-critical applications. Nevertheless, the ability of this approach to generate ultrareliable software cannot be demonstrated by research experiments. The question of whether software fault tolerance is more effective than other design methodologies such as formal verification or vice versa can only be answered for low or moderate reliability systems, not for ultrareliable applications. The choice between software fault tolerance and formal verification must necessarily be based on either extrapolation or nonexperimental reasoning.

Similarly, experiments designed to compare the accuracy of different types of software reliability models can only be accomplished in the low to moderate reliability regions. There is little reason to believe that a model that is accurate in the moderate region is accurate in the ultrareliable region. It is possible that models that are inferior to other models in the moderate region are superior in the ultrareliable region—again, this cannot be demonstrated.

Appendix

In this section, the statistics of life testing are briefly reviewed. A more detailed presentation can be found in a standard statistics textbook such as Mann–Schafer–Singpurwalla [4]. This section presents a statistical test based on the maximum likelihood ratio[9] and was produced using reference [4] extensively. The mathematical relationship between the

---

[9] The maximum likelihood ratio test is the test that provides the "best" critical region for a given α error.

number of test specimens, specimen reliability, and expected time on test is explored.

Let n be the number of test specimens, r the observed number of specimen failures, and $X_1 < X_2 < \ldots < X_r$ the ordered failure times.

A hypothesis test is constructed to test the reliability of the system against an alternative.

$$H_o : \text{Reliability} = R_0$$
$$H_1 : \text{Reliability} < R_0$$

The null hypothesis covers the case where the system is ultrareliable. The alternative covers the case where the system fails to meet the reliability requirement. The α error is the probability of rejecting the null hypothesis when it is true (i.e., producer's risk). The β error is the probability of accepting the null hypothesis when it is false (i.e., consumer's risk).

There are two basic experimental approaches: 1) testing with replacement and 2) testing without replacement. In either case, one places n items on test. The test is finished when r failures have been observed. In the first case, when a device fails a new device is put on test in its place. In the second case, a failed device is not replaced. The tester chooses values of n and r to obtain the desired levels of the α and β errors. In general, the larger r and n are, the smaller the statistical testing errors are.

It is necessary to assume some distribution for the time-to-failure of the test specimen. For simplicity, we assume that the distribution is exponential.[10] The test then can be reduced to a test on exponential means, using the transformation:

$$\mu = \frac{t}{-ln[R(t)]}.$$

The expected time on test can then be calculated as a function of r and n. The expected time on test, D_t, for the replacement case is:

$$D_t = \mu_o \frac{r}{n} \tag{12}$$

where μ_o is the mean time to failure of the test specimen. The expected time on test for the nonreplacement case is:

$$D_t = \mu_o \sum_{j=1}^{r} \frac{1}{n-j+1}. \tag{13}$$

In order to calculate the α and β errors, a specific value of the alternative mean must be selected. Thus, the hypothesis test becomes:

$$H_o : \mu = \mu_o$$
$$H_1 : \mu = \mu_a.$$

A reasonable alternative hypothesis is that the reliability at 10 h is $1 - 10^{-8}$ or that $\mu_a = 10^9$. The test statistic T_r is given by

$$T_r = (n-r)X_r + \sum_{i=1}^{r} X_i$$

for the nonreplacement case and

$$T_r = nX_r$$

[10] If the failure times follow a Weibull distribution with known shape parameter, the data can be transformed into variables having exponential distributions before the test is applied.

for the "replacement case." The critical value T_c (for which the null hypothesis should be rejected whenever $T_r \leq T_c$) can be determined as a function of α and r:

$$T_c = \mu_o \frac{\chi^2_{2r,\alpha}}{2}$$

where $\chi^2_{\nu,\alpha}$ is the α percentile of the chi-square distribution with ν degrees of freedom. Given a choice of r and α the value of the "best" critical region is determined by this formula. The β error can be calculated from

$$T_c = \mu_1 \frac{\chi^2_{2r,1-\beta}}{2}.$$

Neither of the above equations can be solved until r is determined. However, the following formula can be derived from them:

$$\frac{\chi^2_{2r,\alpha}}{\chi^2_{2r,1-\beta}} = \frac{\mu_a}{\mu_o}. \tag{14}$$

Given the desired α and β errors, one chooses the smallest r that satisfies this equation.

Example 1

Suppose that we wish to test

$$H_o : \mu_o = 10^{10}$$
$$H_1 : \mu_a = 10^9$$

For $\alpha = 0.05$ and $\beta = 0.01$, the smallest r satisfying (14) is 3 (using a chi-square table). Thus, the critical region is $\mu_o(\chi^2_{2r,\alpha}/2) = 10^{10}(1.635)/2 = 8.18 \times 10^9$. The experimenter can choose any value of n greater than r. The larger n is, the shorter the expected time on test is. For the replacement case, the expected time on test is $\mu_o(r/n) = (3 \times 10^{10})/n$:

No. of Replicates (n)	Expected Test Duration, D_t, in Hours
10	3×10^9
100	3×10^8
10 000	3×10^6

Even with 10 000 test specimens, the expected test time is 342 yr.

Example 2

Suppose that we wish to test:

$$H_o : \mu_o = 10^{10}$$
$$H_1 : \mu_a = 10^9$$

Given $\alpha = 0.05$ and $r = 1$, the β error can be calculated. First the critical region is $\mu_o(\chi^2_{2r,\alpha}/2) = 10^{10}[0.1026]/2 = 5.13 \times 10^8$. From a chi-square table, the β error can be seen to be greater than 0.50.

Illustrative Table

For $\mu_o = 10^{10}$ and $\mu_a = 10^9$,

$$\frac{\mu_a}{\mu_o} \approx \frac{10^{-9}}{10^{-8}} = 0.1.$$

The following relationship exists between α, r, and β:

α	r	β
0.01	5	≈ 0.005
0.01	3	≈ 0.20
0.01	2	≈ 0.50
0.05	3	≈ 0.02
0.05	2	≈ 0.10
0.10	1	≈ 0.50
0.10	3	≈ 0.005
0.10	2	≈ 0.03
0.10	1	≈ 0.25

The power of the test $1 - \beta$ changes drastically with changes in r. Clearly r must be at least 2 to have a reasonable value for the beta error.

ACKNOWLEDGMENT

The authors are grateful to Dr. A. White for his many helpful comments and to the anonymous reviewers for their careful reviews and many helpful suggestions.

REFERENCES

[1] N. G. Leveson, "Software safety: What, why, and how," *Computing Surveys*, vol. 18, pp. 126–163, June 1986.
[2] I. Peterson, "A digital matter of life and death," *Science News*, Mar. 1988.
[3] E. Joyce, "Software bugs: A matter of life and liability," *Datamation*, May 1987.
[4] N. R. Mann, R. E. Schafer, and N. D. Singpurwalla, *Methods for Statistical Analysis of Reliability and Life Data.* New York: Wiley, 1974.
[5] A. A. Abdalla-Ghaly and A. B. L. P. Y. Chan, "Evaluation of competing reliability predictions," *IEEE Trans. Software Eng.*, pp. 950–967, 1986.
[6] B. Littlewood and P. A. Keiller, "Adaptive software reliability modeling," in *Proc. 14th Int. Symp. Fault-Tolerant Computing*, 1984, pp. 108–113.
[7] B. Littlewood, "Stochastic reliability-growth: A model for fault-removal in computer programs and hardware designs," *IEEE Trans. Reliability*, pp. 313–320, 1981.
[8] P. A. Keiller and D. R. Miller, "On the use and the performance of software reliability growth models," *Reliability Engineering and System Safety*, pp. 95–117, 1991.
[9] B. Littlewood, "Predicting software reliability," *Phil. Trans. Roy. Soc. London*, pp. 513–526, 1989.
[10] P. M. Nagel and J. A. Skrivan, "Software reliability: Repetitive run experimentation and modeling," NASA Contractor Rep. 165836, Feb. 1982.
[11] A. Avizienis, "The n-version approach to fault-tolerant software," *IEEE Trans. Software Eng.*, pp. 1491–1501, Dec. 1985.
[12] R. K. Scott, J. W. Gault, and D. F. McAllister, "Fault-tolerant software reliability modeling," *IEEE Trans. Software Eng.*, May 1987.
[13] D. Miller, "Making statistical inferences about software reliability," NASA Contractor Rep. 4197, Nov. 1988.
[14] J. C. Knight and N. G. Leveson, "An experimental evaluation of the assumptions of independence in multiversion programming," *IEEE Trans. Software Eng.*, vol. SE-12, pp. 96–109, Jan. 1986.
[15] T. J. Shimeall and N. G. Leveson, "An empirical comparison of software fault-tolerance and fault elimination," *IEEE Trans. Software Eng.*, pp. 173–183, Feb. 1991.
[16] J. C. Knight and N. G. Leveson, "A reply to the criticisms of the Knight & Leveson experiment," *ACM SIGSOFT Software Eng. Notes*, Jan. 1990.

Reliability Analysis of Large Software Systems: Defect Data Modeling

YTZHAK LEVENDEL, senior member, ieee

Abstract—System reliability is inversely proportional to the number of unrepaired defects in the system. Improving reliability is a key objective during system development and field deployment, and defect removal is the bottleneck in achieving system readiness.

Defect removal is ruled by the "laws of the physics" of defect behavior that control the defect removal process. The time to defect detection, the defect repair time and the factor of introduction of new defects due to imperfect defect repair are some of the "constants" in the laws governing defect removal. Test coverage is a measure of defect removal effectiveness. A birth–death mathematical model based upon these constants is developed and used to model field failure report data.

The birth–death model is contrasted with a more classic decreasing exponential model. Both models indicate that defect removal is not a cost effective way to achieve quality.

Index Terms—Failure rate, software reliability, software test, test coverage.

I. Introduction

LARGE distributed computer system development presents formidable challenges to the system manufacturer, especially from the point of view of maintaining high system availability in the field. In several segments of the industry (space, telecommunication, military), high system reliability is the cornerstone of product development, since life threatening situations may result from poor product quality. Large systems are subject to high failure rates due to the large number of computing units involved. On the other hand, the distribution of resources provides more flexibility to ensure system availability. The 5ESS® switch [2] represents such a system.

This paper addresses the contribution of software to the reliability of large distributed systems. Large software systems contain several millions of lines of source code, and the sheer size of the product poses unique problems in terms of the ability of the software designers to rapidly achieve product quality. Software errors exist in the system long before they are detected, and they remain unrepaired long after they are discovered. This amplifies the impact of software errors. Driving the system reliability up to acceptable levels becomes the dominant objective during the development process. Here, we analyze and model the software development process, and present field

experience for large distributed systems. Defect removal is shown to be the bottleneck in achieving the appropriate quality level before system deployment in the field. As a result of the long latency of software defects in a system, defect prevention is a far more practical solution to quality than defect removal.

Background is presented in Sections II and III. Defects and failures are categorized in Section IV. A lifecycle reliability model is developed and applied in Section V. This model relates product field readiness to the residual defect level, and allows reliability prediction. The failure data used for validating the lifecycle model of Section V is produced by *random system exercise*, namely an exercise resulting from a pseudo-random combination of planned and unplanned activities. A more classical exponentially increasing reliability model [19], [20] is applied to system testing in Section VI. System testing is a *deterministic system exercise* in that it is generally well planned and executed. It also lends itself easily to a measure of exercise intensity.

II. Incremental Software Development Process

It is impossible to develop software for large size of modern distributed computer systems using a "big bang" methodology [8]. The telecommunication industry represents a typical case of large system development which requires a methodology that encourages partitioning of a job into smaller parts and accommodates the repetitive submission of incremental development segments (*periodic development releases*). Field releases (*generics*) are also produced in increments. The concept of a central software repository is essential for the implementation of such an incremental development environment. A typical large software development follows the process outlined in Fig. 1.

In addition to a set of existing features, each generic includes a set of new features. It is the result of many periodic development releases that are built upon the previous field release. The improvement process of successive development releases results in a field release, when the appropriate quality level has been reached for the new generic.

A distinction is now made between failures and bugs [17]. A *failure instance* is the manifestation of the inability of a program to perform the desired task. A *failure type* is the unique failure representation that corresponds to multiple instances. A *failure (trouble) report* docu-

Manuscript received April 21, 1989; revised September 26, 1989. Recommended by R. K. Iyer.

The author is with AT&T Bell Laboratories, Naperville, IL 60566.

IEEE Log Number 8932231.

®5ESS is a registered trademark of AT&T Bell Laboratories.

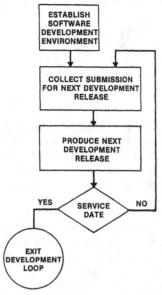

Fig. 1. A typical large software development process.

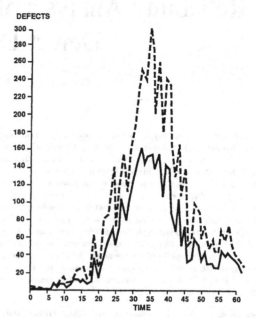

Fig. 2. The raw (dashed) and filtered (solid) defect detection rates.

ments the reporting of one or more failure instances of one or more failure types. A *fault* (*defect*) is the cause of a failure. The reliability of a system is determined both by the nature of a failure (type) and the reoccurrences of that failure (instances). Because of an intense preoccupation for efficiency in the removal of defects, the industry tends to discourage the multiple reporting of all failure instances. Multiple reporting of the same failure is considered as detrimental because of the cost of resolving multiple reports to the same failure type. The industry compensates for this simplification by attaching to the failure report a severity rating that takes into account the frequency of failure reoccurrence. Trouble reports are the source of data used in this paper for modeling.

The "raw" defect detection curve for a certain field release represents the incoming trouble report rate and is given in Fig. 2 (dotted line). The curve includes a large amount of foreign data, such as duplicate trouble reports, false trouble reports, etc. The data can be filtered (solid line) to include only the set of trouble reports that were or are candidates for repairs. The filtering also reduces different instances of the same failure caused by the same fault to one single report. *The filtered data actually represents the defect detection rate.* The defect removal curves are not given here and are similar to the defect detection curves, except that they are skewed in time due to the defect repair delay. In our experience, the ratio between "raw" trouble reports and real defects remains practically constant. This is analyzed in detail in Section IV.

The situation in Fig. 2 represents a development wherein hundreds of thousands of lines of new software are added to a base count of several millions of lines. After field release of a new generic, the residual defects in the current generic go down with time, and they are cumu-

lated with the residual defects in the preceding field generics.

III. THE SOFTWARE DESIGN BOTTLENECK: DEFECT REMOVAL

During the development process, defects are introduced into the central software repository as a function of the size of the software being added or modified [7], [15]. This defect level also depends on the design practices preceding code introduction. Various phases of testing that occur during the development cycle provide the mechanism for defect removal.

The defects introduced at some point in time stay in the system until they are detected and repaired. Unlike hardware defects, most software defects exist in a system as soon as the software is implemented. These defects are latent in the software and manifest themselves as a result of the appropriate system exercise. Critical and "ultra-visible" defects are discovered immediately, whereas less visible latent defects remain longer in the system. The existence of defect latency in large systems has been documented [4], [5], [21].

Although it is essential to achieve quality upfront by better design and development practices [3], it is important to consider the existence of software defects as a reality. From this vantage point, the design process can be reduced to its most significant element, defect elimination, since defect removal is the dominant factor of reliability improvement. As a matter of fact, the success of a development is largely determined by the designer's ability to eliminate defects in the speediest way [1], [18]. The decision of when to deploy a large system hinges primarily on the ability to estimate the quality of the system, namely the current level of (known and unknown) defects and the rate of defects to appear in the future.

IV. FAILURE REPORT CATEGORIZATION

The filtering process of the raw trouble reports is analyzed in this section. A trouble report that persists after the filtering process is generally equivalent to one (single or multiple) defect. This is the reason why no distinction will be made between filtered trouble reports and defects.

A. Catastrophic Failures

Catastrophic failures are the failure that cause a system crash ("outage" in the telecommunication industry). A recent study (Fig. 3) shows that hardware failures are the dominant cause of system crashes followed by procedural errors. Procedural errors are composed of human errors in system operation and incorrect diagnosis of correct operation. The number of software errors seems the lowest. This is somewhat misleading, since some crashes may erroneously be attributed to hardware. This is explained next.

Crashes involving hardware can be a combination of hardware failures, procedural errors and faulty software. The possible paths leading to crash and related to hardware failures are described in the state diagram of Fig. 4. The state diagram assumes duplex hardware arrangement, namely each hardware unit is duplicated. A duplex hardware failure (failure in both units) obviously leads to an outage. A procedural step (e.g., one unit is removed from service) followed by a hardware failure leads to a crash "due to hardware."

B. Noncatastrophic Failures

For the overall deployment, hardware failures are the leading cause of noncatastrophic failures by a wide margin (Fig. 5). However, hardware and software defects manifest themselves in approximately the same number for a single installation [6]. Software errors are more detrimental than meets the eye. Contrary to hardware errors that are immediately corrected by hardware replacement, software errors persist from their detection time until they are repaired. While awaiting repair, the effect of software errors is strongly amplified by repeated detections in a given installation and in multiple sites.

C. Software Trouble Report Attribution

An example of field trouble report rate is given in Fig. 6. The curve represents the sum of the trouble report rates due to all past and present field releases. Obviously, earlier field releases have lower contributions than recent ones.

In Fig. 6, peaks of error detection are caused by the release of new generics, and the curve overall trend is increasing because of the increasing number of installations. Normalizing the data to the number of installations results in a slightly decreasing trend. The normalization to the program size produces a constant trend.

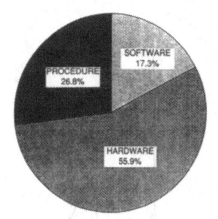

Fig. 3. Crash cause attribution.

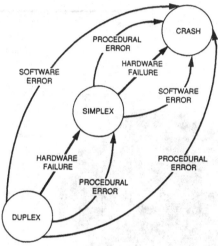

Fig. 4. Crash state diagram.

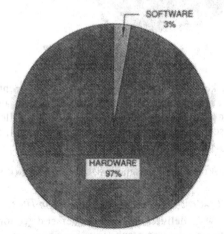

Fig. 5. Noncatastrophic failure attribution.

Less than half of the trouble reports are real software errors as shown in Fig. 7. This is consistent with the observations in Section II.

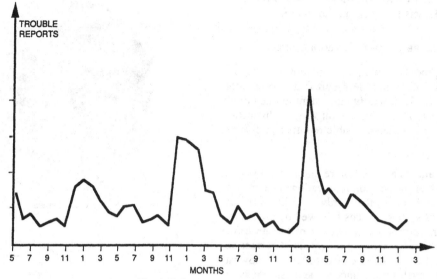

Fig. 6. Software trouble report rate.

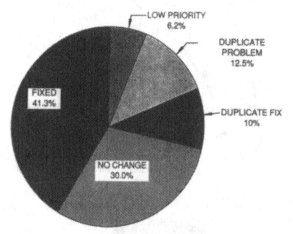

Fig. 7. Software trouble report attribution.

So far, key elements in the software development process for large distributed systems were discussed, and essential defect statistics were presented. In the following section, software quality indicators are introduced, and a reliability model is presented.

V. SOFTWARE RELIABILITY MODELING: RANDOM EXERCISE

A. Defect Latency in the System and Repair Time

The software delivery rate and the defect detection rate are plotted on the same graph (Fig. 8). The software delivery rate is described in Fig. 8(a). The defect detection rate of Fig. 8(b) is the sum of all detection rates produced by random and controlled exercises over the software development life cycle. The average software delivery time and the average defect detection time are separated by approximately four months. This latency is directly derived from the curves in Fig. 8, and it will mathematically be calculated based upon the model of Section V-B.

This fact must have a sobering impact on our thinking. Namely, most of the defects that are introduced at some point in time will be detected much later. This includes the defects introduced close to the service date. Obviously, the defect repair time must be added to the time to detection. This effect is further amplified by the *defect reintroduction factor* (percentage of new defects introduced at defect repair time) as discussed in Section V-E.

Most of the software defects introduced in a system remain in the system for several months before being detected. Therefore, it is essential that enough time elapses between the last software modification and the field deployment.

B. Modeling the Defect Detection and Repair Rates

A time-dependent model [16], [19], [9] developed earlier [12], [13] is used to fit the curves of Fig. 8 and estimate the software quality. The model is a birth–death model [11]. Unlike several models described earlier [10], our model does not assume instant defect repair. The model assumes that defects are introduced incrementally with error density α (number of errors per line of code) when software is added to the system. The defects introduced at some point in time are detected later with an average time to detection δ. The defects are repaired after an average repair time ρ, and improper defect repair introduces new defects at a rate β (defect reintroduction factor). The process is iterative, and the iterations produce probability functions with amplitudes β, β^2, β^3, $\cdots$. As the power i of β increases, the probability with amplitude β^i is skewed in time representing one more round of detection, repair, and defect reintroduction (birth–death model). It is necessary for achieving convergence that β be less than one.

42

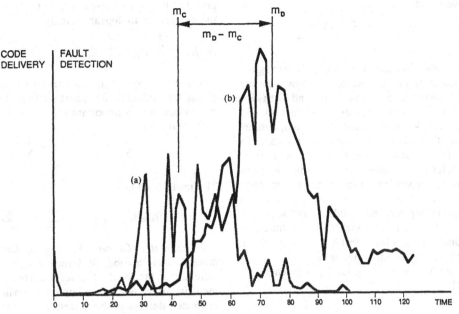

Fig. 8. (a) Software delivery and (b) defect detection rate.

1) Incremental Modeling of Defect Detection and Removal: Given n lines of code, the number of defects appearing during time period i is described by

$$d_i = n\alpha e^{-\delta} \frac{\delta^i}{i!}$$

where α is the defect density (number of defects per line of code). d_i is proportional to a Poisson distribution with mean time δ. Obviously, we have that

$$\sum_{i=0}^{\infty} d_i = n\alpha.$$

If we assume that the defect repair rate is described by a Poisson distribution with mean ρ, the removal rate of the $n\alpha$ defects introduced with n lines of code is described by the new Poisson distribution:

$$r_i = n\alpha e^{-(\delta+\rho)} \frac{(\delta + \rho)^i}{i!}$$

which is the composition of two Poisson distributions, one with mean δ and the other with mean ρ.

2) Analysis with Defect Reintroduction: Let us assume that n_i lines of code are submitted for time period i and that there are $C + 1$ time periods for code submission. The defect detection rate during time period k is obtained by cumulating the defects introduced by repeated and successive code submissions. In addition, the repair of defects will introduce new defects at the rate β (*defect reintroduction*). The process is iterative as illustrated in Table I.

The resulting defect detection rate D_k during time period k is given by:

$$D_k = \alpha \sum_{i=0}^{k} n_{k-i}\Delta_i$$

TABLE I
DEFECT REINTRODUCTION SCENARIO FOR CODE INCREMENT n_i

DEFECTS	DISTRIBUTION
αn_i Introduced at Time i	
αn_i Detected	Mean $\delta + i$
αn_i Repaired	Mean $\delta + \rho + i$
$\beta \alpha n_i$ Reintroduced	
$\beta \alpha n_i$ Detected	Mean $2\delta + \rho + i$
$\beta \alpha n_i$ Repaired	Mean $2\delta + 2\rho + i$
$\beta^2 \alpha n_i$ Reintroduced	
$\beta^2 \alpha n_i$ Detected	Mean $3\delta + 2\rho + i$
$\beta^2 \alpha n_i$ Repaired	Mean $3\delta + 3\rho + i$
$\beta^3 \alpha n_i$ Reintroduced	
.	.
.	.

for $0 \le k \le C$ and

$$D_k = \alpha \sum_{i=k-C}^{k} n_{k-i}\Delta_i$$

for $k > C$.

We also have:

$$\Delta_i = \sum_{j=0}^{\infty} \beta^j e^{-((j+1)\delta+j\rho)} \frac{((j+1)\delta + j\rho)^i}{i!}.$$

Similarly, the defect removed during time k is given by:

$$R_k = \alpha \sum_{i=0}^{k} n_{k-i}\Gamma_i$$

for $0 \le k \le C$ and

$$R_k = \alpha \sum_{i=k-C}^{k} n_{k-i}\Gamma_i$$

for $k > C$.

Similarly, we have:

$$\Gamma_i = \sum_{j=0}^{\infty} \beta^j e^{-(j+1)(\delta+\rho)} \frac{\left((j+1)(\delta+\rho)\right)^i}{i!}.$$

The defect reintroduction rate β produces D_k through an iterative compounding of Poisson distributions with amplitudes β^j decreasing as a function of j and with time constant $(j+1)\delta + j\rho$ increasing as a function of j, which is the iteration variable. The iterative compounding results from the following mechanism. Defects are discovered, and then repaired. The repair of each defect causes β new defects to be introduced, resulting in a new cycle of discovery, repair, etc. (Table I). This produces Δ_i. The same mechanism applied to defect removal results in a compounding with amplitude β^j and with time constant $(j+1)(\delta+\rho)$. This yields Γ_i. The time constants of the compoundings for defect detection and defect removal differ by ρ for the same iteration j.

The mean time to detection m_D for D_k is given by the expression [12]:

$$m_D = \frac{\alpha \sum_{i=0}^{C} n_i \left(\delta \frac{1}{1-\beta} + (\delta+\rho) \frac{\beta}{(1-\beta)^2} + i \frac{1}{1-\beta} \right)}{\alpha \sum_{i=0}^{C} n_i \frac{1}{1-\beta}}.$$

For $\beta \ll 1$, the appropriate simplifications yield:

$$m_D = \frac{\sum_{i=0}^{C} i n_i}{\sum_{i=0}^{C} n_i} + \frac{\delta + \beta\rho}{1-\beta} = m_C + \frac{\delta + \beta\rho}{1-\beta}. \quad (1)$$

Similarly, it can be shown that the mean time to removal:

$$m_R = \frac{\sum_{i=0}^{C} i n_i}{\sum_{i=0}^{C} n_i} + \frac{\delta + \rho + \beta\rho}{1-\beta}$$

$$= m_C + \frac{\delta + \rho + \beta\rho}{1-\beta}. \quad (2)$$

where m_C is the mean time for code delivery.

Also, it appears that:

$$m_R - m_D = \frac{\rho}{1-\beta}.$$

Note that m_D and m_R are independent of α and that the values of $m_D - m_C$, $m_R - m_C$, and $m_R - m_D$ grow with β.

C. Quality Estimates

1) Estimated Number of Defects to Repair: Another important quantity is the predicted number of defects remaining to be fixed after time period T, NDR_T. It is com-

posed of the defects remaining to fix at time period T and the defects yet to appear, namely:

$$NDR_T = \sum_{i=0}^{T} D_i - \sum_{i=0}^{T} R_i + \sum_{i=T+1}^{\infty} D_i = \sum_{i=0}^{\infty} D_i - \sum_{i=0}^{T} R_i.$$

The estimation of the number of defects to repair can be used to project field support staffing needs, and, hence, it may become an important project planning tool.

We have that:

$$\sum_{i=0}^{\infty} D_i = \alpha \frac{1}{1-\beta} \sum_{i=0}^{C} n_i.$$

The result becomes:

$$NDR_T = \alpha \frac{1}{1-\beta} \sum_{i=0}^{C} n_i - \sum_{i=0}^{T} R_i.$$

2) Estimated Current Number of Defects: The estimated current number of defects at time T, CND_T, is an estimate of the level of defects currently in the system inclusive of the number of known unrepaired defects. The estimated defects in the system can be obtained by subtracting the defects that were removed so far, and adding the defects that were reintroduced while removing these defects. The resulting expression is:

$$CND_T = \alpha \sum_{i=0}^{C} n_i - \sum_{i=0}^{T} R_i + \beta \sum_{i=0}^{T} R_i$$

$$= \alpha \sum_{i=0}^{C} n_i - (1-\beta) \sum_{i=0}^{T} R_i.$$

It can be noted that:

$$CND_T = (1-\beta) NDR_T.$$

3) Testing Coverage and Repair Intensity: The testing coverage during time interval k, TC_k, is defined as the ratio of the defects found during interval k and the total amount of defects existing in the system at time k.

$$TC_k = \frac{D_k}{\alpha \sum_{i=0}^{k} n_i - (1-\beta) \sum_{i=0}^{k} R_i}.$$

The testing coverage characterizes the effectiveness of defect detection.

The repair intensity during time interval k, RI_k, is defined as the ratio of the defects removed during interval k and the total amount of defects open at time k.

$$RI_k = \frac{R_k}{\sum_{i=0}^{k} D_i - \sum_{i=0}^{k} R_i}.$$

The repair intensity characterizes the ability of repairing open defects.

Both testing coverage and repair intensity derived from the model vary as a function of k, even if δ and ρ are constant. However, for constant values of δ and ρ, the profiles of TC_k and RI_k are determined for the entire span of the project. It is shown in Section V-F that nonhomogeneous Poisson distributions allow the control of TC_k and RI_k.

4) Testing Process Quality and Effectiveness: The testing process effectiveness, TPE_T, is the ratio:

$$TPE_T = \frac{\text{number of filtered defects found so far}}{\text{number of raw defects found so far}}.$$

This ratio is a measure of the time spent on fixing real defects versus the time spent eliminating "false" defects.

The testing process quality at time $T(TPQ_T)$ is a measure of the success of the defect identification process so far. It is defined as:

$$TPQ_T = \frac{\text{number of defects found so far}}{\text{number of defects introduced so far}}.$$

For $T > C$, the previous formula becomes:

$$TPQ_T = \frac{\sum_{i=0}^{T} D_i}{\alpha \sum_{i=0}^{C} n_i + \beta \sum_{i=0}^{T} R_i}.$$

D. A Case Study: Project P

The filtered data represented in Fig. 2 is used for fitting the mathematical models developed above. The code delivery was measured by a tool that computes the size of the software change requests. The code delivery rate was provided in Fig. 8. In the sequence, the mathematical model (parameters δ, ρ, α, and β) is derived from the curve fitting and the various estimates (NDR_T, CND_T, TPQ_T, TPE_T) are calculated from the mathematical model. The fitting of the analytical model with the cumulative defect detection rate is shown in Fig. 9 (the fitting with the defect removal is phased with time and not shown here). The resulting estimates are summarized in Table II.

E. Impact of Imperfect Repair (Reintroduction Coefficient)

A model simulation was conducted, and it was found that one defect is reintroduced for every three defect repairs. In the long run, this means that 50 percent of the original defects are reintroduced due to imperfect repairs. These defects are introduced later in the process and are subjected to a similarly long time to detection. Also, they may elude detection since a large amount of the test program has already been executed. Using model simulation, the following results were found for a software size of approximately 600 000 lines (Table II):

a) 1140 defects were reintroduced at repair time during the entire project span

b) 626 of these reintroduced defects were found prior to the field release and the remainder, 514 defects, were found by the customer

c) 65 of the defects originally introduced at code submission were found by the customer.

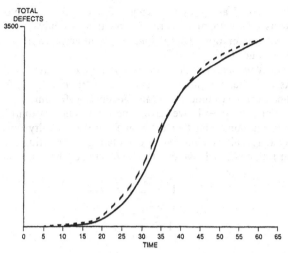

Fig. 9. Filtered (solid) and analytical (dotted) cumulative defect detection.

TABLE II
KEY QUALITY ESTIMATES FOR PROJECT P

Time to Detection δ	8.6 Time Units
Repair Time ρ	2.35 Time Units
Code Delivery	589810 Lines
Initial Error Density α	3.87 Defects per K-line
Defect Reintroduction Coefficient β	33 Percent
Deployment Time T	Time Unit 50
Number of Defects to Repair NDR_T	664 Defects
Current Number of Defects CND_T	445 Defects
Testing Process Quality TPQ_T	90 Percent
Testing Process Efficiency TPE_T	60 Percent

Most of the defects found by the customers were defects reintroduced at repair time. This makes the defect reintroduction coefficient the major cause of customer dissatisfaction. The defect reintroduction coefficient is largely responsible for extending the time to detection. This can be seen from (1).

F. Controllable Test Coverage and Repair Intensity

The defect detection is a direct result of implicit or explicit testing performed during the development cycle. Implicit testing is done when the system is used without the explicit existence of a rigorous set of tests. Implicit testing is also performed in the field during the regular function executed by the system. The testing coverage and the repair intensity do not remain constant during the entire life cycle of a field release. Therefore, irregularities (peaks and lows) are expected in the actual test coverage and repair intensity. These variations cannot accurately be modeled using constant values for δ and ρ.

A nonhomogeneous Poisson distribution with time-varying time "constants" δ and ρ needs to be defined.

This would allow us to decrease δ and ρ during highly focused development periods, and this is equivalent to time acceleration. Our definition is different from previous ones [9].

1) Nonhomogeneous Poisson Distributions [13]: Assume that the time constant of a distribution is λ_i for time i from 0 to time $k-1$, and becomes λ_k for time value k. For $i > k-1$, we have a new Poisson distribution with the constraint that the sum from 0 to infinity must equal 1. This is achieved by calculating a correcting factor f_k that will achieve this result. f_k satisfies the equation:

$$f_k = \frac{1 - \sum_{i=0}^{k-1} f_i p_i(\lambda_i)}{1 - \sum_{i=0}^{k-1} p_i(\lambda_k)}$$

where

$$p_i(\lambda) = e^{-\lambda} \frac{\lambda^i}{i!} \quad \text{and} \quad f_0 = 1.$$

It can be shown that:

$$f_{k+1} = f_k \quad \text{if} \quad \lambda_{k+1} = \lambda_k$$

and that:

$$f_{k+1} > f_k \quad \text{iff} \quad \lambda_{k+1} < \lambda_k.$$

A shortening of the time constant is equivalent to an acceleration of the defect detection rate. In other words, the multiplier will remain the same as long as the time constant does not change. An example is given next. The actual modulated distribution is given by $f_i p_i(\lambda_i)$ in Table III. The resulting graph for $f_i p_i(\lambda_i)$ is plotted in Fig. 10.

2) A Case Study: Project P Revisited: The analysis performed in Section V-D for Project P is redone using nonhomogeneous probability distributions. The graph for time constants δ and ρ are given in Fig. 11. A larger (smaller) value of δ represents a smaller (larger) test coverage, and a larger (smaller) value of ρ represents a smaller (larger) repair intensity. Towards the latter part of the development cycle, the detection time decreased due to increased testing close to and after field release, whereas the repair time increased due to a more cautious defect repair strategy.

The cumulative detection and removal rates are simultaneously fitted with the analytical model. The method is similar to that used in Section V-D. However, the curve fitting is more accurate, because of the ability of controlling δ and ρ. The cumulative defect detection rate only is provided here (Fig. 12). There was no significant change in the estimates of Table II.

G. Residual Defects in the System and Test Coverage

The test coverage during a time interval is defined as the probability that a defect be detected if it exists. It can be measured as the ratio of number of detected defects to the estimated number of total defects in the system during the time interval [13]. For values of δ, ρ, α, and β given

TABLE III
AN EXAMPLE OF NONHOMOGENEOUS POISSON DISTRIBUTION

i	λ_i	f_i	$p_i(\lambda_i)$	$f_i p_i(\lambda_i)$
0	6.0	1.000	0.00248	0.00248
1	6.0	1.000	0.01487	0.01487
2	6.0	1.000	0.04462	0.04462
3	6.0	1.000	0.08924	0.08924
4	6.0	1.000	0.13385	0.13386
5	5.0	1.278	0.17547	0.22421
6	5.0	1.278	0.14622	0.18684
7	5.0	1.278	0.10444	0.13346
8	6.0	0.666	0.10326	0.06874
9	6.0	0.666	0.06884	0.04583
10	6.0	0.666	0.04131	0.02750

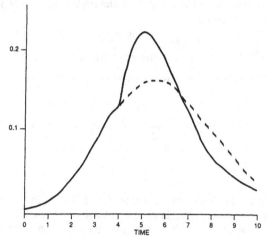

Fig. 10. A nonhomogeneous Poisson distribution.

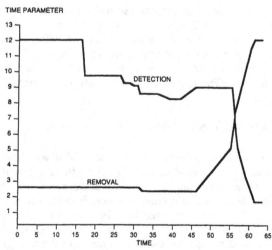

Fig. 11. Detection and repair time parameters.

in Table II, the total estimated number of defects in the system and the defect detection rate are given in Figs. 13(a) and (b), respectively. The estimated test coverage is calculated using the expression provided in Section V-C-3), and it is given in Fig. 14 (solid curve).

The defect introduction rate dominates by far the process of improving software quality. The testing coverage

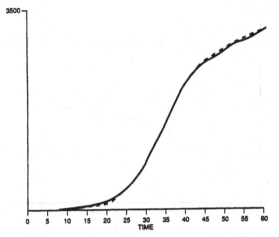

Fig. 12. Filtered (solid) and analytical (dotted) cumulative defect detection.

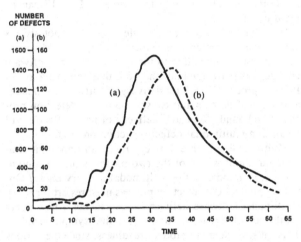

Fig. 13. (a) Number of unrepaired defects and (b) detection rate.

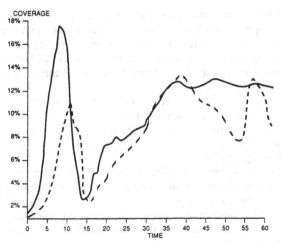

Fig. 14. Estimated test coverage.

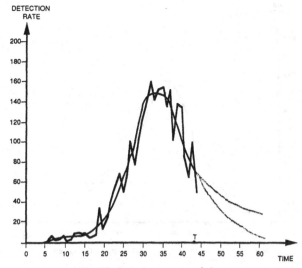

Fig. 15. Detection rate curve fitting.

is generally too weak and insufficient to produce quality fast. The weakness of the test coverage originates from the facts that it represents only a small sample of possible exercises and that it is too costly. By using model simulation, it can be shown that multiplying the test coverage by 1.15 will result in 33 percent less defects found in the field. However, maintaining the increase of test coverage over the entire development interval represents a substantial additional cost. This makes defect prevention a more attractive solution than defect removal. The variable time to detection and repair time of Fig. 11 produce the dotted test coverage curve of Fig. 14.

H. Random System Exercise—Reliability Prediction

The development cycle model introduced in Section V-B allows us to develop a mathematical estimate for the remaining defects in the system. The model is calibrated using actual defect detection and removal rates. Once the model parameters are determined from the curve fitting up to time T, the model can provide an estimate of the detection rate beyond time T (Fig. 15) and of the remaining defects in the system (Fig. 16). These are essential elements for predicting system readiness for field operation.

I. Summary of the Results

Our field experience shows that defect density is a key parameter in deriving a prediction of software reliability. Mathematical modeling of the software design lifecycle is useful in providing reliability prediction and critical parameter (α, β, δ, and ρ) estimation. Modeling can also provide an estimate of the test coverage. In reality, it was found that the defect reintroduction rate is high and that the test coverage is low. Also, defect detection and removal are significantly long and expensive activities that dominate the improvement of system reliability and readiness of field releases.

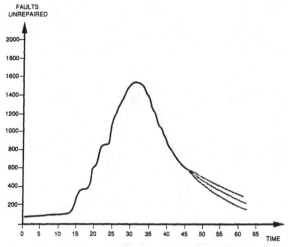

Fig. 16. Projection of defects remaining in the system.

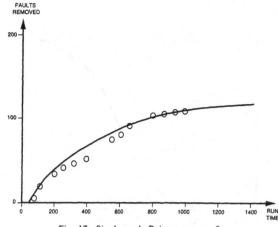

Fig. 17. Single mode Poisson process fit.

VI. SOFTWARE RELIABILITY MODELING: DETERMINISTIC EXERCISE

Two common forms of deterministic exercise consist of comprehensive system test programs and (stability) runs of the system under stress. The system test programs consist of a comprehensive set of functional tests. This exercise enables us to estimate the number of total defects remaining in the system as well as the current system quality. System test metrics reflect the projected level of noncatastrophic failures in the field.

The system runs under stress produce a measure of the system resilience, its ability to maintain operation and an assessment of the system ability to dedicate resources to its main function rather than to error recovery. The system resilience under stress (stability index) is a predictor of catastrophic failures in the field. The defects affecting stability are detected immediately, whereas the residual noncatastrophic defects affect long range customer satisfaction and are more obvious during broad functional coverage.

The system test exercise produces failure data that can be fitted using a more conventional model. The effectiveness of defect removal as a quality improvement method will be examined in this section in order to provide a comparison point to the model of Section V.

A. Noncatastrophic Failure Modeling

The cumulative detected defects are plotted against the run time in Fig. 17. The time is measured in terms of test hours. It can be observed that the cumulative defects grow with time t towards an asymptotic value. The data can be fitted using a Poisson process with exponentially decreasing mean [19]:

$$\mu(t) = \nu_0(1 - e^{-(\lambda_0/\nu_0)t}). \tag{3}$$

This model assumes instant defect repair, and this can be simulated under deterministic system exercise. Also, the actual reliability prediction requires the knowledge of a test coverage estimate. In addition, the deterministic exercise is performed during the phase when the reliability is improving. This is why the curve of Fig. 17 can be fitted using (3).

It can be observed that a single mode fit is not always appropriate. A better fit is achieved using a double mode fit (Fig. 18). This is due to the fact that a large software change was performed at time 460, thus restarting a new Poisson process. The later delivery of software introduces a new set of defects and causes the defect detection process to rebound. Repeated delivery of new software will result in a multimodal defect detection process.

Multimodal software delivery raises an important strategic question: which of the two modes is more economical, the unimodal or the multimodal delivery mode? Obviously, the defect detection process must restart for every multimodal software delivery, thus causing a new delay for the cumulative detection to reach the asymptotic value. This causes a delay in product readiness, since the various phases of the multimodal delivery are not independent.

B. System Stability and Catastrophic Failures

Close to the product release, the size of the periodic development releases is directly related to the defect removal rate, since defect repair is the main activity taking place at that time. Therefore, defect detection and repair estimation is essential to predict the size of the periodic development releases.

Historically, it has been shown that increment size trends and stability measure trends are inversely related in that the larger the increment size trend the lower the index trend. This can intuitively be understood using the following observations:

a) The defects that affect stability are a subset of the defects whose detection is immediate or have been in the system for a short time.

b) The number of defects whose time to detection is short is directly related to the trend in number of changes per time interval.

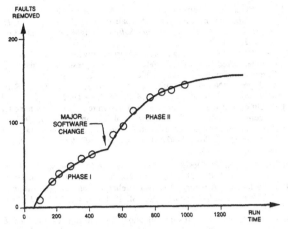

Fig. 18. Double mode Poisson process fit.

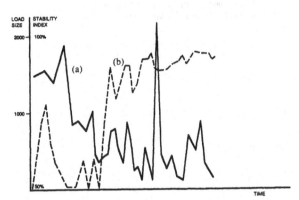

Fig. 19. (a) Number of software changes and (b) stability index.

An example that substantiates this fact is shown in Fig. 19. It shows that our ability to control the system stability is inversely related to the incremental rate of changes. The incremental rate of changes is in turn directly related to the software quality at that moment, since it is related to the number of known defects. Driving the total number of defects down is a key element in converging the quality indicators of a software project, including system stability.

C. Summary of the Results

Multimodality of reliability curves has been observed in a single testing phase (e.g., system test) under multiple product deliveries. Multiple testing phases also cause multimodal behavior of the failure rate curves because of the finite nature of the test programs at each phase.

Several deficiencies of the single mode exponential model above strongly suggest its invalidity. First, a limited size test program will contribute to a premature decrease of the error rate. In addition, rerunning of previously failing tests after defect repair will also create the same effect. Finally, a weak exercise or test environment will reinforce the two previous factors. These three deficiencies will also cause a premature increase of the stability index. Recent system test data analysis [20] that shows a slowdown of the defect finding rate after a very short testing time may indicate a weakness of the exercise and cause an optimistic prognosis. Failure data collected in successive testing phases shows that the initial derivative of the curve $\mu(t)$ in one phase is a better predictor of the initial derivative of $\mu(t)$ in the next phase. This is in line with the dominant result using the model of Section V, namely converging quality by defect removal requires multiple testing phases and is subjected to a large time constant.

VII. CONCLUSIONS

The engineering of large distributed software systems is underlaid by a defect detection and removal process that obeys rigid laws similar to the laws of physics regulating the physical world around us. The laws governing the defect detection and removal process cannot be ignored, and they impose a stringent set of constraints affecting mainly the speed at which defects can be detected (time to detection) and removed (repair time). These laws are modeled in Section V. In addition, the defect reintroduction coefficient acts as a time "decelerator," since it causes an increase in the detection and removal delays. Also, the model developed here provides an estimate of the test coverage. The large size of the software being developed in the context of large distributed systems dominates the ability to fast converge software quality. It has been shown that the complexity underlying the development process is worse than linear [15]. This factor leads to a pessimistic outlook with respect to the industry's ability to control down the residual latent defects in a large software product by relying on defect removal. In fact, the model demonstrates that defect avoidance is more powerful than defect removal. Partitioning of the product into smaller products is the only viable option for reducing the negative effect of complexity on system quality. Product partitioning must also lead to process partitioning [8].

The second model used in Section VI points to similar conclusions. The validity of this model is contingent upon the quality and scope of the system test exercise. This is addressed in another work [14].

ACKNOWLEDGMENT

Our thanks are given to the guest editor, the referees, and R. K. Prasad for their constructive comments, to G. Levendel for programming the model of Section V, and to V. Rinehart for the model application of Section VI.

REFERENCES

[1] J. Abe, K. Sakurama, and H. Aiso, "An analysis of software project failures," in *Proc. 4th Int. Conf. Software Engineering*, Munich, Sept. 17-19, 1979.

[2] J. A. Allers, A. H. Huizinga, J. A. Kukla, J. D. Sipes, and R. T. Yeh, "No. 5ESS—Strategies for reliability in a distributed processing environment," in *Proc. 13th Fault Tolerant Computing Symp.*, Milano, June 1983.

[3] "Quality: Theory and practice," *AT&T Tech. J.*, vol. 65, issue 2, Mar. 1986.

[4] X. Castillo and D. P. Sieworek, "A workload dependent software reliability prediction model," in *Proc. 12th Fault Tolerant Computing Symp.*, Santa Monica, CA, June 1982, pp. 279–286.

[5] R. Chillarege and R. K. Iyer, "The effect of system workload on error latency: An experimental study," in *Proc. ACM SIGMETRICS Conf. Measurement and Modeling of Computer Systems*, 1985, pp. 69–77.

[6] G. Clement and P. Giloth, "Evolution of fault tolerant computing in AT&T," in *Proc. One-Day Symp. Evolution of Fault Tolerant Comput.*, Baden, Austria, June 3, 1986.

[7] J. E. Gaffney, "Estimating the number of faults in code," *IEEE Trans. Software Eng.*, vol. SE-10, no. 4, pp. 459–464, July 1984.

[8] T. Gil, *Principles of Software Engineering.* New York: Wiley, 1988.

[9] A. L. Goel, "A time dependent error detection rate model for software reliability and other performance measures," *IEEE Trans. Rel.*, vol. R-20, pp. 206–211, July 1979.

[10] ——, "Software reliability models: Assumptions, limitions, and applicability," *IEEE Trans. Software Eng.*, vol. SE-11, no. 12, pp. 1411–1423, Dec. 1985.

[11] W. Kremer, "Birth–death and bug counting," *IEEE Trans. Rel.*, vol. R-32, no. 1, pp. 37–46, Apr. 1983.

[12] Y. Levendel, "Quality and reliability estimation for large software projects using a time-dependent model," in *Proc. COMPSAC87*, Tokyo, Japan, Oct. 1987, pp. 340–346.

[13] ——, "Quality and reliability prediction: A time-dependent model with controllable testing coverage and repair intensity," in *Proc. 4th Israel Conf. Computer Systems and Software Engineering*, Tel-Aviv, Israel, June 1989.

[14] ——, "The manufacturing process of large software systems: The use of untampered metrics for quality control," presented at the Nat. Communication Forum 1989, Chicago, IL, Oct. 1989.

[15] M. Lipow, "Number of faults per line of code," *IEEE Trans. Software Eng.*, vol. SE-8, no. 5, pp. 437–439, July 1982.

[16] B. Littlewood and J. L. Verrall, "A Bayesian reliability growth model for computer software," *Appl. Stat.*, vol. 22, pp. 332–346, 1973.

[17] B. Littlewood, "What makes a reliable program: Few bugs or a small failure rate?" in *Proc. 1980 Nat. Computer Conf. 1980*, AFIPS Press, 1980, pp. 707–713.

[18] M. Monachino, "Design verification system for large-scale LSI designs," *IBM J. Res. Develop.*, vol. 26, no. 1, pp. 89–99, Jan. 1982.

[19] J. D. Musa, "A theory of software reliability and its application," *IEEE Trans. Software Eng.*, vol. SE-1, no. 3, pp. 312–327, Sept. 1975.

[20] ——, "Quantifying software validation: When to stop testing?" *IEEE Software*, pp. 19–27, May 1989.

[21] D. J. Rossetti and R. K. Iyer, "Software related failures on the IBM 3081: A relationship with system utilization," in *Proc. COMPSAC 82*, Chicago, IL, Nov. 1982, pp. 45–54.

A MICRO SOFTWARE RELIABILITY MODEL FOR PREDICTION AND TEST APPORTIONMENT

Martin L. Shooman
Polytechnic University
Long Island Campus, Route 110
Farmingdale, NY 11735
PHONE: 516-755-4290; FAX: 5167554404

Abstract

This paper discusses a new micro model which allows reliability estimation to begin at the module test phase, continue during integration testing, and carry over to field deployment. The resulting reliability estimates should improve as the project progresses because more test results are accumulated using more realistic data.

The model first decomposes the structure of the software into a set of execution paths. The failure rate of the software system is related to the frequency and time of path traversal, and the probability of encountering an error during traversal. The software reliability and mean time to failure are obtained from the failure rate.

A second stage of decomposition is necessary to relate the path reliability to the module reliabilities. In the second decomposition the failure probabilities are expressed by combinatorial expressions involving the probabilities of failure of the individual modules. For structured, top-down designs, the modules are largely independent and the probability expressions simplify.

Since the basic model decomposes the structure into execution paths the model can be used to apportion reliabilities and test efforts among the various execution paths. The optimum allocation is computed for a particular effort model and applied to a numerical example.

1. Introduction

Over the past 19 years a number of software reliability models have been proposed [1-15]. Many of these have been applied with some success [3, 10, 16, 25] to practical problems. Most of these models have been used in only one phase of the development life cycle, commonly the integration test phase or early field deployment. This paper discusses a new micro model for software reliability which will allow reliability estimation to begin at the module test phase, continue during integration testing, and carry over to field deployment. In addition, the module allows optimum apportionment of test effort during development.

2.0 Micro Software Reliability Model

Most of the software reliability models developed to date have been macro models, also called black box models and are discussed in [10] Sec. 9.4, and [2], Ch. 5. These models focus on the number of errors in the program ("within the box"), the rate at which the errors are found and removed, and the number of tests which the software fails during some specified test time. A few models [12, 17, 18, 19, 20] have been developed which focus on a simple representation of the software structure and are called micro models. The model developed in this paper [21, 22] will be based on a path oriented micro model [17].

Assume that the program control structure can be represented by i major data flow paths which we call operational cases. Each of these cases is associated with a significant operational mode of the software, and a class of inputs drives the software along an operational path.

The micro model will be developed from the probabilistic viewpoint of relative frequency. We will hypothesize a sequence of tests which either uncover a fault with significant consequences (failure) or run to completion without uncovering a fault (success). We begin our development of the model by defining the following variables and parameters:

N	=	number of tests
i	=	number of software paths (cases, parts, modules, etc.)
t_j'	=	time to run case j (if time is not deterministic we can substitute the mean value of t_j', $\bar{t}_j'$)
q_j	=	probability of failure on each run of case j (probability of no error $p_j = 1 - q_j$)
f_j	=	relative frequency with which case j is run
n_f	=	total number of failures in N tests
H	=	total cumulative test time

We have defined N as the number of tests, thus, we are

modeling actual or simulated operation by a succession of N tests-path traversals-of the system. We also assume that the input data vary on each traversal, therefore, the probability of encountering a bug on a particular run, q_j, varies from run to run. Depending on the code the run time for case j may be fixed at t_j or may vary from run to run in which case we use the average value $\bar{t}_j$.

Since we have assumed a variation in parameters on each run in our model, each test is independent, and the expected number of errors in N tests of path j is given by:

$$\text{Expected number of failures} = Nq_j \quad (1a)$$

where N is the number of runs and q_j the probability of failure along path j.

In general, the N total tests are distributed along each path so that Nf_1 tests traverse path 1, Nf_2 tests traverse path 2, etc. Thus, successive applications of Eq. (1a) to each of the i paths yields the number of failures in N tests:

$$n_f = Nf_1q_1 + Nf_2q_2 + \cdots + Nf_iq_i = N\sum_{j=1}^{i} f_jq_j \quad (1b)$$

We can now compute the system probability of failure on any one test run q_0 as

$$q_0 \equiv \frac{n_f}{N} = \sum_{j=1}^{i} f_jq_j \quad (1c)$$

Similarly we can compute the system failure rate z_0 by first computing the total number of test hours for the successful and unsuccessful runs. We compute the total number of traversals of path j as Nf_j as was previously done. Out of these traversals, Nf_jp_j will be successful and will accumulate a total of $Nf_jp_jt_j'$ hours of successful operation. If we assume that the time-to-failure distribution for the Nf_jq_j traversals which result in failure is rectangular, then each trial which results in failure runs $t_j'/2$ hours on the average before failure (other distributions could be used). Thus, the expected total test time accumulated in N runs is given by

$$H = Nf_1p_1t_1' + Nf_1q_1\frac{t_1'}{2} + Nf_2p_2t_2' + Nf_2q_2\frac{t_2'}{2}$$

$$+ \cdots + Nf_ip_it_i' + Nf_iq_i\frac{t_i'}{2}$$

$$= N\sum_{j=1}^{i} f_jt_j'\left(p_j + \frac{q_j}{2}\right) \quad (1d)$$

Substitution for $p_j = 1 - q_j$ in Eq. (1d) and simplification

yields

$$H = N\sum_{j=1}^{i} f_jt_j'\left(1 - \frac{q_j}{2}\right) \quad (1e)$$

We now compute the system failure rate z_0 as

$$z_0 = \lim_{N\to\infty}\frac{n_f}{H} \quad (1f)$$

and substitution from Eq. (1b) and (1e) into Eq. (1f) yields in the limit

$$z_0 = \frac{\displaystyle\sum_{j=1}^{i} f_jq_j}{\displaystyle\sum_{j=1}^{i} f_j\left(1 - \frac{q_j}{2}\right)t_j'} \quad (2a)$$

Note that the symbol for executed time of path j has been given a prime, t_j' to differentiate it from the system operating time t.

If the q_j values are small as they may be in most cases, then Eq. (2a) simplifies to:

$$z_0 = \frac{\displaystyle\sum_{j=1}^{i} f_jq_j}{\displaystyle\sum_{j=1}^{i} f_jt_j'} \quad (2b)$$

We can interpret Eq. (2) in a simple fashion. The failure rate z_0 is just the ratio of the weighted failure probabilities and the weighted running times (to failure or success), yielding failures per unit time (commonly hours).

Note that the failure rate function z_0 in Eq. (2b) is independent of operating time t. Thus, substituting z_0 into the standard reliability expression [23], yields:

$$R(t) = \exp\left[\int_0^t -z_0\,dx\right] = e^{-z_0t} \quad (3a)$$

The mean time to failure, MTTF, is given by:

$$\text{MTTF} = \int_0^\infty R(t)\,dt \quad (3b)$$

Since z_0 is independent of t, substitution of (3a) in (3b) yields

$$\text{MTTF} = \frac{1}{z_0} \qquad (3c)$$

Also, the density function, which we will need later in our development, can be written as:

$$f(t) = z_0 R(t) \qquad (4)$$

We now discuss how to measure the system parameters which is a necessary step in the application of the model. Note that if the software is under development the above model holds at the point in the development at which the system parameters are measured.

3.0 Estimation of Micro Model Parameters

We now discuss the estimation of the micro model parameters which are the set of f_j, t_j', and q_j values. To simplify the discussion, we will compute these values for $i = 2$ and then generalize for any number of paths.

The best way to evaluate these parameters is to use two approaches, one for f_1, f_2, t_1', and t_2'; and another approach for q_1, q_2. To estimate the frequencies of case execution, the analyst can consult the project specifications and deduce these from the physical problem to be solved. If this is too difficult, one can devise a set of realistic test data, n cases, and examine the relative frequencies f_1 and f_2 either by analysis, or by inserting counters n_1 and n_2 for cases 1 and 2 in the software and executing the set of test data. The frequencies f_1 and f_2 would be (n_1/n) and (n_2/n). Similarly, we could deduce the running times, t_1', t_2', for case 1 and case 2 from the specifications or by timing the execution of the software for a particular instance of case 1 and case 2 test data. If the execution times are not constant, then a number of typical case 1 and case 2 data sets must be used as inputs and the average values of $\bar{t}_1$ and $\bar{t}_2$ are used.

The estimation of q_1 and q_2 is best accomplished via a reliability test. In fact, if the values of relative frequency and execution time are to be determined by instrumenting the software, the same set of realistic test data can be used for the reliability test. The only requirement is that the test data be extensive enough to excite a few errors for each of the cases. We then record the r_1 times to failure of case 1, t_1, t_2, $\cdots$, t_{r1}, and the $n_1 \cdot r_1$ execution times for the successful case 1 executions, T_1, T_2, $\cdots$, $T_{n1-r1} = t_1'$, t_2', $\cdots$, t_{n1-r1}'. (Because of the many different time parameters and measurements required for this model, the reader will appreciate the use of the notations t, t', and T.) A similar set of data is recorded for case 2 executions. We can then use maximum likelihood estimation theory to estimate q_1 and q_2, which we immediately generalize to i cases, (see [2], Sec. A.10.3; [23] Eqs. (8.67) and (8.68); [24]).

The derivation of a maximum likelihood estimator (MLE) for a probability distribution begins by writing the MLE function, L:

$$L(t_{r_i}, T_{n_i}; q_i) = \frac{n_i!}{(n_i - r_i)!} \prod_{k=1}^{r_i} z_0 R(t_k) \prod_{k=1}^{n_i - r_i} R(T_k) \qquad (5)$$

and the natural log of L:

$$\ln(L) = \mathscr{L} = \ln\left[\frac{n_i!}{(n_i - r_i)!}\right] + \sum_{k=1}^{r_i} \ln[z_0 R(t_k)] \\ + \sum_{k=1}^{n_i - r_i} \ln[R(T_k)] \qquad (6)$$

To maximize the log of the likelihood function, one computes the partial derivatives of $\ln(L)$ with respect to each of the i parameters to be estimated (the q_i's) and set them equal to zero. The resulting set of equations is solved for the MLE estimators of the q_i's. We substitute Eqs. (2-4) into Eq. (6) and compute the partial derivatives. After considerable algebra we obtain the following equation in each case after differentiating and simplifying:

$$\sum_{k=1}^{r_i} f_k q_k = \frac{r_i}{H_i} \sum_{k=1}^{r_i} f_k t_k \qquad (7)$$

where

$$H_i = \sum_{k=1}^{r_i} t_k + \sum_{k=1}^{n_i - r_i} T_k$$

The conclusion is that the q_i parameters are not independent and can not be estimated separately from this data. The solution is to run a different type of test. Suppose that we use test data which only excites case 1. We then have the situation where $f_1 = 1$ and $f_2 = f_3 = \cdots = f_i = 0$. In this case after substitution in Eq. (2b) and (3a), Eq. (6) becomes:

$$\ln(L) = \ln\left[\frac{n_i!}{(n_i - r_i)!}\right] + \sum_{k=1}^{r_i} \ln\left[\frac{q_1}{t_1'}\right] \\ - \sum_{k=1}^{r_i} \left(\frac{q_1}{t_1'}\right) t_i - \sum_{k=1}^{n_i - r_i} \left(\frac{q_1}{t_1'}\right) T_i \qquad (8)$$

and after differentiation and equating to zero we obtain:

$$\hat{q}_1 = \frac{r\, t_1'}{H} \qquad (9)$$

and we obtain a similar equation for each of the cases by using test data for only the case in question.

$$\hat{q}_j = \frac{r\, t'_j}{H} \qquad (10)$$

4.0 Combining Module Test and Integration Test Data Via a Control Flow Model

The cases we have been discussing are really execution sequences of the software. We can model these execution sequences by paths in the flow chart or control graph of the software. In general, each such path traverses a number of modules. The failure probability for any case j, q_j, can be related to the probabilities of failure of the modules traversed along path j, using combinatorial reliability methods such as reliability graphs, fault trees, etc. (See [23], Ch. 3). This will allow one to use module test data to determine module failure probabilities, and then use these values in a combinatorial model to determine the q_j values. Then these q_j values are used in Eqs. (1)-(3) to determine the overall software reliability. The combinatorial computations relating q_j values are used in Eqs. (1)-(3) to determine the overall software reliability, and are illustrated via an example.

Consider the flow chart given in Fig. 1 for a program composed of 5 modules (one of which, m_2, is used twice) and two IF THEN ELSE control structures. In this program there are three cases and three control sequences:

CASE 1: $m_1 c_{1T} m_3 m_2'$
CASE 2: $m_1 c_{1E} m_2 c_{2T} m_4$
CASE 3: $m_1 c_{1E} m_2 c_{2E} m_5$

where c_{iT} and c_{iE} mean that the control statement selects the THEN clause or the ELSE clause.

We adopt the notation where M_1 represents successful execution of module m_1 for any one traversal, and $\overline{M}_1$ represents unsuccessful execution of module m_1 for any one traversal. We can write the following expressions for the probabilities of error while traversing the cases (where + indicates union of events)

$$q_1 = P(\overline{M}_1 + \overline{C}_{1T} + \overline{M}_3 + \overline{M}_2') \qquad (11)$$

$$q_2 = P(\overline{M}_1 + \overline{C}_{1E} + \overline{M}_2 + \overline{C}_{2T} + \overline{M}_4) \qquad (12)$$

$$q_3 = P(\overline{M}_1 + \overline{C}_{1E} + \overline{M}_2 + \overline{C}_{2E} + \overline{M}_5) \qquad (13)$$

The above expressions represent the probability of a union of events which can be evaluated in three different ways:

1. The expression can be expanded according to probability theory in terms of the events taken singly, in pairs, in triplets, etc. For example, if all the events in Eq. (11) are independent (which they should be) then the expression becomes

$$q_1 = \begin{aligned} &P(\overline{M}_1) + P(\overline{C}_{1T}) + P(\overline{M}_3) + P(\overline{M}_2') - \\ &P(\overline{M}_1)P(\overline{C}_{1T}) - P(\overline{M}_1)P(\overline{M}_3) - P(\overline{M}_1)P(\overline{M}_2) - \\ &P(\overline{C}_{1T})P(\overline{M}_3) - P(\overline{C}_{1T})P(\overline{M}_2') - P(\overline{M}_3)P(\overline{M}_2) + \\ &P(\overline{M}_1)P(\overline{C}_{1T})P(\overline{M}_3) + P(\overline{M}_1)P(\overline{C}_{1T})P(\overline{M}_2') + \\ &P(\overline{M}_1)P(\overline{M}_3)P(\overline{M}_2') + P(\overline{C}_{1T})P(\overline{M}_3)P(\overline{M}_2') \end{aligned} \qquad (14)$$

2. Since the probability of each module failing is small, Eq. (14) can be bounded (approximated) by the first four terms ([23], Eq. (3.40))

$$q_1 \leq P(\overline{M}_1) + P(\overline{C}_1) + P(\overline{M}_3) + P(\overline{M}_2') \qquad (15)$$

3. The expressions for q_i can be evaluated using any of the computer aided reliability analysis programs which are in use, which do block diagram or fault tree analysis such as those developed for fault tolerant computer systems (e.g. ARIES, CARE III, HARP).

If the control structure contains loops created by DO WHILE or DO UNTIL control structures as is generally the case, then we must establish an algorithm for dealing with the loops. We will use the technique employed in [2] (Ch. 4) and by others to approximately model the loop structure. The loop is executed twice only, once assuming the loop control expression is immediately satisfied and once assuming that one circuit around the loop satisfies the loop control expression. This model represents the majority of errors which occur upon loop initiation or termination, but not those which occur only for a particular number of loop repetitions. For the example of Fig. 2 we obtain 4 cases:

CASE 1: $m_1 c_{1T} m_3 c_{3E}$
CASE 2: $m_1 c_{1T} m_3 c_{3T} m_2'$
CASE 3: $m_1 c_{1E} m_2 c_{2T} m_4$
CASE 4: $m_1 c_{1E} m_{1E} c_{2E} m_5$

The probability expressions are written and evaluated in the same manner as Fig.1 above.

The next step in building our model is to establish how to estimate the module failure probabilities.

5.0 Estimation of Module Failure Probabilities

We now discuss how to measure the various module failure probabilities, e.g. $P(\overline{M}_1)$, which must be substituted into the probability expressions such as Eqs. (11)-(15).

During module test we subject the module to various

test inputs and check to see if the outputs are correct. To estimate the module failure probabilities we can use any of the macro (black box) models which have been developed. Two of the popular macro models ([2] pp. 355-374; [9]) relate the software failure rate to the remaining number of errors. The simplest assumption is to make them directly proportional [1]

$$\lambda = K[E_T - E_c(t)] \qquad (16)$$

where

λ = The software failure rate
K = A constant of proportionality
E_T = The total number of errors present at the start of testing
E_c = The number of errors corrected during interval 0 to t
t = The time variable (to be defined further below)

The constants K and E_T are estimated from test data in a manner similar to that given in Eqs. (5)-(10) above, based upon test data which allows computation of r and H.

Assume that we have applied the above model to test data for module m_1 and have obtained the failure rate λ_1. Then the probability of failure for one traversal of this module is this failure rate times the execution time of this module Δt_1. In the above discussion we have assumed that the time variable t is the actual execution time of a realistic test input stream. This same model has been frequently employed during integration testing for cases where the test times were not recorded by the test team, and the calendar time was used by the reliability analyst instead as an approximation. Since the module tester generally performs his own tests, he has access to the actual execution times and thus better input data is available. However, as Musa ([10], pp. 178, 179, 230-234) has observed, module test cases are often not realistic, since the same inputs are not repeated during testing as they are in real operation. Thus, in operation known good input sets are often repeated, however, this is not the case during on module testing. Musa suggests that a test compression factor, C, be introduced to account for this and that its effect is to lower the measured failure rate. Thus, using a compression factor, our expression for the probability of module failure is

$$P(\overline{M})_1 = \lambda_1 \times \Delta t_1 / C \qquad (16a)$$

Musa has experimental data which show that C is about 10-15 for a number of examples. Furthermore, if one assumes that the inputs fall into a number of discrete classes and that the class execution frequencies are inversely proportional to the rank (this assumption leads to Zipf's frequency law, [2], pp. 159-162) then the constant C is related to the sum of the harmonic series.

Musa shows that for a large range of partition classes, C varies between 8 and 20. In practice the best way to estimate C is from an analysis of the type outlined above or by experimental comparison of the frequency of input occurrences in an actual input stream versus the chosen test input stream.

We now have a model which relates system reliability to a number of parameters including path test frequencies, f_i. If we combine the model developed above with various models for the error removal rate, (see [25] for assumptions which lead to the Shooman or Musa model), we can minimize z_0 in Eq. (2) under constraints and obtain various test strategies [22].

6.0 Optimum Allocation of Test Resources

The effect of testing is to find faults in the code, diagnose the code to find the underlying error, and redesign and test the code so that the error is removed. The effect on our model is to reduce the failure probabilities $q_1, q_2, \cdots q_i$. If the failure probabilities are assumed to decrease with additional test effort, TE (includes redesigning and retest), then our optimization problem reduces to how to apportion the total test effort among the i paths so as to minimize the failure rate z_0. We begin our development by assuming that the test effort is given by

$$TE = TE1 + TE2 + \cdots TE_i \qquad (17)$$

If we further assume that the failure probabilities are inversely proportional to the test effort then

$$q_1 = \frac{K_1}{TE_1}$$
$$q_2 = \frac{K_2}{TE_2} \qquad (18)$$
$$\cdots\cdots\cdots\cdots$$
$$q_i = \frac{K_i}{TE_i}$$

Although it is likely that $K_1, K_2, \cdots K_i$ will differ, for simplicity we set $K = K_1 = K_2 \cdots K_i$, and substituting (18) into Eq. (2b) to obtain

$$z_0 = \frac{\sum_{j=1}^{i} \frac{f_j K}{TE_j}}{\sum_{j=1}^{i} f_j t_j} \qquad (19)$$

To minimize z_0 we will differentiate z_0 with respect to the TE_j values under the constraint of Eq. (17). To facilitate the algebra we substitute Eq. (1e) into Eq. (19).

$$z_0 = \left[\frac{K}{H/N}\right]\sum_{j=1}^{i}\frac{f_j}{TE_j} \qquad (20)$$

For simplicity we assume that $i=3$ thus

$$z_0 = \left[\frac{NK}{H}\right]\left[\frac{f_1}{TE_1}+\frac{f_2}{TE_2}+\frac{f_3}{TE_3}\right] \qquad (21)$$

Introducing the constraint initially in a simple way. (Lagrange multipliers would be more elegant, but are not needed because of the simple nature of the constraint.)

$$TE_3 = TE - TE_1 - TE_2 \qquad (22)$$

and substitution into Eq. (21) yields

$$z_0 = \left[\frac{NK}{H}\right]\left[\frac{f_1}{TE_1}+\frac{f_2}{TE_2}+\frac{f_3}{TE-TE_1-TE_2}\right] \qquad (23)$$

We now compute partials of z_0 with respect to the test efforts and equate to zero

$$\frac{\partial z_0}{\partial TE_1} = \frac{NK}{H}\left[-\frac{f_1}{(TE_1)^2}+\frac{f_3}{(TE-TE_1-TE_2)^2}\right]=0 \qquad (24a)$$

$$\frac{\partial z_0}{\partial TE_2} = \frac{NK}{H}\left[-\frac{f_2}{(TE_2)^2}+\frac{f_3}{(TE-TE_1-TE_2)^2}\right]=0 \qquad (24b)$$

$$\frac{\partial z_0}{\partial TE_3}=0 \qquad (24c)$$

Solving Eqs. 24a, b and using Eq. 22 yields

$$\frac{f_1}{(TE_1)^2}=\frac{f_2}{(TE_2)^2}=\frac{f_3}{(TE_3)^2} \qquad (25a)$$

which is equivalent to

$$\frac{TE_1}{\sqrt{f_1}}=\frac{TE_2}{\sqrt{f_2}}=\frac{TE_3}{\sqrt{f_3}} \qquad (25b)$$

Solving Eqs. 25b and 22 yields

$$TE_1 = \frac{\sqrt{f_1}}{\sqrt{f_1}+\sqrt{f_2}+\sqrt{f_3}}TE \qquad (26a)$$

$$TE_2 = \frac{\sqrt{f_2}}{\sqrt{f_1}+\sqrt{f_2}+\sqrt{f_3}}TE \qquad (26b)$$

$$TE_3 = \frac{\sqrt{f_3}}{\sqrt{f_1}+\sqrt{f_2}+\sqrt{f_3}}TE \qquad (26c)$$

Clearly the general solution for i paths becomes

$$TE_i = \frac{\sqrt{f_i}}{\sum_{j=1}^{i}\sqrt{f_j}}TE \qquad (27)$$

If all the frequencies f_j are equal, the test efforts are all equal, whereas if some of the frequencies are larger than the others such paths will receive more test effort. However, since the apportionment is proportional to $\sqrt{f_j}$, small differences in f_j will result in even smaller differences in apportionment. Of course more realistic models can be made by assuming that the K_j values in Eq. 18 are unequal or by using models which link error removal to test effort (Eq. 18) in a more realistic manner.

6.1 Example Equal Effort

We can better appreciate the impact of optimum allocation if we choose a numerical example. Suppose that at the beginning of integration test the model parameters are

$$f_1=0.1 \qquad t_1'=1\times10^{-2}\text{sec.} \qquad q_1=4\times10^{-7}$$
$$f_2=0.6 \qquad t_2'=3\times10^{-2}\text{sec.} \qquad q_2=1\times10^{-7}$$
$$f_3=0.3 \qquad t_3'=5\times10^{-2}\text{sec.} \qquad q_3=2\times10^{-7}$$

Substituting these values into Eq. 2b yields

$$z_0=0.4706\times10^{-5}\text{ fail/sec.}\times3600\text{sec/hr.} \qquad (28)$$
$$=0.01694\text{ fail/hr.}$$

From Eq. (3c) we compute the mean time to failure as

$$MTTF=59\text{ hours} \qquad (30)$$

Assume that the test effort will be measured in man-hours of testing, debugging, redesign, and retest and that 900 hours (about 1/2 year) are available in the budget. Assume from past experience that we know the constant K is about 10^{-6}. If we apportion the effort equally, each path receives 300 hours and eq. (18) tells us that after this effort is expended

$$q_1=q_2=q_3=10^{-6}/300=3.33\times10^{-9}.$$

Substituting these new values for q_j along with the above f_j and t_j values into Eq. (2b) and (3c) yields

$$z_0=3.53\times10^{-4}\text{ fail/hr.} \qquad (31)$$

$$MTTF=2833\text{ hours.} \qquad (32)$$

Thus, the 900 hours of test, debug, redesign, and retest has reduced the probability of failure and increased the MTTF by about two orders of magnitude.

6.2 Example Effort Proportional to f_j

Suppose we decide to apportion the effort proportional to f_1, f_2 and f_j, then we have 90, 540, and 270 hours respectively and $q_1=11.1\times10^{-9}$, $q_2=1.85\times10^{-9}$, and $q_3=3.70\times10^{-9}$ and substitution in Eqs. 2b and 3c yields

$$z_0=3.408\times10^{-4}\text{ fail/hr.} \qquad (33)$$

$$MTTF = 2934 \text{ hours} \qquad (34)$$

A negligible improvement (3.6%) over equal apportionment.

6.3 Example - Optimum Appointment

Lastly, we partition our effort in the optimum fashion using Eqs. 26a,b,c which yields an apportionment of 174, 425, and 301 hours. Substituting in equations 2b and 3c yields

$$z_0 = 3.1584 \times 10^{-4} \text{ fall/hr.} \qquad (35)$$

$$MTTF = 3166 \text{ hours} \qquad (36)$$

which is a significant improvement (11.7%) over the results given in Eqs. 32. Depending on the numerical values, more dramatic results might be obtained.

7.0 References

1. Shooman, M. L., Probabilistic Models for Software Reliability Prediction," printed in W. Freiberger, Ed., Statistical Computer Performance Evaluation, Academic Press, New York, NY, 1972, pp. 485-502.

2. Shooman, M. L., Software Engineering: Design, Reliability,and Management, McGraw-Hill Book Co, New York, NY, 1983.

3. Shooman, M. L., "Software Reliability - Historical Perspective," IEEE Trans. on Reliability, Vol. R-33, No. 1, June 1984, pp.48-55.

4. Jelinski, Z. and P. Moranda, "Software Reliability Research," printed in W. Freiberger, Ed., Statistical Computer Performance Evaluation, Academic Press, New York, NY, 1972, pp. 465-484.

5. Littlewood, B. and J. L. Verrall, "A Bayesian Reliability Model with a Stochastically Monotone Failure Rate," IEEE Trans. on Reliability, R-23(2), 1974, pp. 108-114.

6. Littlewood, B., "A Semi-Markov Model for Software Reliability with Failure Costs," Proceedings Symposium on Computer Software Engr., Polytechnic Press, New York, 1976, pp. 281-300.

7. Littlewood, B., "Software Reliability Model for Modular Program Structure," IEEE Trans. on Reliability, R-28(3), 1979, pp. 241-246.

8. Littlewood, B., "Stochastic Reliability-Growth: A Model for Fault-Removal in Computer-Programs and Hardware-Design," IEEE Trans. on Reliability, R-30(4), 1981, pp. 313-320.

9. Musa, J., "A Theory of Software Reliability and Its Application," IEEE Trans. Software Eng., Vol. SE-1, No. 3, Sept. 1975, pp 312-327.

10. Musa, J., et al., Software Reliability Measurement, Prediction, Application, McGraw-Hill, New York, NY, 1987

11. Schneidewind, N. F., "Analysis of Error Processes in Computer Software," Proceedings 1975 Int'l. Conference on Reliable Software, Los Angeles, 1975, pp. 337-346.

12. Lloyd, D. K. and Lipow, M., Reliability: Management,Methods, and Mathematics, 2nd Edition, 1977, ASQC.

13. Goel, A. L. and K. Okumoto, "An Analysis of Recurrent Software Errors in a Real-time Control System," Proceedings ACM Conference, 1978, pp. 496-501.

14. Goel, A. L. and K. Okumoto, "A Markovian Model for Reliability and Other Performance Measures," Proceedings National Computer Conference, 1979, pp. 769-744.

15. Goel, A. L. and K, Okumoto, "Time-Dependent Error-Detection Rate Model for Software Reliability and Other Performance Measures," IEEE Trans. on Reliability, R-28(3), 1979, pp. 206-211.

16. Shooman, M. L., "Yes, Software Reliability Can be Measured and Predicted," Proceedings Fall Joint Computer Conference, Oct. 1987.

17. Shooman, M. L., "Structural Models for Software Reliability Prediction," Second National Conference on Software Reliability, San Francisco, CA, October 1976.

18. Littlewood, B., "Software Reliability Model for Modular Program Structure," IEEE Trans. on Reliability, R-28, Aug. 1979., pp. 241-246.

19. Laprie, J.-C., "Dependability Evaluation of Software Systems in Operation," IEEE Trans. on Software Eng. Vol. SE-10, Nov. 1984, pp 701-714.

20. Hecht, H., "Talk on Software Reliability," given at AIAA Software Reliability Committee Meeting, Colorado Springs, CO., August 22-25, 1989.

21. Freedman, R. S. and M. L. Shooman, "An Expert System for Software Component Testing," Final

Report, New York State Research and Development Grant Program, Contract No. SSF(87)-18, Polytechnic University, Oct. 1988.

22. Shooman, M. L., "Optimum Allocation of Test Resources," Polytechnic University, Computer Science Research Memo, Oct. 29, 1989.

23. Shooman, M. L., _Probabilistic Reliability: An Engineering Approach_, McGraw-Hill Book Co., New York, NY, 1968, 2nd. Edition, Krieger, Melbourne, FL, 1990.

24. Hoel, P. G., _Introduction to Mathematical Statistics_, Fourth Edition, John Wiley & Sons, New York, NY, 1971.

25. Shooman, M. L., "Validating Software Reliability Models," _Proceedings IFAC Workshop on Reliability, Availability, and Maintainability_, Bruge, Belgium, 1988.

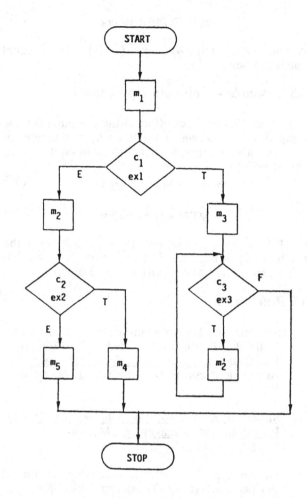

Fig. 2. A Software System with 5 Modules, 2 IF THEN ELSE and 1 DO WHILE control structures.

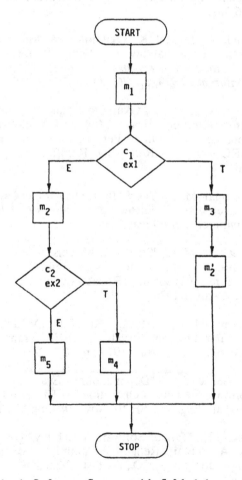

Fig. 1 A Software System with 5 Modules and 2 IF THEN ELSE control structures.

58

Optimization Models for Selection of Programs, Considering Cost & Reliability

Noushin Ashrafi, Member IEEE
University of Massachusetts, Boston
Oded Berman
University of Toronto, Toronto

Key Words — Software reliability, Software cost, Fault tolerance, Optimization, Lagrangian relaxation, Dynamic programming.

Reader Aids —
Purpose: Provide decision-making tool
Special math needed for explanations: Mathematical programming
Special math needed to use results: Same
Results useful to: Software engineers, reliability theoreticians, software managers.

Abstract — This paper presents two optimization models for decision support tools for selecting available programs in the market. Information on reliability and cost of the available programs are considered as basic criteria for the selection. These models apply to software packages that consist of several programs where each, upon execution, performs a different function as required by the user. The objective is to maximize the average reliability of the software package, considering the tradeoff between reliability and cost of the programs. In model 1, redundancy of the programs is not considered; thus we select one program for each function. In model 2, redundancy is considered; thus we identify the optimal set of programs for each function. The paper begins with a discussion of the underlying concepts that rationalize the composition of the models.

1. INTRODUCTION

Software reliability is the most important measure of software quality, and it is very customer-oriented. Software reliability measures how well a software system operates to meet the user requirements [3]. Since, ultimately, it is the user who must be satisfied with the performance of the software, the quality of software should be expressed in terms of its reliability [1].

The relationship between reliability and cost has always been important for software developers. "One can hardly perceive reliability without considering the cost of achieving it" [9, p 2]. Moreover, "the high cost of software development and maintenance is an important reason for emphasis on producing reliable software" [6, p 109]. In order to develop fault-free software, all the latent and known faults in a software must be detected and repaired. This is very difficult, if not impossible, and requires enormous time and money. Since software developers operate within limited resources (time and money), there must be a tradeoff between reliability and cost.

Software reliability and cost are two competing issues, and improvement in one is obtained to the detriment of the other [4].

2. OPTIMIZATION MODELS

This paper presents two models which address the tradeoff between reliability and cost. They apply to large software packages that consist of several programs. Following Pressman [5], we define a program as a set of complete machine instructions (operations with operands) which, upon execution, perform one major function as required by the user. The models can be used as decision support tools for organizations that are in the process of purchasing a variety of computer programs in order to meet the needs of the users, eg, operations people need software packages to perform functions such as scheduling, inventory control, and purchase orders. While the main consideration is to attain high average reliability for the software package, management has to consider both the relative importance of each program to the organization and its associated cost. In this study we define the relative importance of each program in terms of the frequency of the usage of their corresponding function.

Programs can be purchased from software development companies. Several programs are usually available for each function. Each program has a known market cost and an estimated reliability. Ideally, we want to maximize the average reliability of a software package by purchasing the most reliable programs on the market. However, considering the high cost of these programs, a decision must be made regarding the selection of the best program for each function such that maximum reliability for the software package is attained and the total cost of programs remains within the budget.

Two distinct models are addressed:

1. The software package performs several functions but, due to financial limitations and/or noncritical nature of the functions, keeping multiple programs that are functionally equivalent is not possible. The model uses the Lagrangian Relaxation algorithm [2]. The objective is to select one program for each function such that the average reliability is maximized and cost of purchasing programs remains within the budget. This model is presented in section 3.1. Appendix A describes the Lagrangian Relaxation algorithm.

2. The software package performs several functions whose failures must be minimized. The average reliability can be improved by purchasing more than one program for each function. The option of inclusion of more than one program for each function allows fault tolerant operation for any required function. ☐

Reprinted from *IEEE Trans. Reliability*, Vol. 41, No. 2, June 1992, pp. 281–287.

Discussion of Model 2

Suppose several statistically independently designed and functionally equivalent programs are purchased. Since the programs are developed statistically independently by different groups of software developers, each one of them can contain a different (possibly overlapping) set of faults. These faults are triggered by executing a different set of inputs hence causing failures in different programs. We assume that when a function is requested, one of the programs is executed, and the results are examined according to some acceptance criteria. If the results are not acceptable, program 2 is executed. The results are again subjected to acceptance criteria. This process continues until a program with acceptable results is executed. This procedure provides a fault tolerant operation despite the faulty programs in the software packages. All programs, however, could be exhausted with no acceptable results.

This model costs more than model 1; therefore it is aimed at applications where the consequences of failure are severe, eg, software packages used by the military, emergency services, and air traffic control. We analyze this model with a dynamic programming algorithm [8]. The objective is to determine the optimal set of programs for each function, allowing redundancy, so as to maximize the average reliability of the software package while remaining within the budget. Our model is presented in section 3.2. The dynamic programming algorithm is described in appendix B.

We show that by maximizing the average reliability of a software package we minimize the average failure rate for a given package. □

Sections 3.1 & 3.2 present the models, each with a numerical illustration.

3. MODEL FORMULATION & SOLUTION

Notation

K number of functions the software package is required to perform

F_k frequency of use of function k, $k = 1,2,...,K$

m_k number of programs available for function k

R_{kj} reliability of program j, which performs function k

X_{kj} indicator: 1 if program j is selected to perform function k, else 0

$\bar{R}$ average reliability of the software package

C_{kj} cost of developing program j that performs function k

B available budget □

Other, standard notation is given in "Information for Readers & Authors" at the rear of each issue.

Assumptions

     1. Each program has a distinct, known reliability and cost.
     2. The budget is limited.
     3. Usage frequency for each function is known, viz, provided by the user. □

3.1 *Model 1: No Redundancy*

The problem of maximizing average reliability by choosing the optimal set of programs is formulated as:

$$\max \bar{R} = \sum_{k=1}^{K} F_k R_k \tag{P$_1$}$$

subject to:

$$\sum_{j=1}^{m_k} X_{kj} = 1, \; k = 1,..,K \tag{i}$$

$$\sum_{k=1}^{K} \sum_{j=1}^{m_k} X_{kj} C_{kj} \leq B \tag{ii}$$

$X_{kj} = 0, 1$, for $k = 1,...,K$ and $j = 1,...,m_k$.

$$R_k \equiv \sum_{j=1}^{m_k} X_{kj} R_{kj} \tag{1}$$

The objective function of (P$_1$) reflects that we maximize the average reliability of the software package which is a weighted sum of the reliability of the K functions; each reliability is multiplied by the usage frequency of the corresponding function. The set of constraints (i) ensures that exactly one program is selected for each function. Constraint (ii) guarantees that total expenditure does not exceed the budget. Since the functions are required for entirely different purposes (and possibly by different users) they should be considered not as a series of functions but as a set of s-independent functions.

Maximizing the average reliability $\bar{R}$, is equivalent to minimizing the average failure rate $\bar{Z}$ [7, pp 379-381]:

$$\bar{Z} \equiv (N/H) \sum_{k=1}^{K} F_k (1 - R_k) \tag{2}$$

Notation

H operation time

N number of runs during H

$1 - R_k$ probability of failure for function k □

By straight-forward algebra, and noting that $\sum_{k=1}^{K} F_k = 1$, (2) can be rewritten:

$$\bar{Z} = (N/H) \left(1 - \sum_{k=1}^{K} F_k R_k\right) = (N/H)(1 - \bar{R}) \tag{3}$$

To motivate (P$_1$), consider the following real application. A computer center in a university wishes to select programs to perform two functions:

• System editing that requires programs such as Ed & Vi,
• Statistical analysis that requires programs such as SAS, SPSS, MINITAB. □

The objective is to minimize the average failure rate (maximize average reliability) while remaining within the budget.

Problem (P_1) is an integer programming problem that can be solved by using many available software packages (such as Management Scientist). In appendix A we show a Lagrangian Relaxation algorithm [2] that handles the special structure of the problem. This algorithm can be used when the available general purpose integer programming software cannot solve the problem because of its size. Problem (P_1) has sum of m_k, $k=1,...,K$ variables and $K+1$ constraints. If K & m_k are large (say, $K=50$, $m_k > 10$ for all k) the problem might be too complex to solve with the available software. Then, the more efficient algorithm in appendix A can be used. Lagrangian Relaxation is useful here because by replacing constraint set (i) with a penalty term in the objective function involving the amount of violation of the constraints, a Knapsack problem [8] remains that can be solved using a variety of efficient Knapsack algorithms such as dynamic programming.

Example 1. A 2-Function Software Package

Data —

$B = 12$

• Function 1: 4 programs are available.

$F_1 = 0.75$

$R_{11} = 0.90, R_{12} = 0.80, R_{13} = 0.85, R_{14} = 0.95$

$C_{11} = 6, C_{12} = 4, C_{13} = 5, C_{14} = 8$

• Function 2: 3 programs are available.

$F_2 = 0.25$

$R_{21} = 0.70, R_{22} = 0.80, R_{23} = 0.90$

$C_{21} = 2, C_{22} = 4, C_{23} = 6$

Problem —

$$\max \bar{R}^* = 0.675X_{11} + 0.60X_{12} + 0.6375X_{13} + 0.7125X_{14}$$
$$+ 0.175X_{21} + 0.20X_{22} + 0.225X_{23}$$

subject to:

$$X_{11} + X_{12} + X_{13} + X_{14} = 1$$

$$X_{21} + X_{22} + X_{23} = 1$$

$$6X_{11} + 4X_{12} + 5X_{13} + 8X_{14} + 2X_{21} + 4X_{22} + 6X_{23} \leq 12$$

X_{kj} is 0 or 1, for all j,k.

The coefficients of the objective function were computed by multiplying the usage frequency of each function by the reliability of the program available for that function. For example:

$$0.675 = (0.75)(0.9)$$

$$0.60 = (0.75)(0.8).$$

Although the example can be solved by inspection, the rest of this section shows how to solve the problem with the Lagrangian Relaxation algorithm.

problem L_1 is:

$$\max \bar{R}(u_1,u_2) = X_{11}(0.675-u_1) + X_{12}(0.60-u_1)$$

$$+ X_{13}(0.6735-u_1) + X_{14}(0.7125-u_1)$$

$$+ X_{21}(0.175-u_2) + X_{22}(0.20-u_2)$$

$$+ X_{23}(0.225-u_2) + u_1 + u_2$$

subject to:

$$6X_{11} + 4X_{12} + 5X_{13} + 8X_{14} + 2X_{21} + 4X_{22} + 6X_{23} \leq 12$$

$$X_{11},X_{12},...,X_{23} = 0,1$$

Following the steps used to summarize the algorithm in appendix A, we go through 4 iterations to obtain the optimal solution.

Iteration 1. [$i=0$]

Step 0: Begin with $i=0$; then $(u_1^0, u_2^0) = (0,0)$

Step 1: Solve L_1 by inspection for $(u_1^0, u_2^0) = (0,0)$:

$$X_{11}^0 = X_{12}^0 = X_{21}^0 = 1,$$

$$\bar{R}^*(0,0) = 1.45.$$

Step 2: (Compute t_0) Begin with $\bar{R}^* = 0.85$ which is the objective function value of the feasible solution when we arbitrarily choose: $X_{11} = 1, X_{21} = 1$.

$$t^0 = \frac{1(1.45-.85)}{(1-2)^2 + (1-1)^2} = 0.6$$

Step 3: (Find the improved values for vector u). Set:

$$u_1^1 = \max(0; 0-0.6(1-2)) = 0.6$$

$$u_2^1 = \max(0; 0-0.6(1-1)) = 0$$

Iteration 2. [$i=1$]

Step 1:

$$X_{21}^1 = X_{22}^1 = X_{23}^1 = 1 \quad \bar{R}^*(0.6,0) = 1.2$$

Step 2:

$$t^1 = \frac{1(1.2 - 0.85)}{(1-0)^2 + (1-3)^2} = 0.07$$

Step 3:

$$u_1^2 = \max(0; \, 0.6 - 0.07(1-0)) = 0.53$$

$$u_2^2 = \max(0; \, 0 - 0.07(1-3)) = 0.14$$

Iteration 3. [i=2]

Step 1:

$$X_{12}^2 = X_{14}^2 = 1, \quad \bar{R}^*(0.53, 0.14) = 0.9225$$

Step 2:

$$t^2 = \frac{1(0.9225 - 0.85)}{(1-2)^2 + (1-0)^2} = 0.03625$$

Step 3:

$$u_1^3 = \max(0; \, 0.53 - 0.03625(1-2)) = 0.56625$$

$$u_2^3 = \max(0; \, 0.14 - 0.03625(1-0)) = 0.10375$$

Iteration 4. [i=3]

Step 1:

$$X_{14}^3 = X_{22}^3 = 1, \quad \bar{R}^*(0.56625, 0.10375) = 0.9125$$

Step 4: Since $X_{14}^3 = X_{22}^3 = 1$ is feasible for (P$_1$) it is an improved feasible solution.

Since the updated value of $\bar{R}^*$, computed using (P$_1$) is:

$$(0.75)(0.95) + (0.25)(0.80) = 0.9125,$$

$$\bar{R}^* = \bar{R}^*(u^i).$$

Thus we have reached an optimal solution. Program 4 for function 1 and program 2 for function 2 should be selected to provide optimal reliability of 0.9125 at a cost of $8 + 4 = 12$.

Let $N = 100$ and $H = 200$. The optimal failure rate using (3) can be computed:

$$\bar{Z} = 1/2 \, (1 - 0.9125) = 0.04375. \qquad \square$$

3.2 *Model 2. Redundancy Allowed*

The problem can be formulated:

$$\max \bar{R} = \sum_{k=1}^{K} F_k R_k \qquad (\text{P}_2)$$

Subject to:

$$\sum_{j=1}^{m_k} X_{kj} \geq 1, \quad k = 1, \ldots, K \qquad (\text{i})$$

$$\sum_{k=1}^{K} \sum_{j=1}^{m_k} X_{kj} C_{kj} \leq B \qquad (\text{ii})$$

$X_{kj} = 0, 1$, for $k = 1, \ldots, K$ and $j = 1, \ldots, m_k$.

where now:

$$R_k = 1 - \prod_{j=1}^{m_k} (1 - R_{kj})^{X_{kj}} \qquad (4)$$

There are two differences between (P$_1$) and (P$_2$).

- In P$_2$, constraint set (i) ensures that at least one program is selected for each function since redundancy is allowed.
- R_k (reliability of function k in (4)) is the probability that at least one of the programs selected for function k is working, which is one minus the probability that none of the programs selected for function k is working. $\square$

For simplicity, in (ii) we assume that the cost of performing the acceptance test for each program is negligible compared to the purchase cost. This can be easily fixed if the cost of acceptance test is not negligible.

Problem (P$_2$) can be rewritten as a minimization problem by just changing the objective function and using (4) to get:

$$\min \sum_{k=1}^{K} F_k \prod_{j=1}^{m_k} (1 - R_{kj})^{X_{kj}}$$

The objective function value for the optimal solution indicates that the unreliability of the software package must be subtracted from one to give the average reliability.

Like problem (P$_1$), problem (P$_2$), which can be solved by using any integer programming package, has a special structure that can be exploited for solving the problem more efficiently. Since the objective function of (P$_2$) is nonlinear, Lagrangian Relaxation cannot be used to solve the problem. We therefore introduce dynamic programming as presented in appendix B to solve the problem. This approach is particularly helpful when the size of the program is too large to handle with the available software.

Example 2a. [Same data as example 1]

Even though this example can be solved by inspection, we demonstrate the dynamic programming approach in appendix B.

Stage $k = 2$.

Since the cheapest program for function 2 has cost $= 2$ and the cheapest program for the only remaining function has cost $= 4$, (4) is used to calculate $R_k(S)$ for $2 \leq S \leq 8$. Table 1 gives the results.

Table 1
Solution, S, and $R_2(S)$ for Stage 2

S	Solution		$R_2(S)$
2	X_{21}	$= 1$	.0750
3	X_{21}	$= 1$	.0750
4	X_{22}	$= 1$	.0500
5	X_{22}	$= 1$	.0500
6	$X_{21} = X_{22} = 1$		.0150
7	$X_{21} = X_{22} = 1$		.0150
8	$X_{21} = X_{23} = 1$		.0075

For example, $R_2(8)$ is calculated as:

$$R_2(8) = \min\{(0.25)(0.3)^{X_{21}}(0.2)^{X_{22}}(0.1)^{X_{23}}\}$$

where X_{2j} are chosen such that:

$$X_{21} + X_{22} + X_{23} \geq 1,$$

$$2X_{21} + 4X_{22} + 6X_{23} \leq 8.$$

By inspection, the minimization reduces to:

$$\min\{(0.25)(0.30)(0.20), \ (0.25)(0.30)(0.10)\}$$

$$= \min\{0.015, 0.0075\} = 0.0075$$

and thus $X_{21} = X_{23} = 1$.

Now $R_1(12)$ can be calculated:

$$R_1(12) = \min\{(0.75)(0.10)^{X_{11}}(0.20)^{X_{12}}(0.15)^{X_{13}}(0.05)^{X_{14}}$$

$$+ R_2(12 - (6X_{11} + 4X_{12} + 5X_{13} + 8X_{14}))\}$$

where X_{1j} are chosen such that:

$$X_{11} + X_{12} + X_{13} + X_{14} \geq 1,$$

$$6X_{11} + 4X_{12} + 5X_{13} + 8X_{14} \leq 12.$$

By inspection again, the minimization above reduces to:

$$\min\{(0.75)(0.2) + R_2(8), \ (0.75)(0.15)$$

$$+ R_2(7), \ (0.75)(0.1) + R_2(6), \ (0.75)(0.05)$$

$$+ R_2(4), \ (0.75)(0.2)(0.15) + R_2(3), \ (0.75)(0.1)(0.2)$$

$$+ R_2(2)\}$$

$$= \min\{0.1575, 0.1275, 0.09, 0.0875, 0.0975, 0.09\}$$

$$= 0.0875$$

Thus, $X_{14} = 1$; $X_{22} = 1$,

$$R = 1 - 0.0875 = .9125,$$

which is identical to the solution of P_1. In other words with $B = 12$, the model selects program 4 for function 1, and program 2 for function 2 — not using the option of redundancy. □

Example 2b.

[Same data as examples 1 & 2, except $B = 14$]

The critical nature of the software package requires higher reliability, which can be achieved by increasing the budget and introducing redundancy to the system design. With $B = 14$, the $R_2(S)$ must be calculated for $S = 9$ & $S = 10$. Since —

$$R_2(9) = 0.0075, \text{ with } X_{21} = X_{23} = 1$$

$$R_2(10) = 0.0050, \text{ with } X_{22} = X_{23} = 1,$$

the $R_1(14)$ can be calculated:

$$R_1(14) = \min\{(0.75)(0.10)^{X_{11}}(0.20)^{X_{12}}(0.15)^{X_{13}}(0.05)^{X_{14}}$$

$$+ R_2(14 - (6X_{11} + 4X_{12} + 5X_{13} + 8X_{14}))\}$$

The X_{1j} are chosen such that:

$$X_{11} + X_{12} + X_{13} + X_{14} \geq 1,$$

$$6X_{11} + 4X_{12} + 5X_{13} + 8X_{14} \leq 14.$$

By inspection the minimization reduces to:

$$\min\{(0.75)(0.20) + R_2(10), \ (0.75)(0.15)$$

$$+ R_2(9), \ (0.75)(0.10) + R_2(8), \ (0.75)(0.05)$$

$$+ R_2(6), \ (0.75)(0.20)(0.15)$$

$$+ R_2(5), \ (0.75)(0.10)(0.20)$$

$$+ R_2(4), \ (0.75)(0.20)(0.05) + R_2(2)\}$$

$$= \min\{0.155, 0.120, 0.0825, 0.0525, 0.0725, 0.0650,$$

$$\cdot 0.08625, 0.0825\}$$

$$= 0.0525$$

We have —

$$R_1(14) = 0.0525,$$

$X_{14} = X_{21} = X_{22} = 1,$

$\bar{R} = 94.75\%.$

An increase of 2 in the budget allows redundancy; programs 1 and 2 are selected for function 2, and program 4 for function 1. Redundancy of program in function 2 improves reliability from 91.25% to 94.75%. The failure rate is reduced to —

$\bar{Z} = (1/2)(1-0.9475) = 0.02625.$ $\square$

4. CONCLUDING REMARKS

The availability of software packages has eased the burden of software development for the end-users who lack time or technical expertise to analyze requirements and implement their needs. At the same time, the users are faced with the confusing and difficult problem of selecting and evaluating programs.

Future work should be directed towards optimization models dealing with the micro-view of software packages. This view breaks down each function into several tasks where each task is performed by executing a module. Modules can be purchased and each can be used by more than one function. Reusable modules are becoming prevalent. Hence the decisions regarding the purchase of the best available module to be included in a software package is crucial, and need use help from optimization models.

APPENDIX A

The Lagrangian Relaxation Algorithm to Solve P_1

To create the Lagrangian problem, define a non-negative multiplier u_k for $k=1,\ldots,K$, $u = (u_1,\ldots,u_k)$, and add the non-negative term,

$$\sum_{k=1}^{K} u_k \left(1 - \sum_{j=1}^{m_k} X_{kj}\right)$$

to the objective function of P_1 to obtain problem L_1,

$$\max \bar{R}(u) = \sum_{k=1}^{K} F_k R_k + \sum_{k=1}^{K} u_k \left(1 - \sum_{j=1}^{m_k} X_{kj}\right) \quad (L_1)$$

subject to:

$$\sum_{k=1}^{K} \sum_{j=1}^{m_k} X_{kj} C_{kj} = B$$

$for\ X_{kj} = 0,1 \quad k=1,\ldots,K \quad j=1,\ldots,m_k$

Problem L_1 can be rewritten using (1) as:

$$\max \bar{R}(u) = \sum_{k=1}^{K} \sum_{j=1}^{m_k} X_{kj}(\bar{R}_{kj} - u_k) + \sum_{k=1}^{K} u_k \quad (L_1)$$

subject to:

$$\sum_{k=1}^{K} \sum_{j=1}^{m_k} X_{kj} C_{kj} \leq B$$

$X_{kj} = 0,1 \quad k=1,\ldots K \quad j=1,\ldots,m_k$

where:

$$\bar{R}_{kj} = F_k R_{kj}$$

As mentioned above, L_1 is a Knapsack problem for a fixed u. The optimal solution for L_1, $\bar{R}^*(u)$ for a fixed u, is an upper bound on $\bar{R}^*$ the optimal solution value of P_1. Therefore u should be chosen to make $\bar{R}^*(u)$ as small as possible.

To obtain a value for u_k that produces a tight bound on $\bar{R}^*$ we use the subgradient method [2]. It generates a sequence of values for u starting with an initial point u^0 and then follows the steps:

Step 0: choose initial u^0 (eg. $u^0 = (0,\ldots,0)$). set $i=0$

Step 1: solve L_1 (using any procedure to solve the Knapsack problem [8]), using u^i, call the optimal solution X_{kj}^i and the optimal solution value $\bar{R}^*(u^i)$. If X_{kj}^i is a feasible solution of P_1 go to step 4.

Step 2: calculate a scalar t^i

$$t^i = \frac{\lambda^i(\bar{R}^*(u^i) - \bar{R}^*)}{\sum_{k=1}^{K} \left(1 - \sum_{j=1}^{m_k} X_{jk}^i\right)^2}$$

where $\bar{R}^*$ is initially the objective function value of the best known feasible solution to P_1.

For example, $\bar{R}^*$ can be chosen to be equal to the reliability of the system composed of the cheapest program for each function. λ^i is a number between 0 and 2; for this problem we begin with $\lambda^i = 1$ and reduce λ^i by a factor of two whenever $R(u)$ has failed to decrease.

Step 3: set —

$$u_k^{i+1} = \max\left\{0; u_k^i - t^i\left(1 - \sum_{j=1}^{m_k} X_{kj}^i\right)\right\}$$

for $k=1,\ldots,K$. Let $i = i+1$. Go to step 1.

Step 4: if $\bar{R}^* = \bar{R}^*(u^i)$ then X_{kj}^i is the optimal solution. Otherwise set $\bar{R}^*$ equal to the objective function value of P_1 for that solution and return to step 2.

Comments

Since $\bar{R}^*(u)$ is an upper bound for P_1, obviously once an optimal solution to L_1, which is also feasible for P_1, is found then $\bar{R}^*$ must be updated. In general if reaching the optimal solution takes too long, the method can be terminated after reaching a specified iteration limit. $\square$

APPENDIX B

The Dynamic Programming Algorithm to Solve P_2

Define:

- a state of system S to be the budget available,
- stage k to reflect function k for $k = 1,...K$. □

Let $R_k(s)$ be the reliability of the system composed of functions k, $k+1,...,K$ only, given that S is the remaining budget for function k for $k = 1,...,K-1$. The recursive formula for $R_k(S)$ when $k < K$ is:

$$R_k(S) = \min \left\{ F_k \prod_{j=1}^{m_k} (1-R_{kj}) + R_{k+1} \left(B - \sum_{j=1}^{m_k} C_{kj}X_{kj} \right) \right\} \quad (5)$$

where we restrict the solution to variables X_{kj} for which,

$$\sum_{j=1}^{m_k} X_{kj} \geq 1 \; and \; \sum_{j=1}^{m_k} C_{kj}X_{kj} \leq S$$

the recursive formula of $R_k(S)$ when $k = K$ is:

$$R_K(S) = \min F_K \prod_{j=1}^{m_K} (1-R_{Kj})^{X_{Kj}} \quad (6)$$

where again we restrict the solution space to variable X_{Kj} such that —

$$\sum_{j=1}^{m_K} X_{Kj} \geq 1 \; and \; \sum_{j=1}^{m_K} C_{Kj}X_{Kj} \leq S$$

Given stage k and state S, $R_k(S)$ should be calculated for all S in the range:

$$S = \min_{j=1,...,m_k} \{C_{kj}\},...,B - \sum_{i=1}^{k-1} \min_{j=1,...,m_k} C_{ij} \quad (7)$$

For states not in the range above, $R_k(S)$ can be defined as 1. The $R_K(S)$ in (6) is the result of the optimal allocation of budget S to function K. To calculate $R_k(S)$ for $k=1,...,K-1$ in (5) we look for the optimal allocation of budget S to function k taking into account that $B-S$ is allocated to functions $k+1,...,K$ but this is given in $R_{k+1}(B-S)$. In (7) we consider that, for every function k at least one program is selected. Therefore for stage k, state S cannot exceed the minimum budget for stages $1,...,k-1$ and must be at least the cost of the cheapest program in stage k.

REFERENCES

[1] N. Ashrafi, R. C. Baker, J. P. Kuilboer, "Proposed structure for decomposition software reliability prediction models", *Software & Information Technology*, vol 35, num 7, 1989, pp 93–98.

[2] M. L. Fisher, "An application oriented guide to Lagrangian Relaxation", *Interface*, vol 15, num 2, 1985, pp 10–21.

[3] D. J. Musa, "Software quality and reliability basics", *Proc. 1987 Fall Joint Computer Conf.*, IEEE Exploring Technology Today and Tomorrow, Fall Conference, 1987 October 25-29, pp 114–115; Dallas Texas.

[4] D. J. Musa, A. Iannino, K. Okumoto, *Software Reliability: Measurement, Prediction, Application*, 1987; McGraw-Hill.

[5] R. S. Pressman, *Software Engineering a Beginners Guide*, 1988; McGraw-Hill.

[6] R. M. Reiss, "A prediction experience with three software reliability models", *Workshop on Quantitative Software Models for Reliability, Complexity, Cost: An Assessment of the State of Art*, 1979 October 9-11, IEEE Catalog #CH0067-9, pp 190–200.

[7] M. L. Shooman, *Software Engineering*, 1983; McGraw-Hill.

[8] H. M. Wagner, *Principles of Operations Research*, 1975; Prentice-Hall.

[9] F. Zahedi, N. Ashrafi, "Software reliability allocation based on structure, utility, price, and cost", *IEEE Trans. Software Engineering*, vol 17, num 4, 1991, pp 345–356.

Manuscript TR90-123 received 1990 June 29; revised 1991 April 2; revised 1991 August 29.

IEEE Log Number 08069

◄TR►

Software reliability measurement in imperfect debugging environment and its application

Shigeru Yamada, Koichi Tokuno & Shunji Osaki

Department of Industrial and Systems Engineering, Hiroshima University, Higashi-Hiroshima-shi 724, Japan

(Received 23 February 1992; accepted 2 September 1992)

In practice, debugging operations during the testing phase of software development are not always performed perfectly. In other words, not all the software faults detected are corrected and removed. Generally, this is called imperfect debugging. In this paper, we discuss a software reliability growth model considering imperfect debugging. Defining a random variable representing the cumulative number of faults corrected up to a specified testing time, this model is described by a semi-Markov process. Then, several quantitative measures are derived for software reliability assessment in an imperfect debugging environment. The application of this model to optimal software release problems is also discussed. Finally, numerical illustrations for software reliability measurement and optimal software release policies are presented.

1 INTRODUCTION

As computer systems grow in size and complexity, high-quality software systems become necessary for a high degree of system reliability. Therefore, a quality control approach is needed to develop a quality software system efficiently. Software reliability is an essential quality characteristic for a software system. Accordingly, it is of great importance for software development managers to define a reliability objective and its reliability assurance procedures precisely.[1,2] Generally, a mathematical model is a useful tool for grasping and assessing the degree of software reliability. A mathematical software reliability model is called a software reliability growth model and it describes software fault-detection or software failure-occurrence phenomena during the testing phase of software development and during the operation phase.[3,4] A software failure is defined as an unacceptable departure from program operation caused by a fault remaining in the software system. Using the model, we can estimate several quantitative measures such as the initial fault content, the software reliability, and the mean time between software failures.

Most software reliability growth models proposed so far are based on the assumption of perfect debugging, i.e. that all faults detected during the testing and operation phases are corrected and removed perfectly. However, debugging actions in real testing and operation environments are not always performed perfectly. For example, type misses invalidate the fault correction activity or fault removal is not carried out precisely due to incorrect analysis of test results (see Ref. 5). It is interesting therefore, to develop a software reliability growth model which assumes an imperfect debugging environment (cf. Refs 6 and 7). Such an imperfect debugging model is expected to estimate reliability assessment measures more accurately.

In this paper, we discuss a software reliability growth model with imperfect debugging. Defining a random variable representing the number of faults corrected by a given time point, this model is formulated using a semi-Markov process (see Refs 8 and 9). We derive various interesting quantities for software reliability measurement. Further, based on this model, we discuss optimal software release problems by introducing software cost and reliability criteria. Finally, we show numerical illustrations of software reliability measurement and optimal software release policies.

2 MODEL DESCRIPTION

To model an imperfect debugging environment, the software reliability model developed in this paper is based on the following assumptions.

(1) Each fault which causes a software failure is corrected perfectly with probability p $(0 \leq p \leq 1)$; it is not corrected with probability $q(=1-p)$ (see Ref. 7). We call p the perfect debugging rate.

(2) The hazard rate is constant between software failures caused by a fault in the software system, and geometrically decreases whenever each detected fault is corrected.[10]

(3) The probability that two or more software failures occur simultaneously is negligible.

(4) No new faults are introduced during the debugging. (In general, this assumption may not be true. However, Goel[11] claimed that if the additional faults introduced constitute a very small fraction of the fault population, the practical effect on model results would be minimal.) At most one fault is removed when it is corrected and the correction time is not considered.

Now, we consider a stochastic process $(\mathbf{Y}, \mathbf{T})$ where fault count vector $\mathbf{Y} = \{Y(l); l = 1, 2, \ldots\}$ and time series vector $\mathbf{T} = \{T_l; l = 1, 2, \ldots\}$ (see Ref. 9). Let $i = 0, 1, 2, \ldots$ be the state space, where i represents the cumulative number of corrected faults. Then, the events $\{Y(l) = i\}$ means that i faults have been corrected at the lth software failure occurrence and T_l represents the lth software failure occurrence time, where $Y(0) = 0$ and $T_0 = 0$. A sample function of $(\mathbf{Y}, \mathbf{T})$ is shown in Fig. 1. For example, Fig. 1 shows that a fault is detected at T_3 but the fault correction fails (i.e. the fault is imperfectly debugged). Further, let $X(t)$ be a random variable representing the cumulative number of faults corrected up to the testing time t. Then, $X(t)$ forms a semi-Markov process.[8] That is, from assumption 1, when i faults

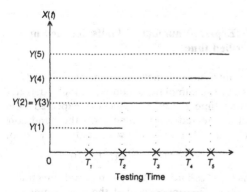

Fig. 1. A sample function of $(\mathbf{Y}, \mathbf{T})$.

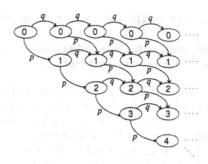

Fig. 2. A diagrammatic representation of transitions between states of $X(t)$.

have been corrected by arbitrary testing time t,

$$X(t) = \begin{cases} i & \text{(with probability } q) \\ i + 1 & \text{(with probability } p) \end{cases} \quad (1)$$

(see Fig. 2). Further, from assumption 2, when i faults have been corrected, the hazard rate for the next software failure occurrence is given by

$$z_i(t) = Dk^i \quad (i = 0, 1, 2, \ldots; D > 0, 0 < k < 1) \quad (2)$$

where D and k are the initial hazard rate and the decreasing ratio, respectively. Noting that some specified functions are executed frequently, eqn (2) reflects that the faults cause software failures with high frequency in execution during the early stage of the testing and the hazard rate decreases rapidly as they are corrected. This assumption is a practically modified one.[12] Early imperfect debugging models such as those of Goel and Okumoto[8] and Ohba and Chou[6] often assume that the hazard rate changes at each fault correction by a constant amount. Then, the distribution function for the next software failure occurrence time is given by

$$F_i(t) = 1 - \exp(-Dk^i t) \quad (3)$$

Let $Q_{ij}(t)$ denote the one-step transition probability that after making a transition into state i, the process $\{X(t), t \geq 0\}$ makes a transition into state j by time t. Then, $Q_{ij}(t)$, which represents the probability that if i faults have been corrected at time zero, j faults are corrected by time t after the next failure occurs, is given by

$$Q_{ij}(t) = P_{ij}(1 - \exp(-Dk^i t)) \quad (4)$$

where P_{ij} are the transition probabilities from state i to state j and are given by

$$P_{ij} = \begin{cases} q & (j = i) \\ p & (j = i + 1) \\ 0 & \text{(elsewhere)} \end{cases} \quad (i, j = 0, 1, 2, \ldots) \quad (5)$$

3 DERIVATION OF RELIABILITY MEASURES

3.1 Distribution of the first passage time to the specified number of corrected faults

Suppose that i faults have been corrected at some testing time. Let $G_{i,n}(t)$ denote a distribution function of the first passage time from state i to state n. In other words, $G_{i,n}(t)$ is the probability that n faults are corrected in the time interval $(0, t]$ on the condition that i faults have been already corrected at time zero. Then, we get the following renewal equation:

$$G_{i,n}(t) = Q_{i,i+1}(t) * G_{i+1,n}(t) + Q_{i,i}(t) * G_{i,n}(t) \quad (i = 0, 1, 2, \ldots, n-1) \tag{6}$$

where $*$ denotes a Stieltjes convolution and $G_{n,n}(t) = 1 \ (n = 1, 2, \ldots)$.

We use Laplace–Stieltjes (L–S) transforms to solve eqn (6), where the L–S transform of $G_{i,n}(t)$ is defined as

$$\tilde{G}_{i,n}(s) \equiv \int_0^\infty e^{-st} \, dG_{i,n}(t) \tag{7}$$

From eqn (6) we get

$$\tilde{G}_{i,n}(s) = \tilde{Q}_{i,i+1}(s)\tilde{G}_{i+1,n}(s) + \tilde{Q}_{i,i}(s)\tilde{G}_{i,n}(s) \quad (i = 0, 1, 2, \ldots, n-1). \tag{8}$$

From eqn (4) the transforms of $Q_{i,i+1}(t)$ and $Q_{i,i}(t)$ are respectively given as

$$\tilde{Q}_{i,i+1}(s) = \frac{pDk^i}{s + Dk^i} \tag{9}$$

$$\tilde{Q}_{i,i}(s) = \frac{qDk^i}{s + Dk^i} \tag{10}$$

Substituting eqns (9) and (10) into eqn (8) yields

$$\tilde{G}_{i,n}(s) = \frac{pDk^i}{s + pDk^i} \tilde{G}_{i+1,n}(s) \quad (i = 0, 1, 2, \ldots, n-1). \tag{11}$$

Solving eqn (11) recursively, we obtain the L–S transform of $G_{0,n}(t)$ as

$$\tilde{G}_{0,n}(s) = \prod_{i=0}^{n-1} \frac{pDk^i}{s + pDk^i} = \sum_{i=0}^{n-1} A_{k,i,n} \frac{pDk^i}{s + pDk^i} \tag{12}$$

where

$$\left. \begin{array}{l} A_{k,0,1} \equiv 1 \\[2mm] A_{k,i,n} = \dfrac{k^{(1/2)n(n-1)-i}}{\displaystyle\prod_{\substack{j=0 \\ j \neq i}}^{n-1} (k^j - k^i)} \\[4mm] (n = 2, 3, \ldots, i = 0, 1, 2, \ldots, n-1) \end{array} \right\} \tag{13}$$

By inverting eqn (12) with respect to t and rewriting $G_{0,n}(t)$ as $G_n(t)$, we have the distribution function of the first passage time when n faults are corrected

$$G_n(t) = \sum_{i=0}^{n-1} A_{k,i,n}(1 - \exp(-pDk^i t)) \tag{14}$$

where $G_0(t) \equiv 1$.

3.2 Distribution of the number of faults corrected up to a specified time

Let $S_n \ (n = 1, 2, \ldots)$ be random variables representing the nth successful correction time of detected faults. Since $X(t)$ is a counting process (see Fig. 1), we have the following equivalent relation:

$$\{S_n \leq t\} \Leftrightarrow \{X(t) \geq n\} \tag{15}$$

Therefore, we get

$$\Pr\{S_n \leq t\} = \Pr\{X(t) \geq n\} \tag{16}$$

Let $P_n(t)$ denote the probability that n faults are corrected up to testing time t. From eqns (14) and (16), we obtain the probability mass function $P_n(t)$ as

$$\begin{aligned} P_n(t) &= \Pr\{X(t) = n\} \\ &= G_n(t) - G_{n+1}(t) \end{aligned} \tag{17}$$

Suppose that the initial fault content in the system prior to testing, N, is known. Using eqn (17), we can derive the expectation and variance of $X(t)$, respectively as

$$\begin{aligned} E[X(t) \mid N] &= \sum_{n=0}^{N} n P_n(t) \\ &= \sum_{n=1}^{N} G_n(t) \end{aligned} \tag{18}$$

$$\begin{aligned} \mathrm{Var}[X(t) \mid N] &= \sum_{n=0}^{N} n^2 P_n(t) - \{E[X(t) \mid N]\}^2 \\ &= \sum_{n=1}^{N} (2n-1)G_n(t) - \left\{\sum_{n=1}^{N} G_n(t)\right\}^2 \end{aligned} \tag{19}$$

where it is noted that $P_N(t) = G_N(t)$ since $G_{N+1}(t) = 0$.

3.3 Expected number of faults detected up to a specified time

We introduce a new random variable $Z(t)$ representing the cumulative number of faults detected up to testing time t. Let $M_i(t)$ be the expected number of faults detected up to time t on the condition that i faults have been already corrected at time zero, i.e.

$$M_i(t) = E[Z(t) \mid X(0) = i] \tag{20}$$

which is called a Markov renewal function. As in Section 3.2, supposing that the initial fault content N

is known, we obtain the following renewal equations:

$$M_i(t) = F_i(t) + Q_{i,i}(t) * M_i(t) + Q_{i,i+1}(t)$$
$$* M_{i+1}(t) \quad (i = 0, 1, 2, \ldots, N-1) \quad (21)$$

where $M_N(t) = 0$. Using the L–S transforms of $M_i(t)$ $(i = 0, 1, 2, \ldots, N-1)$, we get from eqn (12)

$$\bar{M}_0(s) = \frac{1}{p} \sum_{n=1}^{N} \prod_{i=0}^{n-1} \frac{pDk^i}{s + pDk^i}$$

$$= \frac{1}{p} \sum_{n=1}^{N} \bar{G}_n(s) \quad (22)$$

Inverting eqn (22) with respect to t and rewriting $M_0(t)$ as $M(t \mid N)$, we have

$$M(t \mid N) = \frac{1}{p} \sum_{n=1}^{N} G_n(t)$$

$$= \frac{1}{p} \mathrm{E}[X(t) \mid N] \quad (23)$$

Now we consider that all faults detected by the testing are divided into two types: the faults which are corrected successfully, and the faults detected again due to imperfect debugging. Then, the expected number of faults debugged imperfectly is given by

$$D(t \mid N) = M(t \mid N) - \mathrm{E}[X(t) \mid N]$$

$$= \frac{q}{p} \mathrm{E}[X(t) \mid N] \quad (24)$$

3.4 Distribution of the time between software failures

Let X_l $(l = 1, 2, \ldots)$ be a random variable representing the time interval between the $(l-1)$st and the lth software failure occurrences and $\Phi_l(x)$ be a distribution function of X_l. It is noted that X_l depends on the number of the faults corrected up to the $(l-1)$st software failure occurrence, which is not explicitly known.

Further, let C_l be a random variable representing the number of the faults corrected up to the $(l-1)$st software failure occurrence. Then, C_l follows a binomial distribution having the following probability mass function:

$$\Pr\{C_l = i\} = \binom{l-1}{i} p^i q^{l-1-i} \quad (i = 0, 1, 2, \ldots, l-1)$$
$$(25)$$

where $\binom{l-1}{i}$ is a binomial coefficient denoted as $\binom{l-1}{i} = (l-1)! / [(l-1-i)! \, i!]$. From eqn (25), at the $(l-1)$st software failure occurrence, the expected number of corrected faults is given by $p(l-1)$.

Further, it is evident that

$$\Pr\{X_i \leq x \mid C_l = i\} = F_i(x) \quad (26)$$

which is given by eqn (3). Accordingly, we can get the distribution function for X_l as

$$\Phi_l(x) = \Pr\{X_l \leq x\}$$

$$= \sum_{i=0}^{l-1} \Pr\{X_l \leq x \mid C_l = i\} \Pr\{C_l = i\}$$

$$= \sum_{i=0}^{l-1} \binom{l-1}{i} p^i q^{l-1-i} (1 - \exp(-Dk^i x)) \quad (27)$$

Then, we have the reliability function for X_l as

$$R_l(x) \equiv \Pr\{X_l > x\}$$

$$= 1 - \Phi_l(x)$$

$$= \sum_{i=0}^{l-1} \binom{l-1}{i} p^i q^{l-1-i} \exp(-Dk^i x) \quad (28)$$

The expectation of random variable X_l is defined by

$$\mathrm{E}[X_l] \equiv \int_0^{\infty} R_l(x) \, \mathrm{d}x \quad (29)$$

We call (29) the mean time between software failures (MTBF). From eqn (28), we can derive $\mathrm{E}[X_l]$ as

$$\mathrm{E}[X_l] = \frac{(p/k + q)^{l-1}}{D} \quad (30)$$

Apparently, the following inequality holds for arbitrary natural number l:

$$\mathrm{E}[X_l] < \mathrm{E}[X_{l+1}] \quad (l = 1, 2, \ldots). \quad (31)$$

That is, a software reliability growth occurs whenever a software failure is observed.

4 OPTIMAL SOFTWARE RELEASE PROBLEMS

One of the problems for software development managers is deciding the appropriate time to transfer a software system to the user. This decision problem is called an optimal software release problem. Considering evaluation criteria such as achieved software reliability, cost, delivery time and so on, we need to estimate a testing termination time. Using the imperfect debugging model discussed above, we investigate optimal software release problems based on total expected software cost and software reliability criteria.

4.1 Reliability-optimal software release policies

Consider an optimal software release problem that decides the total testing time required to attain a software reliability objective. Suppose that we transfer a software system at the time point when m faults have been detected by the testing. Then, from eqn

(30) the mean time to software release is given by

$$\sum_{l=1}^{m} \mathrm{E}[X_l] = \frac{1-(p/k+q)^m}{pD(1-1/k)} \qquad (32)$$

And from eqn (28) software reliability $R(x_0; m)$ for specified operational time x_0 is given by

$$R(x_0; m) = \sum_{j=0}^{m} \binom{m}{j} p^j q^{m-j} \exp(-Dk^j x_0) \qquad (33)$$

Letting R_0 be a software reliability objective for the operational time x_0, the minimum integer m which satisfies $R(x_0; m) \geq R_0$ is the optimum number of detected faults, m^*, since $R(x_0; m)$ in eqn (33) is a monotone increasing function with respect to the number of detected faults m. That is, if $R(x_0; 0) < R_0$, then there exists a finite and unique $m = m_0$ ($1 \leq m_0 < \infty$) which satisfies the following inequalities:

$$R(x_0; m) \geq R_0 \quad \text{and} \quad R(x_0; m-1) < R_0 \qquad (34)$$

Thus, we have the following theorem for a reliability-optimal software release problem.

Theorem 1. Suppose that $x_0 \geq 0$ and $0 < R_0 < 1$

(1) If $\exp(-Dx_0) < R_0$, then the optimum number of detected faults is $m^* = m_0$, and the optimum software release time is

$$T^* = \frac{1-(p/k+q)^{m_0}}{pD(1-1/k)}$$

where m_0 is an integer number which satisfies (34).

(2) If $\exp(-Dx_0) \geq R_0$, then the optimum number of detected faults is $m^* = 0$, and the optimum software release time is $T^* = 0$.

4.2 Cost-optimal software release policies

The following cost parameters are defined:

c_1: debugging cost per fault during the testing phase,
c_2: debugging cost per fault during the operation phase ($c_2 > c_1 > 0$),
c_3: testing cost per unit time ($c_3 > 0$).

Suppose that the expected number of faults detected eventually is $M = \lceil N/p \rceil$ since $M(\infty \mid N) = N/p$ from eqn (23), where $\lceil x \rceil$ denotes the smallest integer that is not smaller than x. Then, the total expected software cost is given by

$$C(m) = c_1 m + c_2(M-m)$$
$$+ c_3 \frac{1-(p/k+q)^m}{pD(1-1/k)} \quad (0 \leq m \leq M) \qquad (35)$$

(cf. Ref. 13). Therefore, the integer m minimizing $C(m)$ in (35) is the optimum number of detected faults, m^*.

For finding $m = m^*$ minimizing $C(m)$ in eqn (35), we define the following equation:

$$Y(m) = C(m+1) - C(m)$$
$$= -(c_2 - c_1) + \frac{c_3}{D}(p/k+q)^m \quad (0 \leq m \leq M-1)$$

$$(36)$$

It is noted that $Y(m)$ is a monotonically increasing function with respect to the number of detected faults, m, since $p + q = 1$ and $0 < k < 1$. If $Y(0) < 0$, then the minimum m which holds $Y(m) \geq 0$ satisfies inequalities $C(m+1) \geq C(m)$ and $C(m) < C(m-1)$. Accordingly, the optimum number of detected faults, $m^* = m_1$, is given by

$$m_1 = \left\lceil \frac{\ln\{D(c_2 - c_1)/c_3\}}{\ln(p/k+q)} \right\rceil \qquad (37)$$

Thus, we have the following theorem for a cost-optimal software release problem.

Theorem 2. Suppose that $c_2 > c_1 > 0$ and $c_3 > 0$

(1) If

$$D > \frac{c_3}{c_2 - c_1} \geq \frac{D}{(p/k+q)^{M-1}}$$

then the optimal number of detected faults is $m^* = m_1$ ($1 \leq m_1 \leq M-1$) and the optimum software release time is

$$T^* = \frac{1-(p/k+q)^{m_1}}{pD(1-1/k)}$$

where m_1 is given by eqn (37).

(2) If

$$\frac{D}{(p/k+q)^{M-1}} > \frac{c_3}{c_2 - c_1}$$

then the optimum number of detected faults is $m^* = M$, and the optimum software release time is

$$T^* = \frac{1-(p/k+q)^M}{pD(1-1/k)}$$

(3) If

$$D \leq \frac{c_3}{c_2 - c_1}$$

then the optimum number of detected faults is $m^* = 0$, and the optimum software release time is $T^* = 0$.

4.3 Cost–reliability-optimal software release policies

We discuss an optimal software release problem which evaluates both software cost and reliability criteria simultaneously. Consider decision policy on the optimum number of faults to be detected by the release time which minimizes the total expected software cost $C(m)$ in eqn (35) subject to the condition that software reliability $R(x_0; m)$ in eqn (33) satisfies reliability objective R_0. The optimal software release problem can be formulated as follows: For a specified operational time x_0 $(x_0 \geq 0)$,

$$
\left.\begin{array}{ll}
\text{minimize} & C(m) \\
\text{subject to} & R(x_0; m) \geq R_0, \quad 0 < R_0 < 1
\end{array}\right\} \quad (38)
$$

This problem is called a cost–reliability-optimal software release problem.[14] From Sections 4.1 and 4.2, we have the following theorem for a cost–reliability-optimal software release problem.

Theorem 3. Suppose that $c_2 > c_1 > 0$, $c_3 > 0$, $x_0 \geq 0$, and $0 < R_0 < 1$

(1) If

$$
D > \frac{c_3}{c_2 - c_1} \geq \frac{D}{(p/k + q)^{M-1}}
$$

and $\exp(-Dx_0) < R_0$, then the optimum number of detected faults is $m^* = \max\{m_0, m_1\}$, and the optimum software release time is

$$
T^* = \frac{1 - (p/k + q)^{\max\{m_0, m_1\}}}{pD(1 - 1/k)}
$$

(2) If

$$
\frac{D}{(p/k + q)^{M-1}} > \frac{c_3}{c_2 - c_1}
$$

and $\exp(-Dx_0) < R_0$, then the optimum number of detected faults is $m^* = \max\{m_0, M\}$, and the optimum software release time is

$$
T^* = \frac{1 - (p/k + q)^{\max\{m_0, M\}}}{pD(1 - 1/k)}
$$

(3) If

$$
D > \frac{c_3}{c_2 - c_1} \geq \frac{D}{(p/k + q)^{M-1}}
$$

and $\exp(-Dx_0) \geq R_0$, then the optimum number of detected faults is $m^* = m_1$, and the optimum software release time is

$$
T^* = \frac{1 - (p/k + q)^{m_1}}{pD(1 - 1/k)}
$$

(4) If

$$
\frac{D}{(p/k + q)^{M-1}} > \frac{c_3}{c_2 - c_1}
$$

and $\exp(-Dx_0) \geq R_0$, then the optimum number of detected faults is $m^* = M$, and the optimum software release time is

$$
T^* = \frac{1 - (p/k + q)^{M}}{pD(1 - 1/k)}
$$

(5) If

$$
D \leq \frac{c_3}{c_2 - c_1}
$$

and $\exp(-Dx_0) < R_0$, then the optimum number of detected faults is $m^* = m_0$, and the optimum software release time is

$$
T^* = \frac{1 - (p/k + q)^{m_0}}{pD(1 - 1/k)}
$$

(6) If

$$
D \leq \frac{c_3}{c_2 - c_1}
$$

and $\exp(-Dx_0) \geq R_0$, then the optimum number of detected faults is $m^* = 0$, and the optimum software release time is $T^* = 0$.

5 NUMERICAL EXAMPLES

Using the imperfect debugging model discussed above, we show numerical illustrations for software reliability measurement and optimal software release problems.

The distribution functions of the first passage time to the specified number of corrected faults, $G_n(t)$ in eqn (14), are shown in Fig. 3 for various perfect debugging rates, p, where $n = 10$, $D = 0.2$, and $k = 0.9$. We can see that the smaller perfect debugging rate p becomes, the more difficult it is to correct faults.

The expected numbers of faults corrected up to testing t, $E[X(t) \mid N]$ in eqn (18), for various values of p are shown in Fig. 4, where $N = 20$, $D = 0.2$, and $k = 0.9$. The variances of the number of faults corrected up to testing time t, $\mathrm{Var}[X(t) \mid N]$ in eqn (19), for various values of p are shown in Fig. 5, where $N = 20$, $D = 0.2$, and $k = 0.9$. As shown in Fig. 5, $\mathrm{Var}[X(t) \mid N]$ is a convex function with respect to testing time t with

$$
\mathrm{Var}[X(0) \mid N] = \mathrm{Var}[X(\infty) \mid N] = 0 \quad (39)
$$

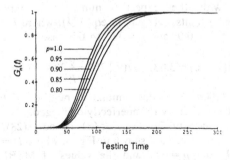

Fig. 3. Dependence of perfect debugging rate p on $G_{10}(t)$ $(D = 0.2, k = 0.9)$.

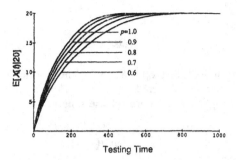

Fig. 4. Dependence of perfect debugging rate p on $E[X(t) \mid 20]$ ($D = 0.2$, $k = 0.9$).

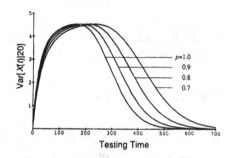

Fig. 5. Dependence of perfect debugging rate p on $\text{Var}[X(t) \mid 20]$ ($D = 0.2$, $k = 0.9$).

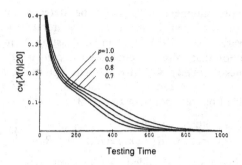

Fig. 6. Dependence of perfect debugging rate p on $\text{cv}[X(t) \mid 20]$ ($D = 0.2$, $k = 0.9$).

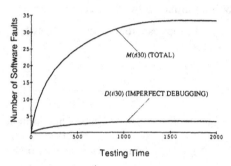

Fig. 7. $M(t \mid 30)$ and $D(t \mid 30)$ ($D = 0.2$, $k = 0.9$, $p = 0.9$).

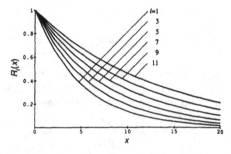

Fig. 8. Dependence of number of failures l in software reliability $R_l(x)$ ($D = 0.2$, $k = 0.9$, $p = 0.9$).

This means that the correctability of faults in debugging is unstable during the early stage of the testing, and as the testing is in progress, it becomes stable. As shown in Fig. 5, we can see that the smaller the perfect debugging rate p becomes, the more difficult it is to stabilize the fault correctability.

The coefficients of variation (cv) of $X(t)$, $\text{cv}[X(t) \mid N]$, defined as

$$\text{cv}[X(t) \mid N] \equiv \frac{\sqrt{\text{Var}[X(t) \mid N]}}{E[X(t) \mid N]} \quad (40)$$

for various values of p are shown in Fig. 6, where $N = 20$, $D = 0.2$, and $k = 0.9$. As shown in Fig. 6, $\text{cv}[X(t) \mid N]$ is a monotone decreasing function with respect to testing time t.

The expected number of faults detected up to testing time t, $M(t \mid N)$ in eqn (23), is shown in Fig. 7 along with the expected number of imperfect debugging faults, $D(t \mid N)$ in eqn (24), where $N = 30$, $D = 0.2$, $k = 0.9$, and $p = 0.9$. In this case,

$$M(\infty \mid 30) = 33.3, \quad D(\infty \mid 30) = \frac{q}{p}30 = 33.3q \quad (41)$$

Then, $(100q)\%$ of the cumulative number of faults detected eventually is imperfectly debugged.

The reliability function, $R_l(x)$ in eqn (28), for various values of l are shown in Fig. 8, where $D = 0.2$, $k = 0.9$, and $p = 0.9$, and the values of MTBF for various values of l are shown in Table 1. Figure 8 and Table 1 show that a software reliability growth during

the testing occurs whenever a software failure occurs.

Next, we show numerical examples of the optimal software release problems. Tables 2 and 3 show relationships between the perfect debugging rate p and the optimum software release time T^* for Theorems 1 and 2 where $x_0 = 2.5$, $R_0 = 0.95$, $c_1 = 1.0$, $c_2 = 10.0$, $c_3 = 0.2$, $D = 0.2$, $k = 0.9$, and $N = 30$. We can see that improving the perfect debugging rate speeds up the optimum software release time efficiently when the perfect debugging rate is low.

Finally, we show a numerical example on the cost–reliability-optimal software release problem. Consider the optimal software release problem formulated as follows:

$$\left.\begin{aligned} \text{minimize} \quad & C(m) \\ \text{subject to} \quad & R(2.5; m) \geq 0.95 \end{aligned}\right\} \quad (42)$$

72

Table 1. MTBF $E[X_l]$ $(p = 0.9,\ D = 0.2,\ k = 0.9)$

l	$E[X_l]$
1	5·000
2	5·500
3	6·050
4	6·655
5	7·321
6	8·053
7	8·858
8	9·744
9	10·72
10	11·79

Table 2. Optimum release time T^* for Theorem 1 $(c_1 = 1,\ c_2 = 10,\ c_3 = 0.2,\ D = 0.2,\ k = 0.9)$

p	m^*	T^*
1·0	22	411·96
0·9	25	491·74
0·8	28	554·22
0·7	32	642·11
0·6	37	741·82
0·5	45	935·40
0·4	56	1 171·99
0·3	75	1 604·38
0·2	113	2 471·52
0·1	226	5 017·14

Table 3. Optimum release time T^* for Theorem 2 $(c_1 = 1,\ c_2 = 10,\ c_3 = 0.2,\ D = 0.2,\ k = 0.9,\ N = 30)$

p	m^*	T^*	$C(m)$
1·0	21	366·26	184·25
0·9	24	442·49	212·50
0·8	26	458·62	237·72
0·7	30	543·84	268·77
0·6	35	642·90	313·58
0·5	41	735·98	378·20
0·4	51	920·99	475·20
0·3	68	1 245·57	636·92
0·2	100	1 801·35	960·27
0·1	199	3 607·86	1 930·37

The minimum satisfying $R(2·5; m) \geq 0.95$ is $m_0 = 25$ and the optimum number of detected faults, m minimizing $C(m)$, is $m_1 = 24$. From Theorem 3 (1), the optimum number of detected faults is $m^* = \max\{25, 24\} = 25$, i.e. though the total expected software cost $C(m)$ is minimized when $m = 24$, the software reliability objective is not satisfied. Accordingly, the optimum software release time is given by

$$T^* = \frac{1 - (p/k + q)^{25}}{pD(1 - 1/k)} = 491·74$$

6 CONCLUSION

In this paper, assuming that whether a fault correction activity succeeds or not is uncertain, we have developed a software reliability growth model based on a semi-Markov process, for an imperfect debugging environment in which the faults detected by testing are not always corrected/removed. Various interesting quantities for software reliability measurement have been derived from the model. Introducing the total expected software cost and software reliability criteria, the application of this imperfect debugging model to optimal software release problems has also been discussed.

In future studies we intend to establish the estimation method of model parameters D, k, p, and N based on actual data observed during software testing.

ACKNOWLEDGEMENTS

Shigeru Yamada is pleased to acknowledge the support of a Grant-in-Aid for Scientific Research from the Ministry of Education, Science and Culture of Japan under Grant no. 04650316.

REFERENCES

1. Kanno, A., *Software Quality Control*. JUSE, Tokyo, 1986 (in Japanese).
2. Yamada, S. & Ohtera, H., *Software Reliability: Theory and Practical Application*. Soft Research Center, Tokyo, 1990 (in Japanese).
3. Yamada, S., *Software Reliability Assessment Technology*. Harcourt Brace Jovanovich (Japan), Tokyo, 1989 (in Japanese).
4. Yamada, S., Software quality/reliability measurement and assessment: software reliability growth models and data analysis. *J. Information Processing*, **14**(3) (1991) 254–66.
5. Shooman, M. L., *Software Engineering: Design, Reliability, and Management*. McGraw-Hill, New York, 1983.
6. Ohba, M. & Chou, X., Does imperfect debugging affect software reliability growth? In *Proceedings of the 11th International Conference on Software Engineering*, IEEE Computer Society Press, Los Alamitos, 1989, pp. 237–44.
7. Shanthikumar, J. G., A state- and time-dependent error occurrence-rate software reliability model with imperfect debugging. In *Proceedings of the National Computer Conference*, 1981, pp. 311–15.
8. Goel, A. L. & Okumoto, K., An imperfect debugging model for reliability and other quantitative measures of software systems. Technical Report no. 78-1, Department of Industrial Engineering and Operations Research, Syracuse University, AFiPS Press, New York, 1978.
9. Ross, S. M., *Stochastic Processes*. John Wiley & Sons, New York, 1983.
10. Moranda, P. B., Event-altered rate models for general

reliability analysis. *IEEE Trans. Reliability,* **R-28**(5) (1979) 376–81.

11. Goel, A. L., Software reliability models: Assumptions, limitations, and applicability. *IEEE Trans. Software Engng* **SE-11**(12) (1985) 1411–23.

12. Musa, J. D., Iannino, A. & Okumoto, K., *Software Reliability: Measurement, Prediction, Application.* McGraw-Hill, New York, 1987.

13. Yamada, S., Ichimori, T. & Masuyama, H., Optimal release problems on software failure time-measuring reliability models. *Trans. IEICE,* **J-73-A**(6) (1990) 1117–22 (in Japanese).

14. Yamada, S. & Osaki, S., Optimal software release policies with simultaneous cost and reliability requirements. *European J. Operational Research,* **31** (1987) 46–51.

Are We Testing for True Reliability?

DICK HAMLET, *Portland State University*

◆ *Conventional reliability theory works fine — if its assumptions hold. But for software, they fail. A new theory of trustworthiness is needed.*

Software engineers are less eager to accept reliability modeling than engineers in other disciplines. Instead, they propose clever methods for developing "defect-free" programs or for testing to eliminate all defects. These methods, although valuable and necessary, are essentially unrelated to reliability.

Reliability is the statistical study of failures, which occur because of some defect in the program. The failure is evident, but you don't know what mistake is responsible or what you can do to make the failure disappear. Reliabilily models are supposed to tell you what confidence you can have in the program's correctness.

But conventional reliability theory — which is taken from the reliability engineering of physical objects — is not satisfactory. It works only when a similar set of operational assumptions hold. It is not tailored for software's quirks. Thus, it rarely provides developers with confidence that they can rely on their software.

TWO KINDS OF MODELS

To understand what a reliability model demands, you must first understand that there are two kinds. *Reliability-growth* models are applied during debugging. They model repeated testing, failure, and correction. Managers can use them to predict when the mean time to failure is large enough to release the software.

Reliability models, in contrast, are applied after debugging, when the program has been tested, and no failures have been observed. The reliability model predicts the MTTF you can expect.

At first glance, the reliability model appears to be just a limiting case of the reliability-growth model in which zero failures are observed. However, these models

Reprinted from *IEEE Software*, Vol. 9, No. 4, July 1992, pp. 21–27. Copyright © 1992 by The Institute of Electrical and Electronics Engineers, Inc. All rights reserved.

differ qualitatively. Because reliability-growth models are used during debugging, as you observe failures, the observations give you direct, nonstatistical feedback on the model's performance: The MTTF you calculate from the model should be roughly the MTTF you actually observe, which for most of the debugging period will be short, say 100 runs. Furthermore, since the reliability-growth model is designed to tell simply when the software's operational quality is at an acceptable level, prediction accuracy can be less than perfect.

The predictions of a reliability model, on the other hand, are purely statistical. Because you do not observe failures, there is nothing to check the predicted MTTF against. Moreover, the MTTF is much larger than any observation data you can obtain, say 100,000 runs. For safety-critical software, the required MTTF may be orders of magnitude higher. For these systems, the calculated MTTF must be precise, because it fulfills a contractual obligation or is related to an inflexible requirement like protecting human lives.

Thus, much more is demanded of a reliability model than a reliability-growth model. And for that reason, you should be careful in accepting the results of a reliability model at face value. These are the models I am concerned with in this article. I want to show that if testing has shown zero failures for enough samples that a model predicts an acceptable MTTF, you can't always trust that model.

WHY CONVENTIONAL RELIABILITY THEORY FAILS

Software reliability is usually modeled by analogy to physical reliability — the engineering of reliability for objects. Physical reliability is concerned with collections (often of apparently identical mechanical parts), whose members differ slightly because of random (as opposed to systematic) fluctuations — such things as manufacturing, operating environment, and durability. The collection is tested, and the destruction times of members are noted; physical reliability theory is concerned with calculating the MTTF.

In the software analogy, a single program is given different inputs to form the collection. A failure rate θ is postulated for each program P as the probability that P will fail on an arbitrary input. Inputs are assumed to be drawn from an operational profile that may weight some more heavily than others, reflecting the actual usage expected of P. Then the statistical theory relates θ to the number of tests N conducted without failure. The MTTF is $1/\theta$, as derived in Martin Shooman's text.[1] If the theory holds, the calculated MTTF will predict observed behavior when inputs come from the operational profile.

TWO DEVELOPMENT MYTHS: DEFECT-FREE SOFTWARE AND TESTING AWAY FAILURES

Some developers seek to avoid testing altogether, claiming that they can develop defect-free software using formal methods. The argument is that software fails only because discrete mistakes were made in developing it. That is, each application has a perfect program — a program that cannot fail. These developers believe that they can create defect-free software.

Other developers acknowledge that perfect programs cannot always be created, but they still hope to remove all defects through testing.

Both these approaches have serious flaws.

Defect-free software. On the surface, the idea of defect-free software seems logical; there is no physical medium in software, as there is in other types of development, to wear out, become flawed during manufacturing, and so on. Of course, the computer executing a program is a physical object, and a physical medium transmits the program text, but these factors are trivial sources of failure compared with program-design mistakes.

Developers, therefore, are tempted to attack failure at its source. But attempts to construct perfect software are doomed to fail for several reasons:

♦ *Intuitive problems.* The problems the software is supposed to solve are imperfectly understood by those who need the solutions. Users communicate this imperfect understanding, imperfectly, to professionals who devise the solutions, who in turn imperfectly communicate the solution's characteristics.

Inevitably, the wrong problem is solved — a difficulty not addressed by improving the development method, particularly by using formal methods, which users do not see or understand.

♦ *Complex problems.* The solution to a complex problem isn't always simple, and the problem may be arbitrarily complex. Computer systems are designed to be general purpose, so more and more complex problem solutions will always be attempted, eventually outstripping the control of any method.

The Strategic Defense Initiative shows that some developers will always be willing to attempt problems acknowledged to be beyond the state of the art.

♦ *Slipshod maintenance.* Once a computer system exists, there is an irresistible pressure to modify it, and unhappily to do so with less care than was used to create it. The fragile nature of languages and of digital computation itself feed the maintenance problem. Programs and their behavior lack any kind of continuity. A very small change to a program can have a very large effect on its behavior; behavior can be arbitrarily different on input that is arbitrarily similar. There are programs for every problem without this discontinuous behavior, but no one knows how to stick to that set of programs, particularly during modification.

But that these problems make defect-free software impossible is no reason to abandon attempts to improve software development or use formal methods. On the contrary, the future will see more formal methods because they are cost-effective. However, more formal development can-

---

The chance that a single test will fail is θ, or $1 - \theta$ that it will succeed. Thus the probability that N independent tests will all succeed is $(1 - \theta)^N$. The largest value of θ such that $(1-\theta)^N > \alpha$ defines the $1 - \alpha$ upper confidence bound on θ — that is, the probability that this value exceeds the correct value for P.

Solving for θ, testing with N independent points from the operational profile gives $1 - \alpha$ confidence that the failure rate is below θ, if $\theta = 1 - \alpha^{1/N}$. For example, one million test points gives 99 percent confidence that the failure rate is below 4.6×10^{-6}, an MTTF of about 220,000 runs.

Unfortunately, this conventional reliability theory is flawed in a number of ways.

Random variables differ. Some software, like a telephone switch, is intended to operate continually, so starting it and waiting for failure is analogous to starting a de-structive test of a physical object. The random variable is execution time, so you can form a collection of objects using a single program by giving it different inputs, weighted according to its operational profile.

However, most programs operate either in a batch mode, in which they are given input then compute and terminate, or in an interactive mode, in which they may be in operation for a long time but spend most of it awaiting human input.

For batch and interactive programs, run count replaces time as the random variable. That is, the MTTF is measured in executions, or number of tests tried. For a batch program, a run is a complete execution; for an interactive program, it is a single I/O interchange.

Program runs aren't always independent. To satisfy the analogy to mechanical parts, program runs must be independent of one another. Otherwise, in the mechanical analogy, the parts being tested would influence one another (the failure of one would depend on the others), fundamentally contravening the statistical theory.

When programs accumulate state information over their runs, they are explicitly compromising run independence. For example, an interactive program can, as a side-effect of responding to an ill-formed command, go into a state in which most subsequent commands fail. Those subsequent runs are statistically meaningless. Dave Parnas cleverly notes that it would be a good idea for safety-critical programs to reinitialize themselves whenever possible to improve the accuracy of reliability theory by avoiding state build-up.[2]

Physical systems fail because defects appear during their use. Design defects are not unknown in established fields such as civil engineering. For example, in the walkway collapse at the Kansas City

not guarantee reliability, which must be independently assessed at the end of any human activity, to catch inevitable mistakes.

Testing away failures. Again, on the surface, testing away all defects seems possible. Each program's code is finite and hence must have only a fixed, finite number of defects. But even clever testing methods are doomed to fail.

Practical systematic testing is a game of coverage. The tester tries to make sure that all the elements of the program or specification have been tried. In partition testing, you divide, or partition, the input space into classes that characterize the elements to be covered and create test sets by selecting points from each class.

The hope is that the input classes will be homogeneous — any point selected from each class will be representative — and that cleverly defined classes will uncover all failures. Partitioning may be based on program structure, as in clear-box methods (named for electronic components in boxes that allow the interior to be examined), or on the specification, as in black-box methods, which do not use the code.

In structural testing, program elements are exercised. Certainly if some part has not been tried at all, you can have no confidence in its quality. The best known structural test method is statement testing, in which tests force the execution of each statement. Statement testing is part of a control-flow hierarchy of methods, including branch testing (tests must force each branch to be taken

both ways), a variety of dataflow methods (tests must cover paths defined by certain definition/use relationships among variables), and full-path testing (tests must force execution of all paths). Path testing has many variants, in which loops need not be executed for each of the infinite ways generally possible. These variants are usually viewed as the most stringent of the practical structural methods.

All the finite, path-based, structural methods are straightforward and relatively inexpensive to implement, and a variety of research and commercial tools have been created for them.

In contrast to control-flow methods, mutation testing is probably the least known structural method. Small individual changes are introduced in the program under test (the most

interesting ones occur in expressions), and test sets must distinguish the mutant program from the original. Mutation testing is often surprisingly difficult because it is hard to think through the extensive bookkeeping required.

The only implementation of mutation testing is the brute-force creation and execution of a vast collection of mutants, which is expensive and slow. So-called "weak mutation" — in which the mutation's effect is detected in the state immediately following — is better in this regard, but still not accepted.

In black-box testing, the specification supplies the organizing information for systematic testing. What is often called functional testing isolates a collection of actions (functions) a program should per-

Hyatt-Regency hotel, construction could not handle the weight of a crowd, and the structure simply waited for its first crowd, then collapsed. However, reliability theory is not applied to such mechanical situations — the objects are one-of-a-kind. Only computer programs have the wealth of design defects that might support a statistical approach.

For a statistical theory, variations must be independent. When one test system fails, it must not imply anything about the failure of others. Programs fail only because of design defects lying in wait for the input that excites them. Test systems differ only in the input each is given. Hence, these inputs must not be correlated. That is, the failure or success of one input cannot force the same behavior for another. Correlated inputs are analogous to cheating on the testing effort by copying one data point several times. If that point is a failure, the reliability will appear worse than it really is; if not, the reliability will appear to be better. In program-release testing, the result is always overly optimistic. Because a release test by definition does not fail, if it contains correlated points, the calculated reliability is too high.

There may be no operational profile. For a telephone switch, you can determine the operational profile empirically from past data, or model the load analytically and derive data from the model. Such a distribution is accurate and appropriate. However, most programs' profiles are not known. What is more in doubt is the validity of any operational profile for a piece of system software. The software may handle an immense number of possibilities, whose frequency and sequence depend on human vagaries. Each execution is more a unique special case than a sample drawn from some distribution. Again, an inappropriate distribution can only work against calculated reliability, because nothing is gained by testing in regions weighted too heavily, but improperly neglected regions give a false security that the software does not in fact support. Thus conventional theory will give overly optimistic results.

There is no appropriate failure rate. A common assumption in software development is that the instantaneous rate of failure — the hazard rate — is constant. For programs that *are* more likely to fail the longer they run, a model might use a time- or run-increasing hazard rate, as in mechanical systems that wear out. (The analogy would be not that the program wears out, but that it accumulates state that increases its likelihood of improper behavior.) Such a model, however extreme for software, gives nearly the same results as for a constant hazard.

form, and requires test data to exercise each function. You can further refine the test sets by including parameters that modify functional behavior, or by requiring that sequences of functions be tested.

Functional testing directly tries what is expected of the software. You can plan tests as soon as you have the specification, which is a plus. Functional testing also protects developers against the embarrassment of a program that doesn't work at all because of an oversight or misunderstanding about some feature.

Why partition testing is misleading. Partition testing has great intuitive appeal, but it is not a panacea. As an absolute method, it is flawed because partition tests can be misleading. For most programs and most testing methods, an infinite number of test sets will satisfy the method. The tester therefore will find it difficult to apply partition testing systematically.

For example, suppose test set T_M is selected, it satisfies a systematic method, and for T_M the tested program does not fail. However, if among the infinite number of other test sets that also satisfy that method, some (or perhaps many) would cause the program to fail, then T_M is misleading.

Unfortunately, misleading test sets are the rule rather than the exception. The following examples for structural and functional methods are common.

♦ *Structural.* A program has several nested conditionals, such that to reach one of its statements S_e, the input must be a singular matrix of rank greater than three, in which one row has elements in strictly increasing order. If S_e contains a complex formula involving the matrix elements, the tests devised for (say) branch testing are not likely to reach it with nontrivial matrix elements — it is too difficult to find data just to reach S_e. Hence if S_e's formula is correct for trivial elements only, most branch-adequate test sets will be misleading.

♦ *Functional.* A program can process read and write commands on random-access files named as a command parameter. A functional test might cover each command, some parameter possibilities for each, and some command sequences. But how likely is the test set to include the sequence write-write, in which two writes address the same record? When this case fails, the program can be thrown into a state in which everything goes wrong. In fact, an acceptance test of an early Digital Equipment Corp. PDP-10 operating system did include such a write-write sequence because record numbers were generated at random. The test failed but was ignored. Testers discovered later that by exciting this bug, a user program could gain unrestricted access to any disk block by absolute address! But no "reasonable" tester would select a set with this sequence, so functional tests, of this system at least, will almost always be misleading.

False comparisons. Misleading test sets confound most of the ways that have been devised to compare the effectiveness of testing methods. For example, the most common comparison uses an inclusion relation: If a test set for method 1 necessarily satisfies method 2, then 1 includes (or subsumes) 2. In the

Furthermore, a growing hazard rate does not really capture failure arising from state accumulation. First, state is not always harmful — it can be used to catch and even correct program problems, and a single program can alternately exhibit beneficial and harmful aspects of state accumulation as it runs. Second, tinkering with the hazard rate does not address the issues of sample independence, nor does it alter the qualitative result that reliability does not depend on program size.

Defects per line should be roughly constant. Conventional theory fails to explain a primary observation about software systems: the MTTF (in runs) in large systems is roughly inversely proportional to program size. That is, the number of defects per line is roughly constant. This software "law," which is observed in practice, is plausible when defects are human mistakes that arise because of the complexity of large programs. But conventional theory predicts that the MTTF does not depend on program size.

TOWARD TRUE RELIABILITY

Conventional reliability is deficient in two significant ways: It relies on an operational distribution that may not exist, and its assumptions about sample independence do not hold. To correct these deficiencies and find a better theory, we must probe the correct sample space and examine the chance of program failure under arbitrary circumstances. Unless we can find a true reliability theory — a theory of what Parnas calls trustworthiness, unlikely to fail catastrophically[2] — developers are building on sand. When they make generalizations like "random system testing should replace unit partition testing," or "inspections are better than testing," they may be setting themselves up for disaster.

Sampling basis. For any reliability theory, you must have a proper sampling basis to infer the probability of failure. Program input is not an appropriate sampling choice because the statistical procedures work only when samples directly probe the sources of failure. For programs, random testing over the input space is only tenuously connected to the design flaws that reside in the code. Input-space sampling also fails to predict the direct relationship between defects and program size because program characteristics are invisible.

The programming analogy to mechanical reliability would be better if the sample space were closer to the source of defects, the program text. If inspections were perfect at detecting failure, it would make more sense to inspect a sample of code, and infer the quality of uninspected code, than to sample executions and infer the quality on unexecuted inputs. Inspec-

best-known inclusion relation among methods, branch testing strictly subsumes statement testing. Intuitively, when method 1 subsumes 2, there is no point in using 2, because method 1 is always at least as good and may be better.

Misleading test sets flaw this inclusion relation, however. The "better" method's test set can always be misleading, while the "worse" method's (different) test set is not. Furthermore, these test sets can be natural for the methods, so the worse method's test set may actually be the right choice for practical testing. To illustrate, consider the Pascal procedure:

```
function misled(x: real): real;
  begin
    misled := x;
    if x > 0 then
      misled := 1.0/sqr(x)
  end
```

Suppose you are trying to compute the reciprocal of the square root function, but if the input is not positive, you wish to return it unchanged. Under the inclusion relation, branch testing is the better method, and statement testing, the worse. A natural statement test set for an electrical engineer would be something like {2}, for which the expected result is 0.707.... Any such test will uncover a failure that results from mistaking the square function "sqr" for the root function "sqrt."

However, if you are trying to attain branch coverage, you are in danger of trying a misleading test set like {-1,1}. The emphasis on branches focuses attention on the predicate rather than on the computation. Thus, the better method isn't better at all. The more elaborate the demands of a systematic testing method, the

greater the danger of trivializing the test set to satisfy it, and hence the more likely that it will mislead.

Obviously then, misleading test sets are the bane of any testing method. Bill Howden attempted to capture their absence by calling a testing method reliable (*not* in the statistical sense of the word) for a program if there are no misleading test sets for that program that satisfy the method.[1] Unfortunately, methods are seldom reliable, and reliability is not in general a property of any algorithmic testing method. Furthermore, the restrictions you must place on programs and methods to guarantee reliability are too stringent to make them practical.[2]

Why partition testing is unreliable. Ross Taylor and I, repeating the 1984 experiments of Joe

Duran and Simeon Ntafos, found that random testing and partition testing are more similar than you might think.[3]

For that reason, you can express an estimate of the quality that can be tested into software with partition testing as an MTTF. A typical unit partition test might contain 100 points. If all succeed, and you assume the test is random, there is 80 percent confidence in an MTTF of about 62 executions. This very modest estimate hardly justifies the usual claim that software has been tested and works.

REFERENCES
1. W. Howden, "Reliability of the Path-Analysis Testing Strategy," *IEEE Trans. Software Eng.*, Sept. 1976, pp. 208-215.
2. R. Hamlet, "Reliability Theory of Program Testing," *Acta Informatica*, 1981, pp. 31-43.
3. D. Hamlet and R. Taylor, "Partition Testing Does Not Inspire Confidence," *IEEE Trans. Software Eng.*, Dec. 1990, pp. 1402-1411.

tions are hard to quantify and control, however, so a different kind of testing is needed. one that samples the space of actual defects.

Sampling the state space. Both Parnas and I have proposed using the program's state space as the sampling domain for trustworthiness,[2,3] but this is not a good practical approach. The argument for using it is that failure results from textual flaws, or faults, when particular circumstances arise at the control point that contains the fault — which describes the state space exactly. It is a tuple of internal-variable values and a value of the location counter. The sampling distribution should be uniform because failure is no more likely for one state location than another. Such a theory correctly predicts that failure probability is proportional to program size.[3]

Unfortunately, the state space of most programs is far larger than the input domain, so a theory that requires sampling this much space is not attractive.

Larry Morell and Jeff Voas suggest an alternative.[4] They argue that points of the state space are themselves correlated. Starting with an input, each program normally goes through a sequence of states (its computation) to reach an output. The computation steps are defined by the operational semantics of the program statements as mappings from state to state.

Hence, when some input leads to program failure, the entire computation has "failed," so sampling states from that sequence overemphasizes failure. States from a single correct sequence are correlated in a similar way. To add to the confusion, the same state may appear in both failed and correct computations.

You don't have to sample variable values in a state if the final result does not depend on them. Although the problem to determine such dependencies is generally unsolvable, dataflow techniques give a

good approximation. Thus, I assume that a computation's data states contain only variable values on which the result depends. Each computation starts with an input, and may have an initial "correct" state subsequence, then the first bad state occurs, followed by a "failed" portion of the sequence. Thus, sampling the input space doesn't work. Inputs that are apparently independent can lead to the same state and thus are not independent samples, relative to failure in that state.

Data fan-in/-out. The crux of appropriate state-space sampling is the idea of state collapse — when different computations contain common sequences of states. State collapse can occur through fan-in — when two paths in a program join or when the values taken on by internal variables are restricted.[5] An example is an assignment statement with a constant right side. This statement produces a kind of ultimate fan-in because after its execution, the assigned variable has lost whatever range of values it might have had; it now can have only a single value.

Fan-out occurs when the possible values in states expand. For example, an input statement is the ultimate fan-out: whatever restricted values the input variable might have had before the statement, after it, any value is possible.

Many program statements do not fan in or out. For example, an assignment statement using an arithmetic operator like + has as many state value possibilities after execution as it did before.

When programs have a good deal of fan-in, their possible data states collapse to a set that can be smaller than the input domain. Many inputs lead to exactly the same computation, and intuitively it is the computations that should be sampled in testing. When programs have a good deal of fan-out, there is a combinatorial explosion of the state space because coverage of early states does not imply coverage of

later states with a wider value range. When programs neither fan out or in, each input leads to a different computation, and appropriate state-space sampling is the same as input sampling. However, the appropriate distribution is uniform, not the operational profile.

Thus, in some cases, far fewer test points are needed to establish trustworthiness than are needed to satisfy conventional reliability. In other cases, the two require about the same number of points, but with different test distributions; And in still other cases, trustworthiness can require vastly more points than reliability, with the full exploration of each state as an upper bound.

Interestingly, computation diversity and fan-out occur when programs read input throughout a computation rather than just at the beginning. Intuitively, such programs are interactive, and make essential use of saved state. The ultimate pathological case is that of real-time programs, in which inputs and state expansion appear at any point in the computation because an interrupt occurs.

HOW SHOULD WE TEST?

Although testing certainly has its limitations, it is unwise to discard it as a useful part of software development. The development process is beginning to be studied and controlled. Capturing the process provides the opportunity to expose likely sources of defects, and to test for them with appropriate partitions. Conventional random testing also has its merits.

Partition testing. The box on pp. 22-25 describes the weaknesses of partition testing to dispel the idea that a successful test means the software is reliable. But I would never recommend that you abandon partition testing altogether — and particularly not in favor of system-reliability testing.

Partition testing is the developer's best tool to probe the software for specific defects. Of particular importance are defects that lead to failures with catastrophic consequences. However infrequent a catastrophic failure may be, it is worth expend-

> Capturing the development process lets us expose likely sources of defects and test for them with appropriate partitions.

ing effort to preclude it, and a partition devised by considering the failure possibilities (for example, using a safety fault tree[6]) is just the way to attack the problem. Indeed, you should use partition testing whenever you suspect a particular source of defects, with a partition emphasizing the defect-prone input. Testing in that partition gives little confidence in overall reliability, but it is the only means of gaining confidence that the particular problem will not arise.

For example, a module that undergoes a specification change late in development, or one that fails an inspection, is an obvious potential defect source. Not only should you heavily exercise its structural and functional unit-test partitions, but when it is integrated into a system, the whole should be tested with a partition that singles out module execution.

Partition testing has many advantages. A functional partition test can be designed beginning in the requirements stage of development. Test data for structural partitions can be automatically generated, and even if hand generated, the tester has a systematic goal and automatic support.

If you have a complex piece of software, whose usage patterns you do not know, and you have a vast nonnumeric input domain, partition testing is probably your only choice.

Random testing. Preliminary results (based on a somewhat doubtful model that uses failures "tagged" by their origin[7]) indicate that uniform-distribution, state-space testing should be much better than partition testing at establishing confidence in apparently defect-free software.

However, random testing is not practical because it requires many orders of magnitude more test points than current practice. Even if you have an oracle — some means of mechanically deciding if program results are correct — random testing is barely feasible. Without an oracle, it is not feasible at all in most cases.

But random testing is the theoretical model that can answer fundamental questions that have too long been ignored. If, in fact, testing for a reasonable reliability is impractical by any means, then testing is

merely a defect-detection method that may not stack up well against others like inspections, and we should be changing our quality-assurance methods accordingly. On the other hand, if we can find a small state space to sample, we can make even trustworthiness practical.

Measuring the state-space coverage a test gives is not impractical. Well-known program-instrumentation techniques can record test penetration and statistically analyze the results. If the state-space theory is correct, such measurements can pinpoint states that have been poorly tested, and leave the difficult problem of how to reach them to the tester.

Voas has given the problem a novel twist with practical promise. He directly probes the state space by perturbing a state, then monitoring whether the perturbation affects program results. If not, that state (or the corresponding statement of the program) is not very "sensitive," since even if the data state were incorrect (as arranged by the perturbation) the results are correct. The lesson for programmers is that faults in insensitive statements will be hard to detect by testing. Perhaps the cleverest part of Voas's idea is that he need not consider the input space, so he doesn't have to reach the data states he perturbs or consider the operational profile.

The main points I have tried to make in this article are

♦ In testing for true reliability, clever partition methods may be no better than random testing, and if they are not, then no practical testing technique exists for guaranteeing software quality.

♦ The analogy to mechanical reliability is a poor one for software.

♦ More research is needed on trustworthiness; it may be that the state explosion is not so important as it seems. Correlated states are grouped into program computations, which may be the appropriate entities to sample.

♦ It may be possible to statically characterize programs for which the combinatorics of testing is not forbidding, giving precision to the desirable quality of "testability." Testability is also dynamically de-

scribed by Voas's idea of sensitivity. Experiments are needed to determine if these theoretically appealing ideas are in fact related to testing difficulty.

If testing for quality is the goal, then we must find a solution to the oracle problem. Until random tests of a million points become practical, testing is only a poor competitor for other heuristic defect-detection methods. ♦

ACKNOWLEDGMENTS
This work was supported by National Science Foundation grant CCR-9110111.

REFERENCES
1. M. Shooman, *Software Engineering Design, Reliability, and Management*, McGraw-Hill, New York, 1983.
2. D. Parnas, A. van Schouwen, and S. Kwan, "Evaluation of Safety-Critical Software," *Comm. ACM*, Sept. 1990, pp. 638-648.
3. R. Hamlet, "Probable Correctness Theory," *Information Processing Letters*, June 1987, pp. 17-25.
4. L. Morell and J. Voas, "Inadequacies of Date State Space Sampling as a Measure of Trustworthiness," Software Eng. Notes, Apr. 1991, pp. 73-74.
5. J. Voas, "Preliminary Observations on Program Testability," *Proc. Pacific Northwest Quality Conf.*, PNQC, Portland, 1991, pp. 235-247.
6. N. Leveson and P. Harvey, "Analyzing Software Safety," *IEEE Trans. Software Eng.*, Sept. 1983, pp. 569-579.
7. D. Hamlet and R. Taylor, "Partition Testing Does Not Inspire Confidence," *IEEE Trans. Software Eng.*, Dec. 1990, pp. 1402-1411.

Address questions about this article to Hamlet at Portland State University, CS Dept., Center for Software Quality Research, PO Box 751, Portland, OR 97207; Internet hamlet@cs.pdx.edu.

Safety Arguments, Software and System Reliability

John A McDermid

University of York,
Heslington,
York, YO1 5DD,
UK

Abstract

Our aim is to discuss the nature of safety arguments, to consider the role of system and software reliability evaluation in these arguments, and to outline an approach to supporting the development of safety arguments. We review some existing work addressing the problems of evaluating systems to high levels of reliability such as 10^{-9} failures per hour using "black box" testing. We also consider ways of achieving confidence beyond testable levels through the use of prior beliefs and discuss some approaches to achieving strong prior beliefs. We use these possible approaches to illustrate a canonical form for representing (safety) arguments, and then to outline the characteristics of a tool which we are constructing for safety argument management.

1 Introduction

It is now widely appreciated that safety and *system* reliability are not synonomous — indeed that safety and reliability are often in conflict [1]. In other words, a high degree of system safety can often only be achieved at the expense of reduction in overall system reliability, or availability. This conflict is perhaps easiest to see in the context of protection systems, such as reactor trip systems, where it is acceptable to have a non-zero probability of false trips (loss of availability) in order to increase the probability of achieving safe shut down when a truly anomalous situation arises. Of course this does not mean that reliability, especially software reliability, is an inappropriate measure for a safety system. Rather we have to realise that we are concerned with reliability in respect of events which are significant for safety, and that software reliability is only one of a number of factors which influence the safety of a software controlled system.

As well as (potential) conflicts between overall system reliability and safety, and difficulties of ascertaining what aspects of system/software behaviour are safety relevant, there are additional problems when considering software reliability for safety critical systems. Many safety requirements state a system (and hence software) reliability figure of 10^{-9} failures per hour, or (approximately) one failure per 100,000 years. In practice it is hard to asses software reliability and gain any measure of confidence that the failure rate is better than 10^{-4} to 10^{-5} per hour, although there are some circumstances where we are concerned with failure on demand and the low level of demand can be used to argue that we will have very low failure rates per unit time. This means that we have to take into account additional factors, e.g. a qualitative analysis of the nature of the development process, if we are to assert (judge) that software has the reliability level required.

Consequently, when assessing the safety of a software controlled system, we have to take into account the evaluation of software reliability — but also many other factors such as the nature of the development process, experience with similar systems, consequences of certain classes of failures, the distribution of failure classes, and so on. In general, safety systems are constructed from a number of different sub-systems of quite different technical natures, and may involve human operators, so we have to produce a multi-disciplinary safety argument, rather than an argument expressed purely in terms of software reliability. Our aim in this paper is to discuss the nature of safety arguments, to consider the role of software reliability in these arguments, and to outline one possible approach to supporting the development of such safety arguments. However we focus on issues of software reliability much more than generalised safety arguments.

We start by amplifying on the problems of evaluating high levels of reliability, especially software reliability, in section 2. In section 3 we discuss the nature of safety arguments and briefly outline a canonical form for arguments which we believe to be suitable for the representation of, and reasoning about, safety. Section 4 discusses requirements for a tool to support the development of safety arguments, and section 5 considers the nature of the process of developing such arguments in the context of system development and certification. We are engaged in the development of a prototype tool for supporting the production and review of safety arguments so we conclude with a discussion of the status of our conceptual framework and prototype.

For the sake of brevity, we have to keep a narrow focus in the paper and this means that we avoid detailed discussion of a number of important topics. However, wherever possible, we give references to relevant discussions. An effect of this focussing is that we say little about the relationship between system and software reliability, but we trust that it is clear that software reliability must always be evaluated in a systems context, i.e. taking into account the operational environment for the software.

2 Evaluating Ultra-High Reliability

It is now well-understood, see for example Littlewood [2], that the levels of software reliability required for safety critical systems cannot be achieved simply by black-box testing. Failure rates of about 10^{-4} to 10^{-5} per hour can be assessed in this way, but the required levels of, say, 10^{-9} failures per hour cannot be assessed within realistic timescales — such levels would require thousands of years' evaluation prior to operational service. We believe that generalised safety arguments may enable us to make valid judgements of reliability (and safety) beyond these levels, but it is worthwhile first briefly reviewing the statistical approaches available to us for extending the limits of statistical reliability assessment, as these will be relevant to our generalised safety arguments. A key issue is what we may infer about a program which has not failed during extensive testing.

Littlewood [2] shows how a Bayesian approach, using notions of prior belief, enables one to gain some formal support for the intuitive notion that if a program has operated without failure for N hours then it has a 50:50 chance of operating without failure for another N hours, assuming prior *ignorance* about the system. The approach adopts the notion that our prior belief about the failure rate, λ, should be represented by a member of the conjugate family as experimental evidence will change the beliefs, but not the nature of the distribution. He adopts a Γ distribution where the changes in belief are represented solely by changes in the parameters.

Littlewood further argues that one requires very strong prior beliefs indeed to be able to assert that a system has a failure rate of, say, 10^{-9} failures per hour given that evaluation has shown more modest levels of reliability such as 10^{-4} to 10^{-5} per hour. It is instructive therefore to consider some possible sources of (very) strong prior beliefs and we consider five different sources of belief which might influence our overall safety arguments.

A very common form of argument is that the nature of software development or evaluation process is such to warrant a high degree of confidence (high prior beliefs) in software reliability. One common claim is that the use of so-called formal methods, that is mathematically based approaches to software specification and verification, gives very high confidence — in fact that, in principle, they can guarantee that programs conform to their specifications. In

other words, using formal methods, programs can have 100% reliability, with respect to their specifications. This view is adopted by a number of influential bodies, see for example the UK Draft Defence Standard 00-55 [3]. The argument in favour of formal methods, as presented above, is, at best, over-simplified as it ignores the "reliability" of the specification but we are not concerned here with the validity of the argument, but with the form[1] as it would appear in a safety argument. The form would be that certain percepts of the development process, e.g. the tools and methods used, gives high prior beliefs and that considerable extrapolations could be made from the reliability figures found through black box testing (this would perhaps only be the case if testing discovered no failures).

Another possible form of argument would be based on a history of reliable operation of similar systems. Here the argument would be, fairly directly, one of analogy. If, for the sake of argument, we assume that a failure rate of 10^{-7} per hour had been observed in operational use for a set of systems in widespread use (taking into account the fact that we have test data from all the systems), then the argument might take the following form:

> "this new system has been developed with similar functionality, to work in a similar environment, by the same company, using similar techniques, using staff with similar qualifications, ... so we can be confident that the new system will also prove to have a reliability of 10^{-7} per hour"

This form of argument could be used directly or it could be used as the basis for prior beliefs in the style of Bayesian argument suggested by Littlewood [2].

Another common form of argument is based on independence of failures and fault tolerance. From the point of view of reliability calculations the form of the argument is that:

> "two components have failure probabilities of 10^{-N} per demand and they can be assumed (guaranteed) to fail independently then the overall failure probability is 10^{-2N} per demand; they can be assumed to fail independently so their failure probability is 10^{-2N} per demand"

The mathematical basis of the argument is sound — the issue is whether or not failure independence, especially in the context of software, is a valid assumption. Interestingly some standards, e.g. DO-178a [6] used for the certification of civil aircraft like the A320, explicitly allow this sort of argument for independently designed and implemented software. This illustrates another aspect of

---

[1] The role and value of formal methods is discussed in a number of papers, e.g. [4, 5], but it is outside the scope of this paper to explore this topic.

the nature of safety arguments — that arguments may be built on other arguments. We return to this point below.

Another form of argument which is sometimes used is that the probability of failure on demand can be quite high yet still give an adequate (acceptable) failure rate, if the rate of demand is sufficiently low. This sort of argument may be appropriate for a protection system, e.g. a reactor trip system[2]. Again, by way of illustration, the argument might take the following form:

"black box testing has shown a failure rate of 10^{-N} per demand (using accelerated testing or deliberate stimulation of demand conditions) and the estimated demand rate is 10^{-M} per hour so the overall reliability is $10^{-(N+M)}$ per hour"

Again we would expect to have further arguments to justify the assumptions, e.g. regarding the predicted demand rate or the authenticity of the test conditions. Perhaps the most important assumption is the independence of the demand and failure processes.

Finally we might expect to gain extra confidence from the use of white box, rather than black box, testing. Here the argument would be in the form that a greater test coverage, and hence confidence, was gained from using structural knowledge about the program. Pragmatically this sort of argument might be based on Markov models of failure and recovery characteristics and perhaps basic software engineering data, e.g. that protection mechanisms prevent certain classes of failure occurring, or faults from propagating. We are investigating this sort of approach for security [7], and have previously made a general study of an "assurance algebra" for combining assurance measures, including reliability, for different system components [8] but this is a topic which requires further study.

In summary, black box testing, on its own, is not enough to evaluate software to the level of reliability required for many safety critical applications and the evaluation has to be supplemented by other arguments. Our aim now is to consider ways in which these additional arguments may be recorded and linked to the reliability evaluation figures. We do this in a relatively informal way as our intention is to illustrate the overall approach, not to present a treatise on Bayesian statistics.

3 Safety Arguments

As we indicated earlier, arguments about reliability and safety of computerised systems tend to be complex and to

involve multiple disciplines, e.g. software engineering, electronic engineering, and cognitive psychology. However the arguments in each field do not stand alone — they inter-relate and, taken together, (should) provide sufficient convincing evidence to show that the system is acceptably safe for its intended use.

In practice safety arguments tend to be presented as large quantities of documentation and it is very hard to trace the dependencies between the different parts of the arguments in the documents, as presented. It is attractive to consider automated support to safety management, but this immediately opens the question of what constitutes an adequate canonical form for argument representation to facilitate the linkage of arguments from the different disciplines. In the following subsections we review what we believe to be a suitable canonical representation, then illustrate it's use on the examples given in section 2.

3.1 Representing Safety Arguments

Our work derives from an analysis of argument structures due to Stephen Toulmin [9]. Toulmin's analysis was aimed at arguments, in general, not specifically technical or scientific arguments. For our purposes we believe that the structure of arguments which he proposed is satisfactory, but that we may need to introduce more restrictive rules about the use of the form (than Toulmin envisaged) for the representation of safety arguments. For the sake of simplicity we restrict ourselves to a straightforward description of the argument representation as developed by Toulmin.

Toulmin divides the constituents of a single argument step into six parts:

- **Claims** are the statements we wish to justify.

- **Data** are the grounds we produce when asked to show what we are basing our claim on and can be such as experimental observations, common knowledge, statistics, personal testimony or previously established claims.

- **Warrants** are step-authorising statements, i.e. laws of nature, legal principles, rules of thumb, engineering formulae and inference rules.

- **Backing** is general information providing reasons for trusting the warrant, e.g. that it is based on well-tried and trusted statistical principles

- **Qualifiers** are modal terms which record the degree of certainty a warrant allows.

- **Rebuttals** are specific circumstances in which the argument will not hold.

In principle arguments presented in this canonical form would have all these components but, in practice, many are often omitted, e.g. it is quite common to omit backing for

---

[2] Again it is far from clear whether or not this would be an acceptable argument as there are issues to do with the ability to predict demand rates, the ability to simulate exactly demand conditions, the ability to carry out realistic tests, and so on. However we are more interested in the argument form, for the purposes of this paper.

warrants from commonly used theories such as reliability theory. In many cases the final backing is simply the scientific process — we would not expect to see explicit justifications for such fundamental principles as the Kolmogorov axioms.

Four our purposes in safety argumentation the Toulmin form can best be thought of as a basis for analysis — to look for hidden assumptions, to expose the dependencies between arguments, and so on. The argument form has ben used relatively rarely, but examples exist in a number of different fields, e.g. safety analysis and resolution of case law.

Toulmin arguments take the form of a "movement" from some data elements to a final claim. This movement is licensed according to a specified warrant. The warrant or the data may include elements of doubt which are made explicit by preceding the claim with a qualification.To show that in general the warrant can be trusted one can produce backing. Specific conditions in which the warrant may not be used can be recorded as a rebuttal. For the purposes of summarising the argument structure it is useful to have a diagrammatic representation of the argument. The layout of a Toulmin argument is:

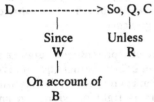

The qualification is expressed in such terms as necessarily, possibly, presumably, probably and so on, and these can be used to represent "strength of belief" although this is not how we will wish to represent prior beliefs. An argument diagram, such as that shown above, might be read as: "given D, so it is probable that C, unless R, since W on account of B". In practice the diagram is a useful summary and we would not necessarily want to make a direct translation into a textual form. The diagrams are also useful when we need to show the structure of chains of arguments, although we will not illustrate this idea here.

In practice it is necessary to build up chains, or nets, of arguments. In the simplest case the claim of one argument may be used as the data of another. As a simple example one can think of establishing chains of reliability calculations, building up from the reliability for simple components, to the overall system reliability figure via subsystems. In a full argument the overall structures would be more complex, e.g. it is possible to have arguments that produce warrants (or more probably backing) as claims. Here qualifiers in backing-establishing arguments might be thought of as representing uncertainty about the model on which the argument is based. Similarly it is possible to have arguments linked through rebuttals.

However, for our purposes here, we do not need to discuss such links in detail.

3.2 Examples using Prior Beliefs

It is easiest to see how to apply such argument structures by considering how we would use the argument form to analyse some of the statements made in section 2 concerning ways of establishing strong prior beliefs (or arguing that high reliability figures can be claimed). We consider three of the examples introduced in section 2.

We first consider an example where the argument involves a direct establishment of the reliability claim, rather than the establishment of prior belief. We take the statement:

> "this new system has been developed with similar functionality, to work in a similar environment, by the same company, using similar techniques, using staff with similar qualifications, ... so we can be confident that the new system will also prove to have a reliability of 10^{-7} per hour"

We can analyse this argument (fragment) and re-represent it in Toulmin form. The argument constituents are:

C   system failure rate will be at most 10^{-7} per hour

D1   failure rates of similar systems are 10^{-7} per hour

D2   the processes have a high degree of similarity

W   (implicit) sufficiently similar processes will yield similar operational reliabilities

B   (implicit) hard to ascertain from the fragment presented – should probably involve instances of other occasions when making this assumption was acceptable, i.e. the failure rates were comparable

The data element, D2, is itself derived from a number of other statements:

C   the processes have a high degree of similarity (D2 above)

D1   systems have similar functionality

D2   systems developed by same company

Dn   ...

W   (implicit) these process attributes are similar, so the processes are similar

B   (implicit/non-existent) the above attributes are sufficient to characterise processes and allow them to be compared in terms of the reliabilities of their end products.

The example not only shows how to use the notation but also indicates the value in exposing hidden assumptions which underlie arguments.

We can now turn to another example which relates more directly to system not software reliability, or more strictly one that relates the two notions:

"black box testing has shown a failure rate of 10^{-N} per demand (using accelerated testing or deliberate stimulation of demand conditions) and the estimated demand rate is 10^{-M} per hour so the overall reliability is $10^{-(N+M)}$ per hour"

This too can be re-expressed in Toulmin form:

C   system failure rate will be $10^{-(N+M)}$ per hour

D1 failure rate on demand is 10^{-N} per hour

D2 demand rate is 10^{-M} per hour

W demand rate x failure rate on demand = failure rate

B (implicit) reliability theory (and the conditions under which the evaluation data was gained)

Again we could consider further levels of argument decomposition investigating the derivation of D1 and D2, but the above fragment suffices for our purposes.

We now turn to our third example:

"two components have failure probabilities of 10^{-N} per demand and they can be assumed (guaranteed) to fail independently then the overall failure probability is 10^{-2N} per demand; they can be assumed to fail independently so their failure probability is 10^{-2N} per demand"

This can be re-expressed in more than one way. We first illustrate an informal approach:

C   system failure rate will be 10^{-2N} per hour

D1 failure rate of component A is 10^{-N} per hour

D2 failure rate of component B is 10^{-N} per hour

D3 components fail independently

W given independent failures of A and B, then failure rate of A x failure rate on B = system failure rate

B (implicit) reliability theory, the conditions under which the evaluation data was gained, and evidence that high levels of independence are achievable (have been achieved).

We could also express some of the above forms of argument more directly in terms of the mathematics of prior beliefs. Specifically we could recast the first and third examples this way. However we sketch the general form, rather than give specific details, as we are more concerned with principles of argument representation than with details of Bayesian statistics:

C   system failure rate will be 10^{-N} per hour

D1 no failures have been observed in M hours ($M < N$)

D2 prior belief is represented by a = .. and b = ... for a Gamma distribution

W using Bayesian inference and the formula in [2]

B see [2]

Again we could build up a chain of arguments which have D1 and D2 as their (final) claim. The chain leading up to D2 would have to result in an estimate of the Gamma distribution parameters based on arguments about the development process (and process similarity) for the first example, and independence of failure of diverse software, for the third. The structure of the second argument is not amenable to such a treatment. Whilst we could illustrate the nature of such arguments we are more concerned with a number of further points regarding the use of the argument form. We discuss these as more general observations since they are not restricted to arguments about prior beliefs.

3.3 Properties of Argument Structures

Argument structures are potentially rich, varied and complex. Our aim here is to identify some of the more interesting facets of the arguments, especially those which influence ways in which we would need to provide automated support for the arguments.

First, there is no unique way of representing an argument. For example we have shown both informal (qualitative) and (outline) formal Bayesian approaches for dealing with prior beliefs. Neither form is right or wrong, in any absolute sense, rather each emphasises different aspects of the argument structure. In many cases one would like to have both the formal and informal version of the argument — the latter acting as a form of "management summary" for the former. In general we need to manage complex argument structures including summaries and to be able to relate the summaries at the different levels so that, for example, we can investigate the ramifications of change.

Second, there is a spectrum of rigour, or formality, to the arguments and this influences the extent to which we can analyse or validate the arguments. In some cases the arguments are purely qualitative and the only checks we can do relate to argument structure, i.e. are all the parts of the argument present, or perhaps we might be able to check adherence to some controlled vocabulary (this is analogous to the notion of a data dictionary in conventional database terminology). In some cases it may be possible to check the validity of the (implicit) computation between data and claim — at least for type or dimensional consistency, if not for numeric accuracy. Finally, in some cases, it would be possible to calculate (derive automatically) the claim from the data, given the warrant. A support mechanism must be able to apply checks or to make automatic derivations where possible.

Third, we need to be able to produce a document which presents the argument in a coherent way — but this document need not present all the argument. For example the argument may make references to published work (as our example did above) or refer to data derived and held by other software tools, e.g. a test system. Thus a support tool needs to deal with the production of high quality documents, but it also needs to be able to control dependencies on "imported" information. However it is not efficient to do all the argument management operations in terms of a text document — there is too much ancillary information which is included for presentational elegance and which doesn't form the core of the technical argument. Thus we need to be able to "factor out" a database for holding the key technical data — it is on this database that consistency checks and claim derivation will be carried out.

One of our aims in this paper is to indicate what role in a general set of safety arguments might be played by software reliability arguments, and to show how such arguments might be managed in practice. It is now appropriate to illustrate some aspects of the intended functionality of the argument management tool we are developing and to say something about how the tool would be used to develop safety arguments, in practice.

4   Support for Safety Arguments

We are currently developing a support system, known as SAM (Safety Argument Manager), which will give support to safety argument management and which will be based on the Toulmin form. SAM can be thought of as a form of hypertext system — albeit one which has some application-specific capabilities, e.g. for analysing arguments and perhaps calculating reliabilities. However thinking of SAM as a hypertext system may lead us to neglect important properties of the relationships between the database held by the tool and the printed document, and between the printed document and the interactive (hypertext) form. The relationships between printed and electronic forms of SAM arguments may well be crucial to the usability and effectiveness of the tool so it is important to consider requirements in this area.

Consequently we will first focus on two of the above views: the internal data structures held by SAM — the *database* view; and the reports produced with the aid of SAM — the *document* view. We use the term database to mean the records of the arguments, and of a model of the system being analysed[3], held by SAM on a semi-permanent basis. We do not imply a commitment to any specific database model, e.g. entity relationship, nor to any database management system. However the tool, when fully developed, will contain a complex database

management system and one of the keys in designing the tool is to establish an appropriate conceptual schema for the tool.

By the term document we mean the printed form of the arguments, including appropriate parts of the system model, produced at any stage whilst using SAM. The view of a document seen through the user interface will be richer than that seen on the printed page — for example because it may be possible to select parts of the displayed document and to raise queries about the selected material. For expository purposes we focus our discussion on "completed arguments", at least in the sense that the arguments are well-formed, rather than intermediate forms of the documents which may contain ill-formed structures. It is intended to be possible to use SAM in a number of scenarios, e.g. in support of certification, in support of systems engineering activities, and in support of evaluation. We will make no specific assumptions about usage in the ensuing discussion, but the breadth of requirements does reflect this broad range of possible uses.

In all modes of use of SAM it will establish and maintain a set of relationships between the database, an associated document, or documents, and a number of associated display views. We will assume that there is a primary document to be produced as part of the process of using SAM[4].

A user of SAM will, in effect, generate a database and a document at the same time. The document will be the printed form of a set of arguments (and associated system model) which the user wishes to be able to give to other people. The database is a (semantically richer) "version" of the document on which there are more operations available through the interactive interface — validity checking, scrolling, zooming, browsing, modification, challenging assumptions, etc. For the time being we assume that all the database contents are available in hypertext form. In using SAM it should be possible to achieve (at least) two distinct objectives:

- produce a convincing document;
- produce a database which can be investigated by a user (who has read the document) through the hypertext interface in order to gain further convincing evidence that the arguments presented in the document are sound, e.g. to investigate the assumptions or to check the validity of arguments[5].

---

[3] In practice the tool would hold a model of the operational environment as well as a model of the system itself, e.g. in order to support hazard analysis.

[4] Really this is a hypothesis about how SAM ought to work but, for the purposes of this paper, it is inappropriate to consider the justification for the hypothesis in any detail.

[5] Of course direct work with the hypertext argument document is also important, but discussion of such interactive capabilities is not our primary concern here, although they will have a significant effect on the usability of the tool.

The above distinction recognises that it will not, in general, be possible to reflect all the information in the database in the document. More importantly it would not be *sensible* to try to do so — the purposes of the document and the database (in it's hypertext presentation) are different and the set of characteristics which make convincing a set of arguments in printed (narrative) form and in interactive (hypertext) form are quite different (although not disjoint). In the printed (narrative) form characteristics such as presentation style and logical order of content will be important. In the hypertext form characteristics such as the ability to find backing for all warrants and the ability to find resolutions of all challenges made to arguments will be important.

Thus, in the terms of the examples illustrated above, it should be possible to express fairly abstract reliability arguments, then to progressively substantiate the arguments by, for example, filling in information on prior beliefs and making explicit the source of the prior beliefs. Clearly the provision of this form of support does not guarantee the appropriateness of safety or reliability claims but it makes the set of arguments explicit and inspectable, and thus aiding the essentially social process in gaining agreement that the form of the argument and its conclusion are both sound. Having seen this as an objective it is now instructive to consider the nature of the process of developing such arguments.

5   Development of Safety Arguments

We have discussed aspects of the way in which argument documents and databases are developed in the previous section. The aim here is to address the process "in the large". We believe that the tool will be used to investigate a rational reconstruction of the argument, in the sense used by Parnas and Clements in their classic paper [10], but that the "real process" will be more complex.

In practice, for large classes of use, we would expect the database and document to be developed in tandem, no doubt with much iteration. Thus, for example, a prose document might be produced containing some informal arguments. Next this would be turned into Toulmin form by indicating the roles in the arguments played by particular phrases, and analysis would be carried out using the tool. If analysis and review found omissions from the arguments then the prose document would be modified, and so on.

In practice it is likely that the user of SAM will develop documents and databases concurrently. Judging by our experience developing Z specifications it is likely that the following orders of derivation will occur. With specialised arguments, such as reliability calculations, it is likely that the formal material will be developed first and later be supplemented with explanatory text. Similarly, with informal arguments it is likely that the prose form will be developed first then it will be annotated to "convert" it into

the analysable Toulmin form. However as there will inevitably be much iteration in developing arguments these observations should not be taken as indicating any desired facilities or constraints on operational modes. In other words the tool should support the user's desired mode of working, not place him under strong procedural constraints about the order of derivation of arguments and supporting text.

6   Summary and Conclusions

Our aim in this paper was to discuss the nature of safety arguments, to consider the role of software reliability in these arguments, and to outline one possible approach to supporting the development of such safety arguments. We have discussed a number of aspects of software and system reliability, together with issues in gaining confidence in high reliability figures as is demanded for many safety critical systems. Specifically we have reviewed some existing work on the problems of evaluating systems to high levels of reliability using "black box" testing and ways of achieving confidence beyond testable levels through the use of prior beliefs. We then discussed some ways of achieving strong prior beliefs — although we made no attempt to argue that these are strong enough to justify reliability figures such as the 10^{-9} failures per hour sometimes demanded and claimed. We used this to illustrate a canonical form for representing arguments and the fundamental characteristics of a support tool for safety management which we are currently constructing

Clearly the provision of this form of support for safety arguments, whether based on prior beliefs or other technical bases, does not guarantee the appropriateness of safety or reliability claims. However it makes the set of arguments explicit and inspectable, and thus should increase confidence that the form of the argument and its conclusion are both sound. In other words our aim is to facilitate the process of developing safety arguments, including those based on software reliability evaluation, but we recognise that we can never produce a fully automatic system which will supplant human judgement.

We are evolving a conceptual framework for safety argument management. Although Toulmin's work gives us a basic structure for representing arguments, there are many additional issues to be addressed. Toulmin didn't address the development of argument chains, nor the ideas of summarising arguments — and clearly both of these concepts must be supported if we are to deal satisfactorily with complex safety arguments. Although this sounds straightforward in fact the structure of typical safety arguments is quite complex, and quite subtle, and it is difficult to produce an adequate framework for handling such arguments. Similarly we need to add notions of validity checks or arguments, dealing with explicit models of the system to be developed, and so on. In order to manage what is an intellectually demanding, and ill-defined, task we are proceeding to develop concepts in parallel with a series of prototypes.

We have developed a first simple prototype of SAM, concentrating on support for the Toulmin-style arguments presented in textual form. The current prototype would be sufficient to support development of the qualitative arguments illustrated above, but not to carry out checks on the validity of reliability calculations. We are currently considering requirements for the next stage of prototype development and hope, *inter alia*, to provide support for some forms of formal argumentation, such as reliability calculations. The final form of the tool will support a range of formal argument styles including fault trees, reliability calculations and probably some form of simple logical inference, perhaps based on formal specifications such as Z or on a causal logic capable of representing the dependencies between, and consequences of, failures.

We strongly believe that this form of tool is necessary to support safety and reliability analysis for complex engineered systems and that it gives a context in which arguments about software reliability can be used as part of an overall system safety assessment. Our hope is that we will be able to give support to realistic safety arguments — including argument steps based on reliability evaluation — covering the range of disciplines and activities necessary for the development and assessment of safety.

7 Acknowledgements

The ideas and concepts set out above have been developed over some time in interactions with colleagues on a number of projects, most notably those engaged in the development of SAM itself, and those involved in the ESPRIT PDCS project. I would particularly like to thank Bev Littlewood of City University, my colleague Chris Higgins and Justin Forder and Graham Storrs of Logica Cambridge, the lead partner on the SAM project.

8 References

[1] N G Leveson, Software Safety: What, Why and How, ACM Computing Surveys, 1986.

[2] B Littlewood, Limits to Evaluation of Software Dependability, Proceedings of the 1990 CSR Conference, Garmisch Partenkirchen (to appear), 1991.

[3] Draft Interim Defence Standard 00-55: Requirements for the procurement of safety critical software in defence equipment, UK MoD, 1989.

[4] J H Fetzer, Formal verification: the very idea, CACM, 1988.

[5] J A McDermid, Formal methods: Use and relevance for the development of safety critical systems, in Safety aspects of computer control, P A Bennett (ed), Butterworth Scientific, 1991

[6] Software considerations in airborne systems and equipment certification, DO-178a, Radio Technical Commission for Aeronautics, 1985.

[7] J A McDermid, Qi Shi, Software Reliability Measurement for Secure Systems, unpublished report, University of York, 1990.

[8] J A McDermid, Principles of an Assurance Algebra, YCS123, University of York, Computer Science Department Report, 1989.

[9] S Toulmin, The Uses of Argument, Cambridge University Press, 1958.

[10] P C Clements, D L Parnas, A Rational Design Process: How and Why to Fake It, IEEE Trans. on SE, 1986.

Application of Software Reliability Modeling to Product Quality and Test Process

Willa K. Ehrlich John P. Stampfel Jar R. Wu

AT&T Bell Laboratories
Holmdel, NJ 07733-1988

ABSTRACT

Software reliability modeling of data collected during the testing of a large-scale industrial system was used to measure software quality from the customer perspective. Specifically, software quality was measured in terms of the system software failure rate expressed as number of failures per hour of system operation. The testing phase analyzed, Stability Test, was an operational profile-driven test in that a controlled load was imposed on the system reflective of the system's busy-hour usage pattern. The usage profile was determined from requirements specifying both the frequency of invocation of each command and the alarm arrival rate for the largest expected user site. For this controlled test environment, a Poisson-type reliability growth model, the Exponential Non-Homogeneous Poisson Process model (or ENHPP) exhibited a good fit to the observed failure data. Furthermore, the model demonstrated predictive power for future failure rates. Differences between model results and observed failure data following release to the Beta site were attributed to differences in these two environments' operational profiles. We conclude that the use of an operational profile to drive System Test is an effective test strategy and that the operational profile must be taken into account when predicting field reliability from reliability measured during test.

1. INTRODUCTION

Software systems whose failures may have severe consequences must be subjected to extensive testing prior to deployment. The testing phase of system development represents a significant cost component, increasing very rapidly with system size. There is a great challenge to conduct the testing in a manner which produces a level of quality satisfactory to the user with minimum cost.

A large-scale software system, System T, has been constructed and deployed. This paper presents our experience in testing that system from the users' point of view.

The System T users' perception of system quality is dominated by system reliability. A widely accepted definition of software reliability is the probability that a computer program performs its defined purpose satisfactorily (i.e., without failure) over a specified time period within a particular execution environment. This execution environment is known formally as the operational profile, which is defined in terms of sets of possible input values together with their probabilities of occurrence. An operational profile was used to drive a portion of System T's system testing. Software reliability modeling was applied to data gathered during this phase of testing and then used to predict subsequent failure behavior during actual system operations (Beta Test.) Data were then gathered during the actual Beta Test phase for comparison.

In this paper, we document the importance of the operational profile in testing software systems for the purpose of measuring software quality from the users' viewpoint. A software reliability model exhibited both model adequacy (i.e.,"goodness-of-fit") and predictive validity for the controlled test environment. However, the model was unable to accurately predict subsequent failure behavior at the Beta site. We also describe an additional analysis documenting differences in the two execution environments and that can explain why additional failures occurred during field use. We conclude that (1) the use of an operational profile to drive System Test is an effective strategy, (2) the operational profile is an important determinant of measured reliability, and (3) the operational profile must be taken into account when predicting field reliability from reliability measured during test.

The paper is organized into eight sections. In Part 2, we describe the system that we studied. The System Test and Beta Test phases of its life cycle are described in Part 3. The Poisson-type reliability growth models used in the present study are presented in Part 4. The statistical results of applying the models to pre- and post- deployment testing are given in Part 5. In Part 6, we indicate how we measured the system's execution environment and then indicate differences between the system's System Test and Beta Test environments. In Part 7, we present the implications of this work for testing software systems in order to measure system quality from the users' point of view while in Part 8, we summarize the conclusions of the study.

2. SOFTWARE SYSTEM PRODUCT

2.1 System T

System T is a network management system which receives data from a geographically large, existing telemetry network and presents events, called alarms, to operators at terminals for action (See Figure 1.) The events are detected by Local Telemetry Interfaces (LTIs) and transmitted through Telemetry Network Interfaces (TNIs). The system is basically driven by failure events occurring in the monitored telecommunications network. These arrive at System T (i.e., at the Central Processor or CPU in Figure 1) as alarm messages. The messages are expanded by reference to stored information in the database, filtered, grouped and presented to the operators at terminals. The operators respond mainly by entering commands to the system for more information, to affect the network or to change data. Database operators update the network description and other data in a system database. The system interacts with other similar and dissimilar systems.

2.2 System Components - Software

The system was built on top of the AT&T UNIX® operating system and environment. A commercial relational database management system was used. Because high availability was required, disk mirroring capability was added to the operating system by the hardware vendor, and all disks were mirrored. In addition, special software was added to the operating system to support a virtual circuit switch through which most communications were routed, a packet network interface front end processor, and other terminal and communications disciplines.

System T includes an administrative log which receives messages about process failures or system status and a separate application related log.

2.3 System Usage Profile

The usage profile for System T was initially determined from requirements specifying the frequency of invocation of each command and alarm arrival rates for an Operations Center. The usage profile was defined for a "busy hour" on the system, which was a mid-morning or mid-afternoon hour on a weekday during the busy month of the year. The absolute rates were for the largest expected user site. This usage profile was used not only to define test scripts for operational profile-driven System Test, but also in the design of the system and in pre-construction performance projections.

A partial list of the usage profile, limited to the "top 10" commands is shown in Table 1. The total command rate was 23.1 per minute.

TABLE 1. TOP 10 USER INVOKED TRANSACTIONS

COMMAND	RATE(PER MINUTE)
es	3.5
sre	3.0
rv	2.8
vi	1.7
rsw	1.5
rfs	1.5
lp	1.1
pri	1.0
vuf	0.8
lilo	0.8
cuf	0.7
lis	0.7
haz	0.7
aup	0.5

Transactions were divided into four groups:

- Application,
- Special,
- DBMS,
- UNIX Operating System.

This division is listed with the expected highest sources of failures first. UNIX operating system code and DBMS code had extensive field experience and so were considered well tested. The application code and special code (e.g., disk mirroring driver) were new and in need of more attention. Application transactions were sub-divided further into alarms, normal operations, database operations and system operations.

3. TEST PROCESS AND ENVIRONMENT

3.1 System Test

The System T System Test phase of development consisted of a variety of testing activities (e.g., functional, regression, stability, stress) with different objectives and strategies for each. The functional testing activity was oriented toward testing of every combination of options for each command or function, to detect departures from command specifications. This form of testing typically ignores simultaneous feature interactions. In contrast, the purpose of Stability Testing was to detect failures following prolonged system usage (i.e., after many cycles of execution of interacting system features) in the expected user mode.

A software failure, as used for analysis in software reliability modeling, was defined to include:

- System goes down due to software fault in code executing on Central Processor; system initialization is required,
- System hangs due to software fault in code executing on Central Processor; initialization *may* be required,
- Process fails due to software fault in code executing on Central Processor; process is purged and then restarted.

The Stability Testing was accomplished in a controlled test environment consisting of a command mix and alarm rate characteristic of the system's typical busy hour. Such testing is of long duration and acts as an amplifier of faults not noticeable in single cycles of a feature, or without competition between features.

The load on the system was provided by testing systems connected to simulate the various external interfaces of System T. Scripts, based on the test operational profile, were used to drive load generators. These load generators simulated user interactions, interactions with the TNI for the generation of alarm load and handling user requests. They also drove lower level simulators of the LTI to send messages through real TNIs connected to the system under test. "Other Systems" to which System T was connected were also simulated. The scripts were a continuous repetition of the one "busy hour" operational profile, varied by starting each TNI simulator or user simulator at slightly different times. The only load on the system under test came from the executing application under test.

Stability Test runs were expected to run approximately 60 hours, although shorter runs were also taken and some failures caused runs to be terminated early. After a run the system was reinitialized. Data were collected over a period of four months (i.e., 08/02/88-12/05/88). UNIX system accounting and process accounting were run at all times. System accounting data were collected at five minute intervals. This provided CPU utilization information as needed for the software reliability analysis in a very inexpensive manner. Process accounting data gave accurate profiles of command and process use and verification of the operational profile. The administrative log provided data on timing of failures, while the application log and load generator logs provided alarm load data. Logs of all interactions were collected on the load generator systems.

Total CPU time in processing transactions was used to index System T program execution. Total CPU time for a given test run--Stability or Beta--was derived from UNIX system accounting files. For each Stability Test run or daily Beta Trial, an average CPU utilization value was obtained. Total elapsed time was then multiplied by this proportionality factor to generate total execution time associated with a given run.

Faults causing failures in a Stability run were repaired as rapidly as possible and corrected software used as soon as available.

3.2 Beta Test Environment

The Beta Test was the first use of the system by the customer. Users were trained in the new system, and development personnel were on site to answer questions. The database started out empty and data from another system was transmitted to System T and reformatted by conversion programs to enter it into the database in bulk. Only gradually, as the database was populated and TNIs connected to the telemetry network did alarms messages begin loading the system. Users had little previous experience with the UNIX operating system and commands and practiced while setting up the system.

Copies of accounting files and all log files, as described above, were transmitted to the development laboratory. Data were collected daily, with nearly four months of data (12/01/88-03/21/89) being included in the analysis.

Failures were reported almost immediately to the development organization where faults were diagnosed. Delivery of corrected software to the Beta system was not immediate, however, with several internal testing phases required prior to release to Beta site.

4. TIME-DOMAIN SOFTWARE RELIABILITY MODELS

4.1 Mathematical Framework

Time-domain reliability models are based on stochastic point processes that characterize system failures (i.e., system actions that depart from specifications) as highly localized events distributed randomly in time (Ascher & Feingold, 1984; Cox & Lewis, 1966).

If $\lambda(t)$ denotes the instantaneous rate of failure occurrence or failure intensity at time t, and M(t) is a random variable that denotes the number of failures in the time interval (0,t), then the mean or expected value of M(t) is:

$$\mu(t) = E[M(t)] = \int_0^t \lambda(s)\,ds. \qquad (1)$$

In one important case of time-domain models, the random variable M(t) is assumed to be generated by a Poisson process. Thus, given $\mu(t)$, $t \geq 0$, the stochastic process specifies a Poisson probability distribution for each value of t. The probability that exactly y failures will be observed by time t, then, is given by the Poisson probability distribution:

$$Pr[M(t)=y] = \frac{\mu(t)^y}{y!}e^{-\mu(t)}. \qquad (2)$$

The reliability or probability of failure-free behavior by time t is given by:

$$Pr[M(t)=0] = \frac{\mu(t)^0}{0!}e^{-\mu(t)} = e^{-\int_0^t \lambda(s)\,ds}. \qquad (3)$$

Note that if $\lambda(t)$ changes over time (i.e., is time-variant), we have a *nonhomogeneous Poisson process (NHPP)*. A *homogeneous Poisson process (HPP)* is a special case of a NHPP, in which $\lambda(t)$ is constant over time (i.e., $\lambda(t)=\lambda$). Note from (1) that, in a HPP, the expected number of failures at time t increases linearly with time:

$$\mu(t) = E[M(t)] = \lambda t. \qquad (4)$$

The reliability at time t is:

$$Pr[M(t)=0] = \frac{\mu(t)^0}{0!}e^{-\mu(t)} = e^{-\lambda t}. \qquad (5)$$

If the assumptions of a Poisson process are satisfied, a homogeneous Poisson process (HPP) model is applicable in the absence of debugging and software correction (e.g., during field operations), whereas a nonhomogeneous Poisson process (NHPP) model with a decreasing $\lambda(t)$ function, that is, a *reliability growth* model, applies when software corrections are made in response to failures (e.g., during test).

4.2 Models Used in Study

In the present study, two types of reliability growth NHPP models were applied to System T's failure data. In one software reliability model, the Exponential Non-Homogeneous Poisson Process model or ENHPP,[1] each fault is assumed to cause failures at the same rate so that faults contribute equally to overall failure intensity. In contrast, in the second model, referred to as the Logarithmic Non-Homogeneous Poisson Process or LNHPP model (Musa, Iannino & Okumoto, 1987; Musa & Okumoto, 1984), the rates at which faults produce failures vary so that overall failure intensity is not necessarily directly proportional to fault content. These two models were selected because they have been found to be applicable to a wide range of execution environments used in testing large, complex industrial software systems. Thus, these models have been applied previously to other software systems, with considerable practical experience being gained in model application (Musa et al, 1987).

In the ENHPP model, failure intensity, $\lambda(t)$, is expressed through parameters, as a family of exponentially decreasing functions over time,

$$\lambda(t) = \lambda_0 \exp\left(-\frac{\lambda_0}{v_0}t\right) \qquad (6)$$

so that the mean cumulative number of software failures increases exponentially to an asymptote with time,

$$\mu(t) = E[M(t)] = \int_0^t \lambda(s)\,ds = v_0\left[1 - \exp\left(-\frac{\lambda_0}{v_0}t\right)\right]. \qquad (7)$$

In the LNHPP model, failure intensity is a family of inverse linear functions with respect to time:

---

1. This model was initially applied by Goel & Okumoto (1979) as a calendar-time model and then by Musa as an execution time model (Musa, Iannino & Okumoto, 1987).

$$\lambda(t) = \frac{\lambda_0}{\lambda_0\theta t+1}, \qquad (8)$$

so that the expected cumulative number of failures is a logarithmic function of time:

$$\mu(t) = E[M(t)] = \int_0^t \lambda(s)\,ds = \frac{1}{\theta}\ln(\lambda_0\theta t+1). \qquad (9)$$

5. APPLICATION OF SOFTWARE RELIABILI-TY MODELING TO SYSTEM T SYSTEM

5.1 Analysis Overview

The best candidates for software reliability model application are system-wide tests in which input conditions are reflective of field usage (Ehrlich & Emerson, 1987). Therefore, software reliability measurement appeared to be most valid for System T Stability Testing. Consequently, software reliability modeling was applied to software failures encountered during System T Stability Testing and a forecast made concerning System T software reliability to be experienced during subsequent Beta usage. Specifically, software reliability model application began with an internal release to System Test, in which all of System T generic functionality was fully integrated into the system.

5.2 Results of Model Fitting

5.2.1 Stability Test Figure 2 presents the results of applying the two reliability growth models, ENHPP and LNHPP, to System T software failures during the Stability Test interval. Both the actual failure data, that is, cumulative observed failures as a function of total CPU time, together with the fitted cumulative software failure counts, are shown. Model parameter estimates were obtained using maximum likelihood statistical estimation and these parameter values were then used to generate fitted reliability curves.

To determine model accuracy, a regression analysis was used to fit the failure intensity function directly. The ENHPP and LNHPP models were first expressed in canonical linear form:

$$y = \beta_0 + \beta_1 t, \qquad (10)$$

by transforming Equations 6 and 8 as follows:

$$\log(\lambda(t)) = \log\lambda_0 - \frac{\lambda_0}{v_0}t \qquad (11)$$

$$\frac{1}{\lambda(t)} = \frac{1}{\lambda_0} + \theta t. \qquad (12)$$

Since, within each test session, fault correction is not occurring, we can model failure behavior within a test session as a Homogeneous Poisson Process (HPP). We can estimate the constant failure rate λ for that test session directly as $\hat{\lambda} = n_0/t_0$ (Cox & Lewis, 1966), where n_0 is the number of failures in the test session's time interval $(0, t_0]$ and t_0 is the test session's total execution time. Because fault correction takes place between any two consecutive test sessions, the estimated failure rate $\hat{\lambda}$ varies from test session to test session and can be modeled by

$$y = \log(\hat{\lambda}) = \log\lambda_0 - \frac{\lambda_0}{v_0}t \qquad (13)$$

or

$$y = \frac{1}{\hat{\lambda}} = \frac{1}{\lambda_0} + \theta t, \qquad (14)$$

depending on whether ENHPP or LNHPP is used. The quantity t is the cumulative (i.e., over the past test sessions) execution time up to and including the current test session. The least squares estimates of β_0 and β_1 can be obtained by regressing the estimated transformed failure intensities on t. Notice that some of the estimates are less precise than others in the sense that their variances are larger.[2] Since the variances of the estimates are not equal, the ordinary least squares estimation formula does not apply and it is necessary to amend the least squares procedure (Draper & Smith, 1981). Therefore, the estimated transformed failure intensity values in Equations 13 and 14 were weighted by quantities that were inversely proportional to their variances[3] and then a regression analysis was applied. The R^2 was 0.7066 for the ENHPP weighted least squares regression analysis and 0.4983 for the LNHPP.[4] Consequently, we decided that the ENHPP model provides a better fit to the data than the LNHPP model, which is also consistent with the observation based on Figure 2. Because of this result, we will only consider the ENHPP model in the following discussion.

To document the predictive validity of the ENHPP model, the derivative of the fitted ENHPP cumulative failures curve, the instantaneous rate of failure occurrence or failure intensity was calculated, together with failure intensity curves for two prior Stability Test intervals: 08/02/88-10/17/88 and 08/02/88-11/03/88 (Figure 3). Our rationale is that if the ENHPP model exhibits predictive capability, then the reliability growth curve obtained from analyzing initial Stability Test failures (i.e., from 08/02/88-

10/17/88 and from 08/02/88-11/03/88) should be similar to the reliability growth curve obtained based on all Stability Test failures (i.e., from 08/02/88-12/05/88). Figure 3 indicates that the curves for the three reporting periods are virtually identical, demonstrating consistency of ENHPP model parameter values over the three time intervals. Hence, by 10/17/88, the System Test organization could have used an ENHPP software reliability growth model to predict failure performance for the remainder of Stability Test (i.e., from 10/17/88-12/05/88).

We conclude that the ENHPP reliability growth model possesses both model adequacy (i.e., good model fit) and predictive validity for System T Stability Test (Iannino, Musa, Okumoto, & Littlewood, 1984). Hence, the ENHPP model characterizes System T Stability Test failure behavior.

5.2.2 Projecting Beta Test Reliability from Stability Test Failures Figure 4 presents the combined Stability and Beta Test data (i.e., from 08/02/88 - 03/21/89) and the results of applying the ENHPP reliability growth model. Again, parameter estimates for the ENHPP model were obtained using maximum likelihood estimation and then these parameter estimates were used to generate the model's fitted failure counts (i.e., cumulative expected failures vs. time). Three software reliability curves are shown in Figure 4:

- The reliability curve fit to Stability Test failure data and then projected into Beta Test,
- The reliability curve fit to Beta Test data only,
- The reliability curve fit to both Stability and Beta Test data.

Based on the ENHPP model fit to Stability Test data only, no additional failures were expected during Beta Test. In fact, ten more failures occurred by the end of Beta Test, causing the reliability growth curve fit to the combined Stability and Beta Test data to differ from the curve fit to Stability Test only. The number of failures (10) is a relatively small number of failures compared to the number uncovered by Stability Test. In addition, reliability modeling applied to failure data collected over approximately 400 Stability CPU time units was able to reasonably predict subsequent failure behavior over 800 field CPU time units. However, a discontinuity in measured failure behavior is readily apparent upon transition from Stability to Beta.

6. OPERATIONAL PROFILE ANALYSIS

Detailed analysis of failures occurring during Beta Test led to a review of the operational profiles of the two test phases. In this section, we compare the operational profiles of these two different phases.

6.1 Measuring Operational Profile

The operational profiles were measured using process accounting and alarm message logging data, the former data being automatically recorded by the UNIX operating system. In the case of Stability Test, alarm message load was validated against the load generator logs. System usage within a given environment was converted to an operational profile as follows. Each program executed or alarm event processed was considered a transaction.[5] Transactions' absolute rates for a 24 hour period were computed and then converted into relative frequencies.

6.1.1 Test Operational Profile. To construct the Stability Test operational profile, we analyzed the transaction load for just one day of Stability Test. We choose an arbitrary day of Stability Test since the test scripts were a constant repetition of the same "busy hour" time period. Figure 5 presents a histogram portraying the Stability Test operational

---

2. This can be shown as follows. Let X = Number of failures observed in $(0, t_0]$ where X is distributed as a Poisson variable with $E(X) = \lambda t_0$ and $Var(X) = \lambda t_0$.

To estimate λ, we will use $\hat{\lambda} = \frac{X}{t_0}$, where $E(\hat{\lambda}) = \lambda$ and

$$Var(\hat{\lambda}) = Var\left(\frac{X}{t_0}\right) = \frac{1}{t_0^2} Var(X) = \frac{1}{t_0^2} \lambda t_0 = \frac{\lambda}{t_0}. \quad (15)$$

Equation 15 indicates that estimates of failure intensity based on long test intervals will have less variation than estimates based on shorter test time intervals.

3. The appropriate weights for the transformed ENHPP and LNHPP models are derived as follows:

Let $f(\hat{\lambda})$ represent transformed failure intensity. We can express $f(\hat{\lambda})$ as:

$$f(\hat{\lambda}) = f(\lambda) + f'(\lambda)(\hat{\lambda} - \lambda) + \frac{f''(\lambda)}{2}(\hat{\lambda} - \lambda)^2 + \cdots \quad (16)$$

where

$$E(f(\hat{\lambda})) = f(\lambda) \quad (17)$$

and

$$Var(f(\hat{\lambda})) = [f'(\lambda)]^2 Var(\hat{\lambda} - \lambda) = [f'(\lambda)]^2 Var(\hat{\lambda}) = [f'(\lambda)]^2 \frac{\lambda}{t_0}. \quad (18)$$

If $f(\hat{\lambda}) = \log(\hat{\lambda})$ as in the ENHPP model, then

$$f'(\lambda) = \frac{d}{d\lambda} \log(\lambda) = \frac{1}{\lambda} \quad (19)$$

and

$$Var(f(\hat{\lambda})) = \left[\frac{1}{\lambda}\right]^2 \frac{\lambda}{t_0} = \frac{1}{\lambda t_0}. \quad (20)$$

If $f(\hat{\lambda}) = \frac{1}{\hat{\lambda}}$ as in the LNHPP model, then

$$f'(\lambda) = \frac{d}{d\lambda} \frac{1}{\lambda} = -\frac{1}{\lambda^2}, \quad (21)$$

hence,

$$Var(f(\hat{\lambda})) = \left[-\frac{1}{\lambda^2}\right]^2 \frac{\lambda}{t_0} = \frac{1}{\lambda^3 t_0}. \quad (22)$$

4. The β estimates were obtained by minimizing a quadratic error function with R^2 being a measure of the proportion of this error function explained by the model. If the assumption of normality is true, then β has the further desirable property of being the maximum likelihood estimate of β, with statistical tests of significance and confidence intervals on β being able to be obtained. The assumption that the estimated transformed failure intensity values are independently and approximately normally distributed (i.e., $\varepsilon_i \sim N(0, \sigma^2)$) is reasonable since the normal distribution is the limiting distribution of the Poisson distribution, the latter distribution being the one that is assumed to characterize the random variable, number of failures observed in $(0, t_0]$.

5. The transactions described here represent internal transactions as opposed to user commands described in the system usage profile in Section 2.3. These include other transactions such as the backend transaction that is invoked by several of the commands given in Table 1.

profile. The histogram has been truncated at the highest and lowest ends in order to more clearly portray the data. Thus, the alarms, which represent 53% of the transactions, together with certain transactions with 0% contributions, are not shown.

6.1.2 Beta Operational Profile

The operational profile for Beta Test was based on system weekday usage during 02/01/89 to 03/06/89. Weekends had very light activity so this exclusion should not bias the results. For each transaction, the average absolute rate over this time period was computed and then these absolute rates converted into relative frequencies.

6.2 Comparison of Test *vs.* Beta Operational Profiles

Figure 6 presents the Stability Test operational profile together with the Beta Test operational profile. As in Figure 5, the alarm transactions are not shown because they dominate the plot. (The alarms' relative frequency was 53% in Stability Test *vs.* 21% during Beta.) Figure 6 is also truncated on the right with some transactions with 0% relative frequencies during Stability not being shown.

In addition to the large disparity in alarm transactions between Stability and Beta Test there is also a disparity between Stability and Beta Test in database operations, normal operations, and UNIX operating system transactions. The increase in database transactions during Beta Test is attributed to the large frequency of transactions needed in Beta to load the database so that normal operations could be sustained. The increase in UNIX operating system transaction frequency in Beta Test is attributed to users with little experience with the UNIX operating system needing to familiarize themselves with that system. Finally, since a smaller fraction of Beta load came from alarm message processing, there is a corresponding decrease during Beta in the relative frequency of commands that operators enter in response to alarms.

A chi-squared analysis indicated that the observed transaction frequencies during Beta differed significantly from the expected frequencies derived from Stability Test (probability value less than 0.001). We conclude that the two operational profiles are statistically different.

6.3 Explanation of Field Failures

During Beta, the system was only beginning to be used. Consequently, there was a much higher relative frequency of use of some database commands that initialized the system's databases. An additional consequence of system start-up was that there was a considerably smaller fraction of load coming from alarm message processing, as well as from commands that operators entered in response to alarms. In this section, we demonstrate how these factors resulted in System T exhibiting unpredicted failures during Beta.

Figure 4 presents Beta site failure data with a data point for each day. In actuality this data represents ten independent failures, mnemonics for which are:

dk	fmas
mos	etups
bc	eal
logit	xt
inst	mirror

Of these, two were determined to be operational problems with no fault existing in the software, but resulting from improper invocation. The other eight were attributed to transactions that were executed during Beta Test but that had been excluded from the Stability Test operational profile. An example of one of these failures is described below.

Mos is a process which is started at system initialization and is not supposed to terminate. It is part of a sequence of processes which handle alarm messages, and has a DBMS back end process which interacts with the database (see Figure 7.) *Mos*'s back end process opens a transaction when started and leaves it open, even though it does few database reads and no updates. The DBMS maintains in shared memory a set of "log buffers" to record all database update transactions, so they can be backed

out in event of failure or abort. An asynchronous DBMS process (flush) periodically inspects these "log buffers" and if close to full, flushes them to disk. If a transaction is open so the buffers can not be cleanly disposed of, the flush process *kills* the process with the open transaction. The *mos* back end was such a victim. This had not been detected in Stability Testing because insufficient database update transactions were performed to fill up the log buffers prior to the system being reinitialized. During busy hour usage, this flush transaction was unexpected, whereas it occurred once per day during Beta, because of the high database update activity associated with the system deployment.

7. IMPLICATIONS FOR SYSTEM TESTING

The empirical work demonstrates that the operational profile is an important component of pre-deployment testing of large-scale industrial software systems. Thus, when a software system is not tested against a specific field environment, it is possible for software reliability experienced in the field environment to differ from that measured during test. There are several implications of this work for measuring software quality from the users' point of view.

First of all, software engineers should recognize that a software system can operate in several different *operational modes* or characteristic operational profiles. In the case of System T, there was *an* operational profile characteristic of the system's busy hour and that was used to drive Stability Test, *another* operational profile characteristic of system start-up that contained transient or one-time events such as database provisioning, and a steady-state operational profile that included off hours report generation, load extremes and database backup situations. Alternatively, in the case of the AT&T 5ESS® switch that is expected to serve both urban and rural communities, a city operational profile would contain call types such as credit card calls, conference calls, and international calls, in addition to residential calls.

Secondly, the empirical work demonstrates the importance of an operational profile when measuring a software system's reliability. Given the potentially large number of different usage patterns for a software system, however, a System Test organization may be unable to implement and test all possible field usage patterns. Thus, a second implication of this work is that it indicates a need in software reliability theory to extend software reliability measurements taken during test to customer environments not being tested in the system laboratory. Such an extension would be extremely desirable since it would enable software engineers during test to estimate software reliability under a change in the system input distribution without retesting the actual computer code. Given that n_0/t_0 is a point estimate of failure intensity, λ, where n_0 is the number of failures in $(0,t_0]$ and t_0 is the total execution time, the "test problem" becomes one of relating or transforming the estimates of the components, n_0 and t_0, obtained under one operational profile, $f_T(x)$, into corresponding estimates that would apply under a second operational profile, $f_F(x)$, without executing the software in this latter environment. A theoretical framework, based on a statistical method for producing an unbiased estimate of the expected value of an output variable under a new distribution of inputs, based on the original outputs (Beckman & McKay, 1987), has been proposed. This method is applicable both to estimating expected failure outcome under $f_F(x)$ given input sampled from $f_T(x)$, and estimating expected execution time under $f_F(x)$ given an input distribution of $f_T(x)$.[6] However, the amount of needed information about testing is so

---

6. The procedure is as follows:

Let X_1, X_2, ..., X_n be a sample of input states selected at random from the input space characterized by the test operational profile, $f_T(x)$. Let $Y_i = H(X_i)$ be the number of failures observed following presentation of input state X_i, and let $S_i = G(X_i)$ be the execution time associated with exercising input state X_i. The expected value of Y (expected number of failures resulting from an input state) and the expected value of S (expected execution time associated with executing an input state) are the parameters to be estimated. The expected number of failures and expected execution time are denoted by $\mu_{Y_T} = E_T(Y)$ and by $\mu_{S_T} = E_T(S)$ when the inputs come from the test operational profile, and by $\mu_{Y_F} = E_F(Y)$ and $\mu_{S_F} = E_F(S)$ when the input states come from the field operational

enormous that it is not practical to implement the proposed framework. Therefore, further work is required to determine how this method can be practically applied.

It should be emphasized that although System T's test operational profile differed significantly from the Beta operational profile, the test profile was still able to detect approximately 90% of the failures occurring by the end of Beta Test. Thus, the use of an operational profile proved to be an effective test strategy for directing test effort in the interest of producing a high user- perceived quality software system. Pre-deployment system testing performed with an operational profile that more closely matched the Beta profile, in conjunction with software reliability modeling, would most likely measure user perceived quality even more accurately. Consequently, we recommend operational profile-driven testing, together with software reliability modeling, as a rational mechanism for determining when to terminate testing.

8. CONCLUSIONS

In this paper, we have documented the use of software reliability modeling together with operational profile-driven testing, in measuring software quality from the users' point of view. We have demonstrated that software reliability models are applicable to software products such as System T tested in a controlled environment. We have indicated how software reliability measurement can be used for predicting software failure behavior later in System Test, and for estimating additional test effort required to attain a particular software quality level. Consequently, we recommend that software development projects should consider applying software reliability measurement in real-time for the purpose of monitoring user-perceived software quality during controlled load testing.

9. ACKNOWLEDGEMENTS

We would like to acknowledge Mario Garzia and Keith Lee for many valuable comments and Wei-Ho Chen for much work during the Stability runs.

REFERENCES

[1] H. Ascher and H. Feingold, *Repairable Systems Reliability: Modeling, Inference, Misconceptions, and Their Causes*. New York, NY: Marcel Dekker, Inc., 1984.

[2] R. J. Beckman and M. D. McKay, "Monte Carlo Estimation Under Different Distributions Using the Same Simulation," *TECHNOMETRICS*, 29(2), pp. 153-160, 1987.

[3] D. R. Cox and P. A. Lewis, *The Statistical Analysis of Series of Events*. New York, N.Y.: John Wiley & Sons, Inc., 1966.

[4] N. R. Draper and H. Smith, *Applied Regression Analysis, Second Edition*. New York, N. Y.: John Wiley & Sons, Inc., 1981.

[5] W. K. Ehrlich and T. J. Emerson, "Modeling Software Failures and Reliability Growth During System Testing," *Proceedings of the Ninth International Conference on Software Engineering*, March 30-April 2, 1987, pp. 72-82.

[6] A. L. Goel and K. Okumoto, "Time-dependent error-detection rate model for software reliability and other performance measures," *IEEE Trans. on Reliability*, R-28(3), pp. 206-211, 1979.

[7] A. Iannino, J. D. Musa, K. Okumoto, and B. Littlewood, "Criteria for software reliability model comparisons," *IEEE Trans. on Software Eng.*, SE-10(6), pp. 687-691, 1984.

[8] J. D. Musa, A. Iannino and K. Okumoto, *Software Reliability: Measurement, Prediction, Application*. New York: McGraw-Hill, Inc., 1987.

[9] J. D. Musa and K. Okumoto, "A logarithmic Poisson execution time model for software reliability measurement," *Proceedings of the 7th International Conference on Software Engineering*, Orlando, Florida, pp. 230-238, 1984.

profile with a different density function, $f_P(x)$. Given that the inputs are sampled from the test operational profile $f_T(x)$, we can estimate μ_{Y_P} and μ_{S_P} from $H(X_i)$ and $G(X_i)$ obtained using $f_T(x)$ from a weighted average of the original outputs:

$$\hat{\mu}_{Y_P} = \frac{\sum_{i=1}^{n} w_i H(X_i)}{n} = \frac{\sum_{i=1}^{n} w_i Y_i}{n} \quad (23)$$

$$\hat{\mu}_{S_P} = \frac{\sum_{i=1}^{n} w_i G(X_i)}{n} = \frac{\sum_{i=1}^{n} w_i S_i}{n} \quad (24)$$

where $w_i = \dfrac{f_P(x_i)}{f_T(x_i)}$.

To estimate failure intensity under $f_P(x)$, we would compute

$$\hat{\lambda}_P = \frac{\sum_{i=1}^{n} \frac{f_P(x_i)}{f_T(x_i)} Y_i}{\sum_{i=1}^{n} \frac{f_P(x_i)}{f_T(x_i)} S_i}. \quad (25)$$

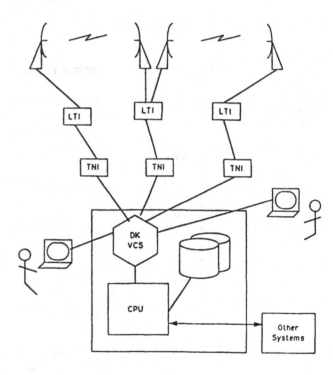

Figure 1. SYSTEM T CONFIGURATION AND ENVIRONMENT

SYSTEM T STABILITY TEST: 08/02/88 - 12/05/88

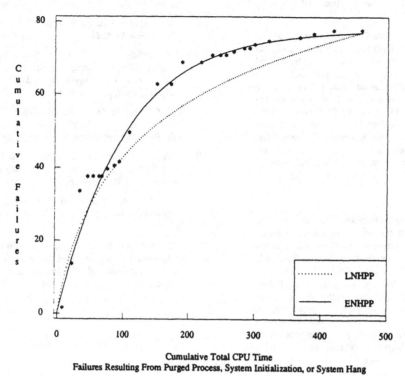

Cumulative Total CPU Time
Failures Resulting From Purged Process, System Initialization, or System Hang

Figure 2. MEASURED FAILURES DURING STABILITY TEST WITH FITS

SYSTEM T STABILITY TEST (08/02/88-12/05/88)

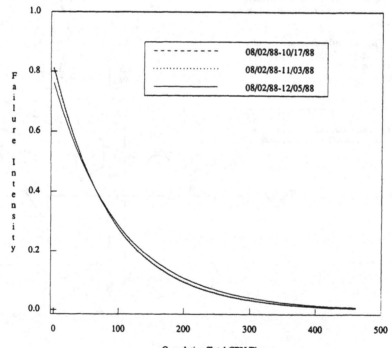

Cumulative Total CPU Time
Failures Resulting From Purged Process, System Initialization, or System Hang

Figure 3. ENHPP PREDICTIVE VALIDITY FROM STABILITY TEST DATA

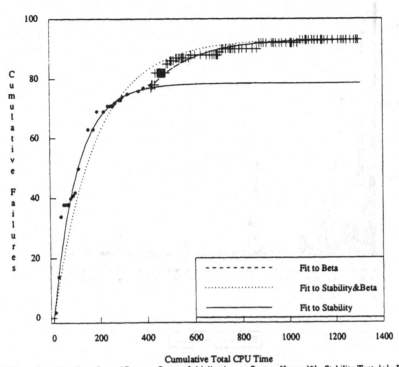

SYSTEM T STABILITY (08/02/88-11/27/88) AND BETA TEST (12/01/88-03/21/89)

Cumulative Total CPU Time

Failures Resulting From Purged Process, System Initialization, or System Hang: '*'= Stability Test, '+'= Beta Test

Figure 4. FAILURE PREDICTION FROM STABILITY, AND BETA TEST FAILURE DATA

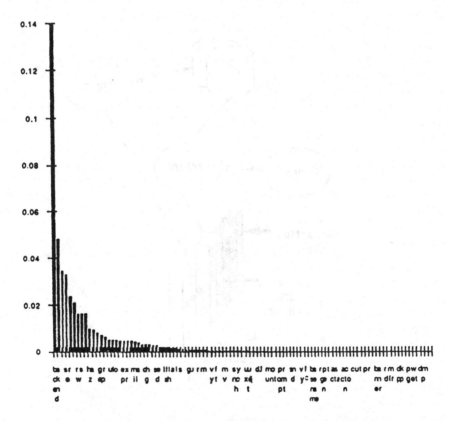

Figure 5. SYSTEM T TRANSACTION RELATIVE FREQUENCY HISTOGRAM FOR STABILITY TEST

Note: Alarm transactions are the highest contributor at 53% and have not been shown in this graph to emphasize smaller components. The abscissa is labeled with transaction mnemonics.

97

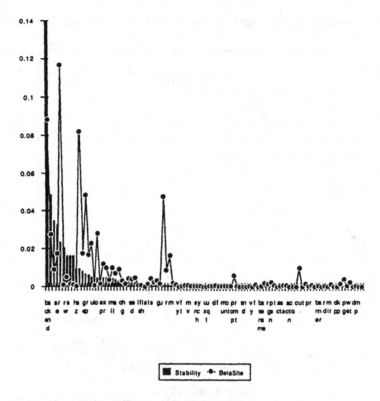

Figure 6. SYSTEM T TRANSACTION RELATIVE FREQUENCY HISTOGRAM, STABILITY AND BETA

Note: Alarm transactions are the highest contributor at 53% for Stability and 21% for Beta and have not been shown in this graph to emphasize smaller components. The abscissa is labeled with transaction mnemonics.

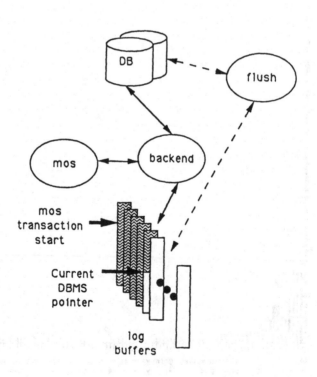

Figure 7. *mos* FAILURE SCENARIO - *back end* DIES

Some New Models of Software Testing
with Performance Comparisons

T. Downs
 University of Queensland, Queensland
P. Garrone
 University of Queensland, Queensland

Key Words — Software testing, Software reliability, Stochastic models, Performance models

Reader Aids —
Purpose: Advance state of the art
Special math needed for derivations: Probability and statistics
Special math needed to use results: Same
Results useful to: Software reliability theoreticians and analysts

Abstract — Two models of software testing, developed previously by T. Downs, are generalised to incorporate a greater degree of realism. This generalisation leads to three new models. A fourth (new) model, which has been developed using a rather different line of reasoning, is also presented. The performance of these models as reliability predictors is then assessed by applying them to 16 sets of failure data collected from various software development projects. Comparisons of performance are made with the two earlier models and with two variants of another model that has appeared frequently in the literature. Three distinct measures of performance are employed. The performance of the new models is generally superior to that of the older models with one model showing outstanding performance under all three measures.

1. INTRODUCTION

A large part of the software industry is governed by market forces and, as a consequence, the majority of software development projects are governed by quite severe time and cost constraints. Within these constraints, a project manager is obliged to produce as reliable a product as possible. Thus, reliability is not always considered a primary parameter and, as was pointed out by Evans [1], this is because producers prefer not to spend resources, especially calendar time, producing quality software when their competitors are not doing so and are making all the sales. Warranties for software are extremely rare; more commonly software is released with the ominous "as is" disclaimer.

As software development techniques become more mature, we must all hope that the setting of reliability goals for software systems will become more the rule than the exception. There are, of course, a good many situations already in which reliability is of primary importance and in these situations, time and cost are secondary. Obvious examples concern life-critical situations and these arise in military, medical, and other applications. For applications such as these, it is highly desirable to be able to make an accurate assessment of software reliability but, at the present time, the problem of reliability assessment appears to be very difficult.

Over the past 15 years or so, more than 100 (statistical) models of software reliability have appeared in the literature. The number of models that have actually been employed to assist with software development projects is, however, much smaller and of those that *have* been employed, there are none to our knowledge that have provided important assistance. The reason for this is that none of these models give sufficiently accurate estimates of reliability. This seems to us to be chiefly due to the fact that the authors of the various models have all treated software as a black box and have paid little or no attention to the manner in which a software system is tested. T. Downs has sought to develop a software reliability model by modelling testing directly [2, 3]. Adequate modelling of testing is likely to require models with a good many parameters and it is our contention that a many-parameter model[*] should exhibit much greater predictive ability than existing models which attempt to capture the very complex reliability behaviour of software in models having only two or three parameters.

This paper extends the modelling work in [2, 3]. In part 2, the two main models considered in [3] are briefly described and three generalisations of these models are derived. A fourth new model, which is derived from purely qualitative arguments, is also presented in part 2. In part 3 the performance of all 6 models is compared to that of two variants of the Littlewood-Verrall model [4]; the predictive ability of all 8 models is measured (using three different measurement techniques) on application to 16 sets of software failure data compiled by Musa [5].

The models in [2, 3] were developed using lemma 1 [2]; it is based upon the path-testing strategy and is used several times in part 2.

Lemma 1. If the execution profile of a software system is invariant in the intervals between fault removals, then the software failure rate in any such interval is:

$$\lambda = -r \cdot \log[\Pr\{\text{a path selected for execution is fault-free}\}]$$

$$r = \text{number of paths tested per unit time.} \tag{1}$$

2. THE MODELS

2.1 *The non-uniform path-selection model* (*NU*)

Of the models whose performance was compared in [2], the best predictive ability (on application to 3 of the Musa data

---

[*]Individual parameters could be estimated at those stages of the software development process where they have influence.

sets) was exhibited by a model on non-uniform testing. This model was developed under the assumption that a software system can be partitioned into two sections, one of which is heavily tested, the other lightly tested. We refer to these sections as 1 & 2 respectively. The testing profile is then defined as: On any test run, a path through section 1 is executed with probability p and a path through section 2 is executed with probability $1-p$.

Notation

N_i number of faults initially in section i
M_i number of paths through section i
c_i number of paths affected by each fault in section i

Other, standard notation is given in "Information for Readers & Authors" at the rear of each issue.

In the development of this model, the very strong assumption is made that each fault in section i affects the same number, c_i, of paths. This assumption is relaxed in some of the models considered below. For the model in hand, use of lemma 1 leads to the following expression for software failure rate, prior to the removal of any faults from the software:

$$\lambda_0 = -r \log[p(1-\phi_1)^{N_1} + (1-p)(1-\phi_2)^{N_2}] \qquad (2)$$

Notation

ϕ_i c_i/M_i
r rate of path testing

The subscript on λ indicates that this is the failure rate when zero faults have been removed.

In [2], the fact that the ϕ_i are usually very small was used to reduce (2) to the simplified form:

$$\lambda_0 = K[N_1 + CN_2] \qquad (3)$$

where K and C are positive constants.

After j faults have been removed, the failure rate is:

$$\lambda_j = K[N_1^{(j)} + CN_2^{(j)}] \qquad (4)$$

$$N_1^{(j)} = N_1^{(j-1)} \left[1 - \frac{1}{N_1^{(j-1)} + CN_2^{(j-1)}} \right]$$

$$N_2^{(j)} = N_2^{(j-1)} \left[1 - \frac{C}{N_1^{(j-1)} + CN_2^{(j-1)}} \right] \qquad (5)$$

2.2 The non-uniform model with an infinite number of faults in one section (NUI)

Numerical experience with the NU model of part 2.1 showed that in many cases the model indicated a much larger number of faults in section 2 than in section 1, that is $N_2 \gg N_1$. Since section 2 is executed less frequently than section 1, faults tend to be found (and removed) more rapidly from sec-

tion 1 than from section 2. Consequently, as faults are removed from the software (as j increases) we find $N_1^{(j)}$ reducing much more rapidly than $N_2^{(j)}$. A simplified model, in which the number of faults in section 2 is assumed constant throughout the debugging process, therefore seems worthy of investigation. Thus, we set $N_2^{(j)} = N_2$ for all j, and (4) becomes:

$$\lambda_j = K[N_1^{(j)} + CN_2] = K[N_1^{(j)} + Q] \qquad (6)$$

$$N_1^{(j)} = N_1^{(j-1)} \left[1 - \frac{1}{N_1^{(j-1)} + Q} \right] \qquad (7)$$

Q is a constant.

With the assumption that debugging makes no difference to the number of faults in the lightly-used part of the software, we are effectively assuming that the number of faults in this part of the software is infinite. This is not an entirely unreasonable assumption, at least for larger and more complex software systems. In the development of such systems, it is usual for the code which is destined to be heavily used, and any other supporting software that is perceived *a priori* as critical to system performance, to be afforded much greater care than the remainder of the code. Very often the non-critical software is vast, so that the number of faults it contains can be very large indeed. Certainly the assumption that N_2 remains fixed leads to a model that exhibits improved performance when applied to Musa's data sets (see part 3).

2.3 A model in which faults affect random numbers of paths (RP)

In the two models in parts 2.1 & 2.2, the very strong assumption is made that each fault in a given section of code affects the same number of paths. In [3] this assumption was relaxed by allowing the number of paths affected by an arbitrary fault to be a random variable. For mathematical tractability it was necessary to exclude the possibility of any path containing more than one fault and this, in turn, imposed a restriction on the number of paths that can be affected by any fault. Suppose there are initially N faults distributed over the M paths of the software system and let the random variable X_0 represent the number of paths affected by an arbitrary fault prior to any debugging. Then the restriction on X_0 is that it cannot take on a value larger than gilb(M/N). Let $m \equiv$ gilb(M/N), then —

$$\text{Pr\{an arbitrary path is fault-free\}} = 1 - N\mathrm{E}\{X_0\}/M \qquad (8)$$

$$\mathrm{E}\{X_0\} = \sum_{i=1}^{m} i \, \mathrm{Pr}\{X_0 = i\}$$

Using lemma 1, the failure rate prior to any debugging is:

$$\lambda_0 = -r \log[1 - N\mathrm{E}\{X_0\}/M] \qquad (9)$$

In [3], a fault affecting i paths was termed a "type i" fault.

Notation

$P_i^{(k)}$ probability that an arbitrary path contains a type i fault after k faults have been detected and removed from the system (under uniform testing)

The following recursive relationship exists [3]:

$$P_i^{(k)} = \frac{P_i^{(k-1)}}{N-k} \left[N-k+1 - \frac{i}{E\{X_{k-1}\}} \right] \tag{10}$$

$$E\{X_{k-1}\} = \sum_{i=1}^{m} i\, P_i^{(k-1)}$$

The failure rate after k faults have been removed is:

$$\lambda_k = -r \log \left[1 - \frac{N-k}{M} E\{X_k\} \right] \tag{11}$$

2.4 The RP model under non-uniform execution (NURP)

This model is simply an amalgamation of the NU & RP models. As in the NU model we assume that the software can be partitioned into two sections with section 1 being more heavily executed than section 2. But for this model we further assume than an arbitrary fault affects a random number of paths.

Notation

N_j number of faults initially in section j

M_j number of paths through section j

$X_{0,j}$ number of paths affected by an arbitrary fault in section j prior to any debugging; a r.v.

K rp/M_1

C $\dfrac{(1-p)}{p} \dfrac{M_1}{M_2}$

Let the testing profile be defined such that on any test run a path through section 1 is executed with probability p and a path through section 2 is executed with probability $(1-p)$. The failure rate of the software system, prior to any debugging, is:

$$\lambda_0 = -r \log \left\{ p \left[1 - \frac{N_1 E\{X_{0,1}\}}{M_1} \right] \right.$$
$$\left. + (1-p) \left[1 - \frac{N_2 E\{X_{0,2}\}}{M_2} \right] \right\} \tag{12}$$

Using the fact that M_1 and M_2 are large numbers, (12) can be simplified to obtain:

$$\lambda_0 \approx K[N_1 E\{X_{0,1}\} + CN_2 E\{X_{0,1}\}] \tag{13}$$

Now, the probability that an arbitrary path through section j contains a fault is:

$$P_{fj}(0) = N_j E\{X_{0,j}\}/M_j, \; j=1,2 \tag{14}$$

When the first fault is found, the probability that it lies in section 1 or 2 is:

$$P_{f1}(0) = \frac{pP_{f1}(0)}{pP_{f1}(0) + (1-p)P_{f2}(0)} \tag{15}$$

$$P_{f2}(0) = 1 - P_{f1}(0). \tag{16}$$

Then, using the information in (14)-(16), the following recursive relationships are readily derived:

$$N_1^{(k)} = N_1^{(k-1)} \left[1 - \frac{E\{X_{k-1,1}\}}{N_1^{(k-1)}E\{X_{k-1,1}\} + CN_2^{(k-1)}E\{X_{k-1,2}\}} \right]$$

$$N_2^{(k)} = N_2^{(k-1)} \left[1 - \frac{CE\{X_{k-1,1}\}}{N_1^{(k-1)}E\{X_{k-1,1}\} + CN_2^{(k-1)}E\{X_{k-1,2}\}} \right].$$
$$\tag{17}$$

Notation

$N_j^{(k)}$ number of faults in section j after k faults have been removed from the software system

$X_{k-1,j}$ number of paths affected by an arbitrary fault in section j after $k-1$ faults have been removed from the system

The manner in which the $E\{X_{k-1,j}\}$ are calculated is described in the appendix. The failure rate, after the removal of k faults, is:

$$\lambda_k = K[N_1^{(k)} E\{X_{k,1}\} + CN_2^{(k)} E\{X_{k,2}\}]. \tag{18}$$

2.5 The NURP model with an infinite number of faults in one section (NURPI).

For completeness we consider nonuniform execution where: 1) faults affect random numbers of paths, and 2) the number of faults in one section of the software is constant (changes negligibly) during the debugging process. As before, we consider the software to be in two sections with section 1 heavily executed and section 2 lightly executed; we assume that the number of faults in section 2 remains constant during debugging. The software failure rate, after removal of k faults, is:

$$\lambda_k = K[N_1^{(k)} E\{X_{k,1}\} + Q] \tag{19}$$

$$N_1^{(k)} = N_1^{(k-1)} \left[1 - \frac{E\{X_{k-1,1}\}}{N_1^{(k-1)} E\{X_{k-1,1}\} + Q} \right] \tag{20}$$

$E\{X_{k-1,1}\}$ is defined in part 2.4.

2.6 *A piecewise linear hazard rate model (PLHR)*

All the models we have considered so far have been derived using lemma 1 which contains the implicit assumption that the software failure rate is constant between fault removals. A constant failure rate implies that failure times are exponentially distributed. It was argued in [3] that a model in which failure times were hyperexponentially distributed would be likely to exhibit improved predictive ability. The main reason advanced in support of this argument was that although reliability growth is usually evident from a set of failure data, it is not uncommon to find a fair number of relatively long intervals between failures early in the data collection period and also a fair number of short intervals between failures late in the data collection period. This can occur because, during testing, a particular line of attack leads to gradually diminishing returns (longer time intervals) and a change in the line of attack leads to new types of faults being discovered, often providing a spate of short intervals between failures. We have not yet been successful in modifying lemma 1 to accommodate failure time distributions other than the exponential and so an *ad hoc* approach to the development of a model in which failure times are hyperexponential was adopted.

The PLHR model has the piecewise linear characteristic in figure 1. The model reflects the fact that testing personnel usually have a good idea where to look for errors and, quite often, several errors are located close together due to a badly designed section of code. This implies that one can anticipate a good number of short time intervals between failures and explains the initially high value of the hazard rate $\lambda(t)$ in figure 1. When a poorly designed section becomes reliable, testing is likely to be continued for some time until the tester feels sure that all faults have been removed. This causes $\lambda(t)$ to decrease with t. When the tester feels that he has cleared all faults from a section of code he will "move on", looking for more errors elsewhere, and the hazard rate will rise again, but it will not rise to the level attained immediately after a failure (for small t) because the tester is now effectively searching for another section of bad code and is not in the process of debugging one.

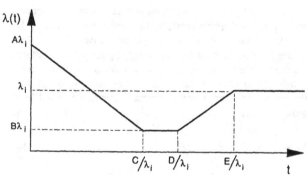

Figure 1.   Piecewise-Linear Hazard Rate

In this model we assume that the hazard rate maintains the basic shape indicated in figure 1 throughout the test phase. The

model must, of course, take account of the fact that there is, on the average, a downward trend in failure rate as debugging proceeds, and this is achieved as follows. It is assumed that the hazard rate function ultimately levels off to a value λ_i, as indicated in figure 1. λ_i is the (constant) failure rate predicted by the NUI model after the removal of i faults. (The next part shows that the NUI model provides the best predictions for failure rate out of all the models based upon the constant failure rate assumption.) In this way, we ensure that the level λ_i gradually decreases as faults are removed. Thus, the estimation process for $\lambda(t)$ involves two steps:

1. λ_i is estimated using the NUI model
2. The parameters A, B, C, D, E, which define the piecewise linear curve, are estimated in a manner which we briefly describe next.

The 5 parameters A, B, D, C, E have been chosen in such a way that they are dimensionless. Figure 1 indicates the following constraints on these parameters: $A > 1$, $0 < B < 1$, $0 < C < D < E$. The problem of estimating them is very easily formulated by defining:

$$I(t) \equiv \int_0^t \lambda(u)\,du$$

from which the pdf of the time to next failure is:

$$f(t) = \lambda(t)e^{-I(t)}.$$

The pdf is used to form a likelihood function in the usual way. The integral $I(t)$ is obtained by simply evaluating the area under the piecewise-linear curve in figure 1. Thus, maximum likelihood estimation of the model parameters is quite straightforward.

3.   COMPARATIVE PERFORMANCE OF THE VARIOUS MODELS

The data sets compiled by Musa [5] provide a convenient means of assessing performance of models of software testing and software reliability. In [3] the NU and RP models were applied to 3 of Musa's data sets and their performance compared with that of the Littlewood-Verrall (LV) model [4]. In this section we assess the performance of all 6 models described in the previous section on application to all the major data sets compiled by Musa (that is, 16 data sets) and compare performance with two versions of the LV model.

Performance assessment is essentially measurement of how well a model fits a given set of data. By and large, we are interested in how well, on the basis of a given set of failure data, a model will predict future reliability behaviour. Thus, the assessment procedure employed here is to fit a model to the first m data points in a given data set and then to see how well the model predicts data point $m + 1$. The value of m is then increased by unity and the procedure repeated. The process continues until m is equal to the number of data points in the set. For each data set, the initial value of m was chosen as the nearest integer to 25% of the total number of data points in the set. Thus, predictive ability was measured over approximately 75% of the data for each data set.

We have employed 3 distinct methods of assessing the predictive ability of the various models. We used the Kolmogorov-Smirnov (KS) test [3], and the related Cramer-von Mises (CvM) test, which has been similarly employed by Troy & Moawad [6].

And finally we have used the prequential statistic of Dawid [7]; its use in this context has been described by Abdel-Ghaly et al [8]. The KS & CvM tests are based upon the same data transformation and give highly correlated results. The prequential statistic is based upon a rather different premise and Dawid argues [7] that it has greater validity than either the KS or CvM statistics. We do not need to debate the relative merits of the three assessment techniques here because, as can be seen from the results in tables 1-7, there is one model which performs outstandingly according to all three techniques.

TABLE 1
Kolmogorov-Smirnov Statistics

Data set	NU	NUI	RP	NURP	NURPI	PLHR	LV2	LV3
1	0.082	0.123	0.181	0.076	0.172	0.060	0.129	0.178
2	0.101	0.147	0.164	0.103	0.180	0.153	0.238	0.162
3	0.269	0.200	0.276	0.146	0.227	0.286	0.334	0.339
4	0.134	0.094	0.147	0.098	0.110	0.106	0.117	0.238
5	0.217	0.209	0.236	0.227	0.161	0.090	0.097	0.083
6	0.260	0.241	0.268	0.257	0.225	0.096	0.123	0.136
14	0.225	0.169	0.192	0.222	0.193	0.176	0.334	0.247
17	0.206	0.201	0.171	0.189	0.119	0.107	0.182	0.134
27	0.295	0.222	0.281	0.227	0.150	0.134	0.301	0.207
40	0.279	0.123	0.300	0.141	0.194	0.069	0.300	0.217
ss1a	0.158	0.152	0.158	0.158	0.156	0.079	0.155	0.114
ss1b	0.217	0.203	0.247	0.239	0.184	0.122	0.129	0.118
ss1c	0.207	0.202	0.212	0.202	0.173	0.132	0.130	0.152
ss2	0.255	0.187	0.187	0.243	0.299	0.100	0.184	0.143
ss3	0.288	0.287	0.286	0.286	0.271	0.078	0.237	0.187
ss4	0.246	0.245	0.244	0.250	0.247	0.069	0.213	0.216

Tables 1-3 show the three statistics computed for the 6 models described in section 2 along with two variants of the LV model, each applied to 16 of the Musa data sets. The Musa names for the systems from which the data sets were obtained appear in column 1 of each table. The two variants of the LV model differ in the type of ψ function [4] employed. For the model designated LV2 the ψ function $\beta_0 + \beta_1 i$ was used and in LV3 the ψ function $\beta_0 + \beta_1 i + \beta_2 i^2$ was used.*

For each of the 3 statistics used in computing the entries in tables 1-3, a good model gives a low value of the statistic

---

*In [6] Troy & Moawad chose the best ψ function (from 6 possibilities) for each data set. We disagree with this approach arguing that each choice constitutes a different model.

TABLE 2
Cramer von Mises Statistics

Data set	NU	NUI	RP	NURP	NURPI	PLHR	LV2	LV3
1	0.0012	0.0035	0.0115	0.0013	0.0120	0.0011	0.0045	0.0091
2	0.0026	0.0051	0.0131	0.0016	0.0097	0.0071	0.0217	0.0078
3	0.0190	0.0102	0.0310	0.0064	0.0128	0.0336	0.0468	0.0362
4	0.0069	0.0025	0.0072	0.0025	0.0037	0.0041	0.0029	0.0278
5	0.0163	0.0149	0.0207	0.0180	0.0083	0.0024	0.0030	0.0024
6	0.0280	0.0238	0.0321	0.0228	0.0166	0.0018	0.0046	0.0062
14	0.0113	0.0112	0.0114	0.0127	0.0105	0.0060	0.0411	0.0267
17	0.0092	0.0089	0.0075	0.0078	0.0039	0.0019	0.0109	0.0044
27	0.0290	0.0150	0.0297	0.0162	0.0068	0.0032	0.0302	0.0114
40	0.0253	0.0052	0.0275	0.0059	0.0100	0.0008	0.0289	0.0177
ss1a	0.0067	0.0063	0.0060	0.0059	0.0055	0.0007	0.0080	0.0040
ss1b	0.0176	0.0153	0.0271	0.0231	0.0114	0.0038	0.0045	0.0051
ss1c	0.0159	0.0136	0.0193	0.0148	0.0082	0.0059	0.0043	0.0085
ss2	0.0221	0.0129	0.0203	0.0334	0.0214	0.0027	0.0123	0.0054
ss3	0.0231	0.0232	0.0232	0.0212	0.0200	0.0012	0.0234	0.0097
ss4	0.0163	0.0163	0.0163	0.0185	0.0160	0.0010	0.0172	0.0179

TABLE 3
Prequential Statistics

Data set	NU	NUI	RP	NURP	NURPI	PLHR	LV2	LV3
1	773	769	781	766	791	743	766	782
2	369	371	373	369	382	416	372	371
3	295	255	267	259	258	283	265	297
4	335	332	323	328	331	333	315	371
5	7065	7044	7058	7057	7063	6772	6975	6975
6	315	314	316	314	310	307	292	315
14	394	395	396	394	400	393	429	432
17	300	300	300	300	306	317	300	298
27	429	428	427	424	445	415	437	435
40	1092	987	1035	994	1075	988	996	1023
ss1a	1113	1115	1114	1116	1113	1076	1108	1116
ss1b	3652	3651	3662	3672	3686	3538	3629	3664
ss1c	2657	2657	2661	2659	2667	2571	2632	2701
ss2	1962	1963	1963	1968	1962	1894	1992	1994
ss3	2780	2780	2782	2781	2812	2618	2801	2816
ss4	1994	1995	1995	1995	2003	1894	2003	2053

TABLE 4
Win Matrix for KS Statistic

	NU	NUI	RP	NURP	NURPI	PLHR	LV2	LV3	wins
NU	0	2	10	5	3	2	6	5	33
NUI	14	0	13	11	9	4	8	6	65
RP	7	3	0	4	4	1	6	3	28
NURP	11	6	12	0	5	3	7	6	50
NURPI	13	7	12	11	0	1	7	7	58
PLHR	14	12	15	13	15	0	15	14	98
LV2	10	8	11	9	9	1	0	6	54
LV3	11	10	13	10	9	2	10	0	65

103

TABLE 5
Win Matrix for CvM Statistic

	NU	NUI	RP	NURP	NURPI	PLHR	LV2	LV3	wins
NU	0	4	13	6	2	2	10	6	43
NUI	13	0	14	9	6	3	11	7	63
RP	4	4	0	4	2	1	9	4	28
NURP	10	8	12	0	5	3	10	6	54
NURPI	14	10	14	11	0	2	9	8	68
PLHR	14	13	15	13	14	0	14	16	99
LV2	6	5	7	6	7	2	0	6	39
LV3	10	9	12	10	8	1	10	0	60

TABLE 6
Win Matrix for Prequential Statistic

	NU	NUI	RP	NURP	NURPI	PLHR	LV2	LV3	wins
NU	0	5	10	8	9	2	6	13	53
NUI	11	0	11	9	12	5	8	13	69
RP	6	5	0	6	12	4	5	11	49
NURP	9	8	10	0	12	4	8	13	64
NURPI	7	4	4	4	0	4	4	9	36
PLHR	14	11	12	12	12	0	11	14	86
LV2	10	8	11	8	12	5	0	12	66
LV3	3	3	5	3	7	2	4	0	27

TABLE 7
Models in Order of Performance

	KS Statistic	CvM Statistic	Prequential Statistic
1	PLHR	PLHR	PLHR
2	LV3,NUI	NURPI	NUI
3		NUI	LV2
4	NURPI	LV3	NURP
5	LV2	NURP	NU
6	NURP	NU	RP
7	NU	LV2	NURPI
8	RP	RP	LV3

and a poor model a high value. Tables 4-6 are "Win Matrices" which indicate, for each model, the number of data sets for which it out-performed each of the other models.* Thus, row 1 of table 4 indicates that the NU model out-performed model NUI on 2 data sets, and so on. The final column in each of tables 4-6 indicates the total number of "wins" for each model. Table 7 ranks the models according to the number of wins for each model under the 3 assessment statistics. The striking result is that the PLHR model is clearly superior, regardless of the statistics employed.

---

*The entries in tables 1-3 have been rounded down to a few figures; the "win matrices" were computed using 8-figure statistics.

4. DISCUSSION & CONCLUSIONS

The tables show that the KS & CvM statistics give quite similar results. These two statistics, which are both based upon the probability integral transform, indicate that the refinements to the models derived using lemma 1, which are described in parts 2.1-2.5, led to improvements in predictive performance. They also indicate that the LV3 model outperformed the LV2 model, the latter model using the less complex ψ function. Some of these indications are, however, contradicted by the results obtained using the prequential statistic. As explained in [8], such contradictions tend to occur when a model gives "noisy" (highly variable) predictions for a data set. The prequential statistic is quite sensitive to noisy predictions but the KS & CvM statistics are not. Thus, a model that gives noisy predictions can perform well under the KS & CvM tests but is likely to perform less well under the prequential test. An examination of the predictions (of mean time to failure) obtained from the models considered in this paper confirms that noisy predictions tend to be present in those cases where a model performs well under the KS & CvM tests and less well under the prequential test.

More importantly, all three statistics indicated that the PLHR model outperformed the other models by a substantial margin. This is very promising, especially considering its *ad hoc* nature. There are several ways in which the model can be generalised, with every likelihood that performance will be improved. This is under investigation. We remain hopeful of generalising lemma 1 so as to accommodate models of the PLHR type. This is important as it should allow this type of model to be placed on a firmer footing from both a theoretical and a practical point of view.

ACKNOWLEDGMENT

We are pleased to thank Nick Redding and Matthew Gallagher for their assistance in computing the results. This work was supported by the Australian Research Council and the Australian Telecommunications and Electronics Research Board.

APPENDIX

Calculation of s-Expectations Required for (17)

Let $P_{i,j}$ represent the probability that, at the commencement of testing, an arbitrary path through section 1 contains a type i fault. Then, using the notation of part 2.5,

$$\Pr\{\text{First fault detected in section } j \text{ is type } i\} = \frac{iP_{i,j}}{E\{X_{0,j}\}}$$

(A.1)

Therefore $\Pr\{\text{First fault detected lies in section } j \text{ and is type } i\}$

$$= \frac{iP_{i,j}}{E\{X_{0,j}\}} - P_{ij}(0)$$

(A.2)

Then, after the first fault is removed,

s-Expected number of type i faults remaining in section j

$$= N_j P_{i,j} - \frac{iP_{i,j}}{E\{X_{0,j}\}} \, P_{lj}(0) \qquad (A.3)$$

$$= P_{i,j} \left[N_j - \frac{iP_{lj}(0)}{E\{X_{0,j}\}} \right] \qquad (A.4)$$

Now let $P_{i,j}^{(k)}$ denote the probability that an arbitrary path through section j contains a type i fault after k faults have been removed from the software system. Then, (A.4) may be rewritten

$$[N_j - P_{lj}(0)]P_{i,j}^{(1)} = P_{i,j} \left[N_j - \frac{iP_{lj}(0)}{E\{X_{0,j}\}} \right] \qquad (A.5)$$

giving

$$P_{i,j}^{(1)} = \frac{P_{i,j}}{N_j - P_{lj}(0)} \left[N_j - \frac{iP_{lj}(0)}{E\{X_{0,j}\}} \right] \qquad (A.6)$$

After k faults have been removed, we find

$$P_{i,j}^{(k)} = \frac{P_{i,j}^{(k-1)}}{N_j^{(k-1)} - P_{lj}^{(k-1)}} N_j^{(k-1)} - \frac{iP_{lj}(0)}{E\{X_{k-1,j}\}} \qquad (A.7)$$

Then, the s-expectations required in (17) are:

$$E\{X_{k-1,j}\} = \sum_{i=1}^{m_j} iP_{i,j}^{(k-1)} \qquad (A.8)$$

$$m_j \equiv \text{gilb}(M_j/N_j)$$

REFERENCES

[1] R. A. Evans, "Sad software", Editorial, *IEEE Trans. Reliability*, vol R-35, 1986, p 129.

[2] T. Downs, "An approach to the modelling of software testing with some applications", *IEEE Trans. Software Engineering*, vol SE-11, 1985, pp 375–386.

[3] T. Downs, "Extensions to an approach to the modelling of software testing with some performance comparisons", *IEEE Trans. Software Engineering*, vol SE-12, 1986, pp 979–987.

[4] B. Littlewood, L. Verrall, "A Bayesian reliability growth model for computer software", *Applied Statistics*, vol 22, 1973, pp 332–346.

[5] J. D. Musa, "Software reliability data", Data and Analysis Center for Software, RADC, Rome, NY.

[6] R. Troy, R. Moawad, "Assessment of software reliability models", *IEEE Transactions on Software Engineering*, vol SE-11, 1985, pp 839–849.

[7] A. P. Dawid, "Statistical theory: The prequential approach", *J. Royal Statistical Society,A*, vol 147, 1984, pp 278–292.

[8] A. A. Abdel-Ghaly, P. Y. Chan, B. Littlewood, "Evaluation of competing software reliability predictions", *IEEE Trans. Software Engineering*, vol SE-12, 1986, pp 950–967.

Manuscript TR88-055 received 1988 February 17; revised 1991 January 15.

IEEE Log Number 43761   ◄TR►

Software Fault Content and Reliability Estimations for Telecommunication Systems

BO LENNSELIUS AND LARS RYDSTRÖM

Abstract—One of the major problems of software engineering is the lack of objective measures of software quality. This paper is concerned with the problem of software fault content and reliability estimations. Estimations that can be used to improve the control of a software project are emphasized. A model of how to estimate the number of software faults is presented, which takes into account both the development process and the developed software product. A model of how to predict, before the testing has started, the occurrences of faults during the testing stage is also presented. These models, together with software reliability growth models, have been evaluated on a number of software projects.

I. INTRODUCTION

SOFTWARE is today a major component in large and complex telecommunication systems. The development of such software systems normally takes several years and involves hundreds of people at different sites, often in different countries. Even with the help of advanced methods, modern software design support systems [1], and a fault avoiding program structure, it is in practice impossible to make these systems completely correct. Although the software is carefully reviewed and tested before release, some faults still remain when the software is put into operation. It is well known that these faults sometimes cause severe failures.

Efforts are continuously made to make the systems more correct and fault tolerant. To assess the results of such efforts and to achieve more reliable systems, it is necessary to improve the methods to control the process and to have methods that estimate the correctness and the reliability of the software [2]. Good software quality measures are needed already during the early stages in the software life cycle, in order to allocate resources for detailed design and test. This may be years before the software is put into operation at a customer's site.

Our study of these issues started in 1984 at ELLEMTEL and Lund Institute of Technology. The aim of our study is to develop methods and tools for the following.

• *Early Software Fault Content Estimation:* It is very important to estimate the fault content as early as possible

in the software life cycle. Therefore, we chose to develop an estimation model which takes into account both the development process and the developed software product. This model includes software structure metrics. These metrics can be measured from the source code or, in some cases, from the design descriptions [3]. In this paper, we only consider measures of the software structure obtained from the source code.

• *Software Reliability Estimation:* An estimate of the fault content is not enough to estimate the reliability of the software, i.e., the probability that the software will operate without failure for a specified time under specified conditions. Because of that, we have evaluated a number of software reliability growth models.

Whereas knowledge gained from earlier software products and projects (knowledge about how many faults that are typically introduced during the development) is used for the early estimation of the software fault content, reliability growth models use the knowledge gathered from the failures during test and operation of the product for which we are trying to make an estimation. Both of these sources of knowledge are needed. However, in this paper we emphasize estimations that can be used early in the development process.

Our study of fault content and reliability estimation is based on seven industrial projects, which are presented in Section II. In Section III we give a brief discussion of our experiences of software reliability growth models before proceeding to the main problem of early estimation. A model of how to make an early estimation of the initial number of faults is presented in Section IV. If we have an estimate of the initial number of faults, it is also desirable to be able to predict when these faults occur during the testing phase. A method to make such a prediction is suggested in Section V.

II. ANALYZED PRODUCTS (PROJECTS)

In our study we have analyzed seven products (projects). The projects are below called project A–project G. The software products are new subsystems of larger telecommunication switching systems. Reused or modified software has not been considered. The products were all developed in a very stable development environment. The same programming language is used in all products, and very similar development methodologies and design languages have been used. Approximately 30–70 man-years

Manuscript received June 16, 1989; revised September 29, 1989. This work was supported at ELLEMTEL by Swedish Telecom and Ericsson Telecom, and at Lund Institute of Technology by Swedish Telecom and TeleLogic AB.

B. Lennselius was with the Department of Communications Systems, Lund Institute of Technology, S-221 00 Lund, Sweden. He is now with E-P Telecom Q-Labs, Research Park IDEON, S-223 70 Lund, Sweden.

L. Rydström is with ELLEMTEL Telecommunications Systems Laboratories, P.O. Box 1505, S-125 25, Älvsjö, Sweden.

IEEE Log Number 8932731.

have been spent on the development of the software for each product.

The software was tested with a bottom-up strategy comprising unit, function, integration, and system test. The unit test is done by the programmer. The other tests are done by independent test groups. Failure data are collected from the independent testing stages. The fault density, as defined in Section IV-C, considers only faults detected during the independent testing stages. However, the collection of failure data is continued when the products are taken into operation. (One reason for this is to evaluate the applicability of the model presented in Section V.) All trouble reports were carefully examined to extract the number of relevant faults.

For each project, the following data were collected: software structure metrics, project and product data (see Section IV), failure data, and testing time. To use calendar time as a measure of testing time was in many cases not sufficiently accurate, because the test effort could vary considerably. We had no possibility to measure testing time in CPU-time. Instead, we recorded the number of test shifts that were booked each day at the test equipment, and used this number as a measure of testing time. Unfortunately, we have only been able to calculate this measure for projects A and D. For projects A and C, we could use calendar time, because the test effort was rather constant during the test period.

III. Experience of Reliability Growth Estimation

Reliability growth models use the history of failures recorded during test and/or operation. The more the software is used, the more faults are discovered and corrected and the more reliable the software becomes. Before a reliability growth model can be applied, the program must have been tested for some time and a certain number of failures must have been recorded. The observed times of failure occurrences can then be used to estimate the parameters of the model. The estimation of these parameters cannot be done without the help of computer programs. We have mostly used programs for Goel-Okumoto's Non-Homogenous Poisson Process Model (NHPP) [4], Goel's Modified NHPP Model [5], and the Jelinski-Moranda De-Eutrophication Model [6]. Throughout this paper, the Goel-Okumoto NHPP model is called the GO model, and the Jelinski-Moranda model is called the JM model.

The reliability growth models usually regard the program as a black box. Assuming that the reliability of the program is growing with time (this may not necessarily be the case), the models can only try to fit a smooth curve (the mean value function) to the observed number of failures (or interfailure times) as a function of time and then extrapolate it to make predictions. This accounts for the fact that many reliability growth models are more or less equivalent. They differ mainly in the form of the mean value function and in the estimation of the parameters. If the observed curve is far from smooth, they may, however, differ considerably in their predictions.

The curve in Fig. 1 is obtained from project A and shows the observed accumulated number of discovered faults as a function of the number of test shifts. The crosses represent estimations of the initial number of faults. These estimations are made each calendar week with the help of the GO model. The parameters of the GO model were estimated with the maximum likelihood method. From the figure we can observe that the estimates change a lot, even though the shape of the observed curve for the cumulative number of detected faults comes quite close to the shape expected by the GO model [see (4)]. One reason for the unstable estimates is that the mean value function is, by the maximum likelihood estimation method, constrained to pass through the last observed point. This example shows that it is very difficult to obtain good estimates from reliability growth models early in the test period. Because of that, we have emphasized models which use the knowledge gained from earlier products and projects (see the next section).

Most reliability growth models assume that the software is executed randomly. But the testing is intended to be systematic, not random. This may cause problems for the reliability growth models. This is further discussed in [7].

IV. A Software Fault Density Estimation Model

A. A Structure of Factors That May Influence the Fault Content

To develop a model for software fault content estimation, we need to find factors that are likely to influence the number of faults introduced into the software and to organize these factors into a general structure. It is natural to assume that many of the factors that influence the software fault content can be sought among the factors that influence the software development effort, and vice versa. This does not mean that *all* the factors that influence the effort also influence the fault content, or that their impact on the fault content is equal to their impact on the effort. From the literature on software cost estimation [8]-[10], and fault content estimation [11], we have compiled a structure of factors that are likely to have a major impact on the software fault content (see Fig. 2). This structure consists of three main groups: the *complexity*, the *project ability*, and the *applied tools and methods*. (For a detailed description and motivation of the obtained structure, see [12].)

For each factor, we have to identify and define measurable attributes which, for a specific environment, can represent the factor and, consequently, its impact on the number of software faults. For each attribute, one or several metrics can be defined. Several metrics may occur when we want to measure the attribute at different stages in the software life cycle, and when the information about the attribute increases with the progress of the project. This leads to the factor, attribute, metric model presented in Fig. 3.

Even if the factors in the obtained structure are not completely independent of each other, the structure

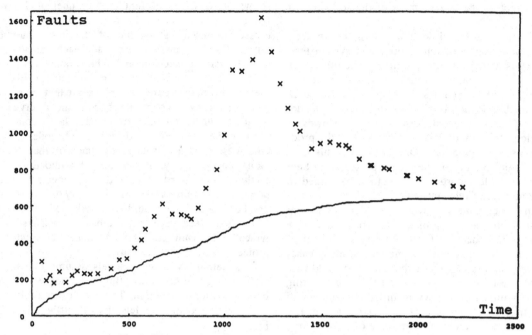

Fig. 1. The curve shows the observed cumultative number of observed faults as a function of the number of test shifts. The crosses show the initial number of faults as estimated by the GO model at corresponding times.

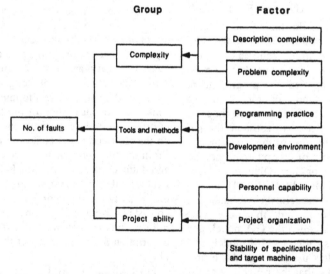

Fig. 2. The structure of factors that are likely to have a major impact on the software fault content.

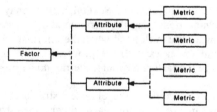

Fig. 3. Factor, attribute, metric model.

makes, for a specific environment, the identification of critical factors and the definition of attributes and metrics easier.

B. Tailoring the Structure

The structure of factors, discussed above, was used as a guideline to identify factors and define attributes which are, in the actual environment at ELLEMTEL, assumed

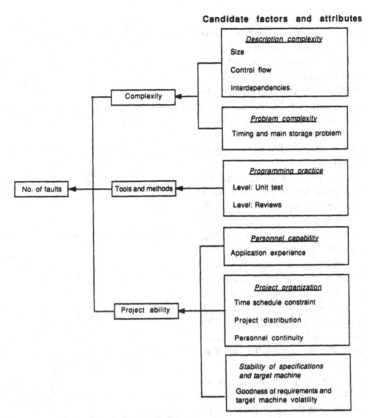

Fig. 4. Candidate factors and attributes used in the study.

to have a major impact on the number of faults (see Fig. 4 and [12]). The candidate attributes are presented below.

• *Description Complexity:* Attributes of the description complexity are chosen, namely, *size, control flow*, and *interdependencies (coupling) between different modules*. McCabe's Cyclomatic Complexity metric [13] and Halstead's Software Science metrics [14], together with more simple software structure metrics such as "number of lines of code," "number of signals," etc., are used as candidate metrics of these attributes. Because of the lack of automated tools for measuring data structure metrics, it was not possible to choose the attribute *data structure* in the study.

• *Problem Complexity:* A candidate attribute was chosen, namely, *timing and main storage problems*. Since the products are similar and belong to the same application, it was decided that no other attributes of the problem complexity should be incorporated in the model at this stage of the study.

• *Development Environment:* This factor is similar between the projects. Hence, the factor is omitted from the study.

• *Programming Practice:* The software products are developed with very similar methods. Since the estimation is assumed to be done at the end of the coding phase (including unit test), it is possible to define attributes which consider how well the methods were used. The attributes which are assumed to have the largest impact on the software fault content are: how well the reviews were performed (*Level: Reviews*) and how well the tests of the different modules were done (*Level: Unit test*).

• *Personnel Capability:* An attribute of this factor is chosen, namely, *application experience*, which is defined as the project members experience of software development for the actual telecommunication system.

• *Project Organization:* The attributes of this factor that are assumed to have the largest impact on the number of software faults are *time schedule constraint, personnel continuity*, and *project distribution*. The latter attribute measures how the project is shared between different offices and companies.

• *Stability of Specifications and Target Machine:* For our products, the requirement specifications cover both software and hardware in the case of parallel development of software and hardware. This makes it difficult to divide the factor into several attributes. Hence, the following attribute is chosen: *goodness of requirements* and *target machine volatility*.

The chosen attributes are subjectively measured (rated) according to ranking lists (see the Appendix), except the software structure metrics.

C. Experiences

Due to the stable development environment at ELLEMTEL and to the fact that all the analyzed products belong to the same application, our initial assumption was that a fault content estimation model could be based only on attributes belonging to the description complexity factor, that is, on software structure metrics. Within each product, the correlation ratios between the number of faults per module and the software structure metrics used were calculated. No structure metric had a consistently superior correlation ratio with the number of faults, and all metrics showed a very high correlation with each other. Furthermore, the differences in fault content between the seven products could not be explained by any combination of software structure metrics.

Because of the above result, we chose to use only one structure metric, Halstead's program length (number of operands and operators), in the subsequent analysis. We define the *fault density* as the number of faults detected during the independent testing stages divided by Halstead's program length. (Fault density is often defined with respect to the number of lines of code. We chose Halstead's program length as a size measure since it is less sensitive to the programming style than the number of lines of code.) In Fig. 5, the fault density for each project is shown. Since the differences in fault density between the projects could not be explained by the software structure metrics, we studied the impact of the other attributes proposed above.

We have analyzed only a few projects, and it is not possible to apply any statistical analysis to determine the impact of the different attributes on the fault density. Instead, we have used the three oldest projects, that is, projects A, B, and C, to identify the attributes which differ between the three projects. The following attributes showed large differences between the projects:

- application experience,
- level: unit test, and
- project stability.

The attribute "project stability" is a combination of the attributes "timing and main storage problems" and "goodness of requirements and target machine volatility."[1] How the three identified attributes are measured is presented in the Appendix.

The other attributes showed very small differences between the three projects. That is, we had no possibility to analyze their impact on the fault density. Since we could not use any statistical analysis (e.g., regression analysis) to determine the impact of the attributes on the fault density, we used a simple estimation model as a hypothesis of how the differences in fault density can be explained by the attributes. The estimation model is presented in the Appendix. The three attributes which differ between the projects A, B, and C were chosen to be parameters in the estimation model, and the three projects were chosen to be reference projects. The reference projects were used to calculate the mean fault density (λ_{ref} in the estimation equation, see the Appendix). The mean fault density is

[1]This was done due to the small number of analyzed projects and in order to simplify the analysis.

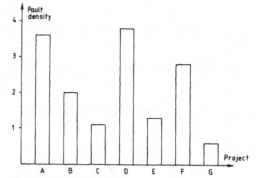
Fig. 5. Fault densities (relative values) of the projects.

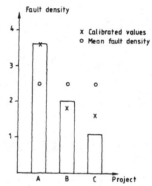
Fig. 6. Observed fault densities (relative values) of the reference projects compared to the calibrated values and the mean fault density.

represented in Figs. 6 and 7 by circles. The reference projects were also used to calculate the mean values of the attributes ($\alpha_{j,ref}$ in the estimation equation), and to determine the value of the proportionality constant in the estimation equation (calibration of the model). The chosen value of the constant is the value that, for the three reference projects, minimizes the mean relative error between the observed fault densities and the values calculated by the model ("estimated" values).

With the three identified attributes, the model can be adjusted (calibrated) to explain a large part of the differences in fault density between the reference projects. The calculated fault density values are represented in Fig. 6 by crosses. The bars in the figure show the observed fault densities. The mean relative error between the observed values and the mean fault density (λ_{ref}) is 58%. With the calibrated model, the mean relative error between the observed and calculated values is 17%.

The calibrated reference model is used to estimate the fault densities of the other four projects. In Fig. 7, the estimated values (denoted by crosses) are compared to the observed values (denoted by bars). For three projects, the accuracy of the estimation is better than 20%, with a mean estimation error of 16%. This should be compared to an accuracy of 84% and a mean estimation error of 44%, when only the mean fault density is considered (λ_{ref}, denoted by circles in Fig. 7). The fourth project unfortu-

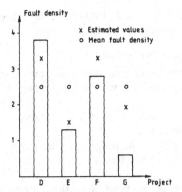

Fig. 7. Fault density (relative values) actuals versus estimates obtained by the developed estimation model. These values are also compared to the mean fault density of the three reference projects.

nately had an estimation error of 245%. However, this estimation error should be compared to an estimation error of 333% when the attributes were not considered (λ_{ref}).

The fact that this model gave improved estimates indicates that the three chosen attributes have an impact on the fault density. We are not able to show this statistically, since so few projects were analyzed. However, in [11], it is statistically shown that "programmer's experience," "frequency of program specification changes," and "volume of program design documents" have an impact on the number of faults. The first two attributes are very similar to our attributes "application experience" and "project stability." In our environment, the volume of design documents was regarded as an irrelevant attribute, due to the applied development methods and tools. It is obvious that the number of faults detected during the independent testing stages is dependent of how well the unit test was performed (even though the quantitative impact is unknown).

Even though we obtained better estimates of the fault density by applying the estimation model, it can happen for single projects (for example, project G) that the estimated fault density is far from the observed fault density. This implies that the obtained estimate has to be continuously evaluated (and refined) during the testing phase. Unfortunately, this cannot be done during the early testing phase by applying a software reliability growth model, due to the unstable estimates. In the next section, we propose a method to predict the fault occurrences during the testing phase. This method may be used to evaluate the estimate given by the model used in this section.

V. Prediction of the Fault Occurrences During Testing

A. Fault Detection Process

If we, before the test has started, want to predict the occurrences of faults during testing, we have to assume that the faults are detected according to a mathematical formula which relates the expected number of failures to testing time (or interfailure times). Such a formula can be found in many of the software reliability models which have been proposed during the last two decades. However, two constraints must be put on the software reliability models if they shall be used to predict fault occurrences before having actual failure data. These constraints are that

1) the models must be valid for the specific testing method, and

2) the models must have parameters which can be established from characteristics of the software, the development process, or the testing process.

Several software reliability models have parameters which can be established according to the second constraint. The most well-known models are the JM model, the GO model, and the Musa execution time model [15]. The latter model assumes that testing time is measured in CPU-time. This model is not further discussed here since we had no possibility to measure CPU-time. However, the method presented in this section can easily be extended to the case when CPU-time is used.

The JM model and the GO model differ only in their assumption of the distribution of the number of faults observed by time t. The expected number of faults observed by time t is equal for both models [16]. The JM model assumes that the failure intensity is proportional to the remaining number of faults, while the GO model assumes that the failure intensity is dependent of testing time. The JM model is chosen as a model of fault occurrences during testing, because it directly relates the failure intensity to the number of remaining faults (the GO model can be derived from a modification of the JM model as discussed in Section V-C).

We have to discuss the derivation of the JM model in some detail to show how it can be applied to predict fault occurrences before having actual failure data. The JM model is based on the following assumptions.

1) The initial software fault content is an unknown fixed constant N.

2) The faults are independent of each other and the times between failures are independent of each other. Each fault is equally likely to cause a failure.

3) A detected fault is removed with certainty at the end of each testing interval and the fault removal time is negligible. No new faults are introduced during the fault removal process.

4) The failure rate between two consecutive failures is constant and proportional to the number of remaining faults.

These assumptions give us the following basic formulas:

$$p(k) = \lambda(k)e^{-\lambda(k)t}$$
$$\lambda(k) = \phi(N - (k - 1))$$

where

$p(k)$ the probability density function of the time between failures $k - 1$ and k

$\lambda(k)$ the failure rate during the interval between failures $k - 1$ and k

111

N   initial number of faults

ϕ constant of proportionality, which can be interpreted as the per-fault hazard rate.

The appropriateness of these assumptions is to some extent discussed in Sections III and V-E and in [7]. Below, we assume that these assumptions are not critical.

B. Estimation of the Parameter ϕ

The JM model has the Markov property, that is, the future of the fault detection process depends only on its present state and is independent of its history. Hence, we can identify the transition probabilities as

Pr(one failure in $t, t + \Delta t \mid k - 1$ failures have occurred)

$$= \lambda(k)\Delta t + o(\Delta t)$$

Pr(no failure in $t, t + \Delta t \mid k - 1$ failures have occurred)

$$= 1 - \lambda(k)\Delta t + o(\Delta t)$$

Pr(more than one failure in $t, t + \Delta t \mid$

$$k - 1 \text{ failures have occurred}) = o(\Delta t). \quad (1)$$

If we assume that the faults are equally likely to occur and that the faults are equally distributed in the software, then we can make the following approximation:

Pr(one failure in $t, t + \Delta t \mid k - 1$ failures have occurred)

$$\approx T\frac{N - (k - 1)}{S}\Delta t \quad (2)$$

where

S   program size (measured as the number of operands and operators, number of lines of code, or a similar metric)

T   proportionality constant, which can be interpreted as the efficiency of the test to detect a specific fault.

By combining (1) and (2), we can estimate the per-fault hazard rate[2]

$$\phi \approx T/S.$$

If the testing process and the software structure remain similar between different projects (products), we can assume that the constant *T* is equal for these projects. In this case, the per-fault hazard rate for a new software product can be estimated as

$$\phi_{New}^{*} = \phi_{Ref}S_{Ref}/S_{New}. \quad (3)$$

where

ϕ_{New} estimated per-fault hazard rate during the test of the new software product

S_{New} size of the new software program

ϕ_{Ref} known per-fault hazard rate obtained from the test of an old program (or several old programs)

S_{Ref} size of the old program (or the equivalent size of several old programs).

C. Initial Number of Faults

During the development process, errors are made that result in a number of faults in the product. Let us assume that[3]

• a fault is introduced into the product independently of other faults, and

• a size unit of the program either has one fault or no fault; the probability that a size unit contains one fault is called *p*.

These two assumptions imply that for each size unit developed, a fault is introduced with probability *p*. Hence, the initial number of faults is a random variable ($\tilde{N}$), which is binomially distributed. The expected number of faults is equal to

$$E\{\tilde{N}\} = \overline{N} = Sp.$$

If $S > 10$ and $p \leq 0.1$, then the binomial distribution can be approximated with a Poisson distribution. This approximation can be made for most large software products, thus, the initial number of faults is approximately poisson distributed ($\tilde{N} \in Po(\overline{N})$).

The JM model assumes that the initial number of faults is equal to an unknown fixed constant. If instead we assume that the initial number of faults is Poisson distributed, it can be shown that the failure process during testing is a nonhomogeneous Poisson process [17]. The expected number of faults detected by time *t* is given by

$$m(t) = \overline{N}(1 - e^{-\phi t}) \quad (4)$$

and the failure intensity is given by

$$\lambda(t) = \overline{N}\phi e^{-\phi t}. \quad (5)$$

These formulas are identical to the formulas given by the GO model.

The failure intensity is often proposed as a stopping rule for the testing, that is, the testing shall be continued until the failure intensity of the software is equal to (or less than) a given constraint [18], [19]. This value of the failure intensity is below called Λ. Let us assume that failures occur according to (4). The necessary testing time can be calculated from (5) as

$$T = -\left(\ln\frac{\Lambda}{\overline{N}\phi}\right)\Big/\phi. \quad (6)$$

The expected number of detected faults by time *T* is equal to

$$m(T) = \overline{N}(1 - e^{-\phi T}) = X. \quad (7)$$

Combining (6) and (7) gives

$$\overline{N} = X + \frac{\Lambda}{\phi}. \quad (8)$$

---

[2]In [17], a method to calculate the per-fault hazard rate is presented when execution time is used as a measure of testing time.

[3]These assumptions do not take into account the existence of faults due to omission and the possibility of multiple faults due to one specific error. However, if we assume that the distribution of multiple faults and faults due to omission is similar for different products, then the two assumptions may not be critical.

D. Prediction of Fault Occurrences

In Section IV, a model was proposed to estimate the fault density of a product before the test has started. This model was calibrated with respect to the number of detected faults in historical products during the independent testing period, without considering the number of remaining faults in these products. If we assume that the above discussed stopping rule for the testing has been applied to the historical projects and that the stopping rule will be applied on the new project, then we get the following estimate:

$$X* = Sp'$$

where

$X*$ expected number of observed faults during the test
p' estimated fault density

and the estimate of the initial number of faults is given by

$$\overline{N}* = X* + \frac{\Lambda}{\phi*}.$$

The occurrences of faults during testing are predicted as

$$m*(t) = \overline{N}*(1 - e^{-\phi*t})$$

where $\phi*$ is given by (3). If the required failure intensity (Λ) at the end of the testing is very low, then we can use $X*$ instead of $\overline{N}*$ in the formulas above.

E. Experiences

We have only been able to test the method presented above on two projects. Project A has been used as a reference project in order to estimate the parameter ϕ for the projects C and D. The fault density estimation model has been used to estimate the parameter $\overline{N}$.

The initial estimate of the parameter ϕ has been compared to the estimate of ϕ given by the GO model. The latter estimate was obtained when the testing was completed. This comparison showed that the initial estimates of the parameter ϕ were very good. The estimation error for each project was 2%. In Fig. 8, the predicted fault occurrences during testing are compared to the observed fault occurrences for project C (the fault density of project C was estimated when the other 6 projects were reference projects; the estimated fault density was 18% higher than the observed fault density).

In order to check the initial estimates $\phi*$ and $\overline{N}*$, we have tried to use hypothesis testing, that is, we have used the estimates given by the GO model at different times during the testing and compared these to the initial estimates. But this approach did not work well, due to the unstable estimates given by the GO model. During the early part of the testing, we can, today, only evaluate the initial estimates by a subjective comparison between the estimated fault occurrences as a function of time and the observed fault occurrences. It is desirable to have a statistical method for this comparison. Further research is needed to obtain such a method.

The applicability of the method discussed in this sec-

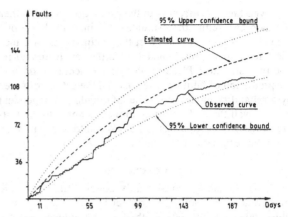

Fig. 8. Predicted occurrences of faults during testing versus observed fault occurrences for project C.

tion has to be further analyzed. Two possible objections are presented below. These objections have also to be evaluated in order to analyze the applicability of different software reliability growth models. First, the impact of different test methodologies on the assumption of random execution has to be investigated. Second, there is a discontinuity in the use of the software between test and operation. Most of the time during operation, only a few traffic modules are active, whereas during test, modules performing less frequent functions are executed. This indicates that the estimated failure intensity during test is not the same as the failure intensity during operation. This problem is independent of how the testing time is measured, but it is obvious when the testing time is measured in number of test shifts. The proposed method can be used to control the software reliability only if the assumption of random execution is not critical and if there is a (known) relationship between failure intensity during test and failure intensity during operation.

VI. ESTIMATIONS THROUGHOUT THE LIFE CYCLE

Below we summarize how the presented models can be applied throughout the software life cycle as a project control tool.

- *Specification and Design:* During these stages in the development, we can only measure some of the attributes (for example, "application experience") used in the fault density estimation model. The values of the other attributes have to be estimated (for example, by an expert judgment method). From the model, we can, in this case, get rough estimates of the fault content and the required testing time. In the design phase, it may be possible to use structure metrics obtained from the design descriptions, if a well-defined design language, like SDL [20], is used. These metrics can give us good estimates of the size of the final software [3].

- *Implementation:* In this phase, we can measure all the attributes used in the fault density estimation model. Hence, we can get refined estimates of the fault content and of the required testing time.

- *Test:* During the early testing phase, we compare the

113

observed fault occurrences to the prediction. We can then evaluate and refine the estimates obtained in the implementation phase. At the end of the testing phase, we may use a reliability growth model to further evaluate and refine the estimates. Please note that the accuracy of both the prediction of fault occurrences and the estimates given by a reliability model (e.g., the GO model) is dependent on how well the underlying assumptions apply to the testing process. This fact has to be taken into account when the initial estimate of the fault density is evaluated.

VII. CONCLUSIONS

We have obtained considerably better estimates of the fault content in a software product by applying a model which takes into account both the development process and the developed software product, compared to a model which only considers software structure metrics. This promising result has led us to the decision that this is one of the main directions to go in the future. This approach will improve the control of the process and help us to achieve more reliable software. Such a model also improves our understanding of the software development process. It should be noted that we, so far, only have analyzed a small number of projects (products). Further research has to be conducted to *statistically determine* the

factors (and attributes) that *significantly* affect the number of faults. Studies have to be done, similar to those done to develop software cost models.

We have presented a method to estimate the fault occurrences during testing, as well as the required testing time to fulfill a given constraint on the failure intensity. This method was evaluated on two projects and showed a promising result. However, the applicability of the method has to be further analyzed and tested. The method can also be used to evaluate the accuracy of the early estimate of the fault content. Today, this evaluation is done by a subjective comparison between the estimated and observed occurrences of faults. A statistical evaluation method is necessary.

Our experiences of software reliability growth models are less promising. However, we do need models that can estimate the reliability of the software. Further work is needed in order to make the models more useful for the software industry. For example, to obtain better estimates, we will need better measures of how the program has been tested and of how it will be used in operation. We will need models that can interpret this more detailed knowledge and that can make more stable and robust estimations.

It is hoped that further research and experiments will be devoted to these challenging issues. At ELLEMTEL and Lund Institute of Technology, we are continuing to evaluate and study these issues according to the directions outlined above.

APPENDIX
FAULT DENSITY ESTIMATION EQUATION

We assume that each attribute has a multiplicative influence on the fault density:

$$\lambda_i = \lambda_{min}(1 + k_1\alpha_{1,i})(1 + k_2\alpha_{2,i})$$
$$\cdot (1 + k_3\alpha_{3,i}) \cdots (1 + k_n\alpha_{n,i})$$

where

λ_i fault density of product (project) i

λ_{min} the lowest possible fault density, that is, the fault density when all $\alpha_{j,i} = 0$

k_j constant proportional to the impact of α_j on the fault density

$\alpha_{j,i}$ value of metric (attribute) j for project i

n number of attributes (metrics) which have an impact on the fault density.

This hypothesis leads to the following estimation equation:

$$\hat{\lambda}_i = \lambda_{ref} \frac{(1 + k_1\alpha_{1,i})(1 + k_2\alpha_{2,i})(1 + k_3\alpha_{3,i}) \cdots (1 + k_n\alpha_{n,i})}{(1 + k_1\alpha_{1,ref})(1 + k_2\alpha_{2,ref})(1 + k_3\alpha_{3,ref}) \cdots (1 + k_n\alpha_{n,ref})}$$

where

$\hat{\lambda}_i$ estimated fault density of project i

$\alpha_{j,ref}$ mean value of metric (attribute) j for the reference projects (historical data)

λ_{ref} mean fault density of the reference projects (historical data)

$$\alpha_{j,ref} = \sum_{a=1}^{m} \alpha_{j,a} W_a \Big/ \sum_{a=1}^{m} W_a$$

$$\lambda_{ref} = \sum_{a=1}^{m} Fault_a \Big/ \sum_{a=1}^{m} W_a$$

m number of reference projects

$\alpha_{j,a}$ value of metric j, reference project a

W_a Halstead's program length, reference project a, or number of project members, reference project a (for the attribute "application experience")

$Fault_a$ number of faults, reference project a.

Please observe that for reasons of simplicity, and due to the small number of reference projects in our study, we assumed that the constants in the estimation equation are equal. That is, $k_1 = k_2 = k_3$ for the three identified attributes chosen to be parameters in the estimation model.

Below is presented how the three identified attributes are measured.

$Rank_i$ rank of program unit i

N_i Halstead's program length, program unit i

n number of program units.

Level: Unit Test: Each program unit is ranked according to the following ranking list:

Rank = 0: extended unit test

Rank = 1: complete unit test

Rank = 2: not complete unit test

Rank = 3: not tested.

The unit test is performed in a simulated environment. The unit test is complete when all the specified test cases have been performed. "Extended unit test" signifies a "complete unit test" and that the program unit has been tested on the target machine.

$$Metric = \sum_{i=1}^{n} Rank_i N_i \bigg/ \sum_{i=1}^{n} N_i.$$

Project Stability: The attribute "project stability" is a combination of the two subattributes "timing and main storage problems" and "goodness of requirements and target machine volatility." The problems originating from each of these two subattributes are ranked according to the following list.

Rank = 0: very small problems

Rank = 1: minor problems; only changes in the

source code

Rank = 2: 1–2 redesigns

Rank = 3: ≥ 3 redesigns.

The changes in the software product affect a number of program units. The metric for the whole product is calculated as the average weighted with the sizes of the units affected.

$$Metric = \sum_{i=1}^{n} Rank_i N_i \bigg/ \sum_{i=1}^{n} N_i.$$

The metric for the attribute "project stability" is the sum of the metrics of the two subattributes.

Application Experience: The application experience of each project member is ranked according to the following list.

Rank = 0: more than 5 years experience

Rank = 1: 3–5 years experience

Rank = 2: 1–2 years experience

Rank = 4: less than 1 year experience.

Please note that we assume that the relation between the personnel capability and the experience is nonlinear. We also assume that a large number of beginners is very critical for a project.

$$Metric = \sum_{i=1}^{k} Rank \text{ project member } i / \text{total number of}$$

project members $(= k)$.

ACKNOWLEDGMENT

The authors would like to thank O. Viktorsson of EL-LEMTEL and C. Wohlin of Lund Institute of Technology for their participation and helpful suggestions throughout this project. C. Wohlin contributed many valuable suggestions for improving an earlier draft of this paper. The authors would also like to thank the many people who have provided project and product data.

REFERENCES

[1] C. Johansson and I. Svenle, "Handling of AXE 10 software," *Ericsson Review*, vol. 1, no. 2-10, 1985.
[2] B. Lennselius, C. Wohlin, and C. Vrana, "Software metrics: Fault content estimation and software process control," *Microprocessors Microsyst.*, vol. 11, no. 7, pp. 365-375, 1987.
[3] B. Lennselius, "Software complexity and its impact on different software handling processes," in *Proc. 6th Int. Conf. Software Eng. Telecommun. Switching Syst.*, 1986, pp. 148-153.
[4] A. L. Goel and K. Okumoto, "Time-dependent error-detection rate model for software reliability and other performance measures," *IEEE Trans. Reliability*, vol. R-28, pp. 206-211, 1979.
[5] A. L. Goel, *A Guidebook for Software Reliability Assessment*, Syracuse Univ., Syracuse, NY, 1983.
[6] Z. Jelinski and P. Moranda, "Software reliability research," *Statistical Comput. Performance Evaluation*, pp. 465-484, 1972.
[7] L. Rydström and O. Viktorsson, "Software reliability prediction for large and complex telecommunication systems," in *Proc. 22nd Annu. Hawaii Int. Conf. Syst. Sci.*, 1989, pp. 312-319.
[8] B. Boehm, *Software Engineering Economics*. Englewood Cliffs, NJ: Prentice-Hall, 1981.
[9] J. Vosburgh, B. Curtis, R. Wolverton, B. Albert, H. Malec, S. Haben, and Y. Liu, "Productivity factors and programming environments," in *Proc. 7th Int. Conf. Software Eng.*, 1984, pp. 143-152.
[10] C. E. Walston and C. P. Felix, "A method of programming measurement and estimation," *IBM Syst. J.*, vol. 16, no. 1, pp. 54-73, 1977.
[11] M. Takahashi and Y. Kamayachi, "An empirical study of a model for program error prediction," in *Proc. 8th Int. Conf. Software Eng.*, 1985, pp. 330-336.
[12] B. Lennselius, "Guidelines on how to develop a software fault content estimation model," Tech. Rep., Dep. Commun. Syst., Lund Inst. Technol., Lund, Sweden, 1988.
[13] T. J. McCabe, "A complexity measure," *IEEE Trans. Software Eng.*, vol. SE-2, pp. 308-320, 1976.
[14] M. H. Halstead, *Elements of Software Science*. New York: Elsevier North-Holland, 1977.
[15] J. D. Musa, "A theory of software reliability and its application," *IEEE Trans. Software Eng.*, vol. SE-1, pp. 312-327, 1975.
[16] C. Wohlin, "A comparison between two software reliability models: Jelinski-Moranda's de-eutrophication model and Goel-Okumoto's non-homogeneous Poisson process model," Tech. Rep. 4, Dep. Commun. Syst., Lund Inst. Technol., Lund, Sweden, 1986.
[17] J. D. Musa, A. Iannino, and K. Okumoto, *Software Reliability: Measurement, Prediction, Application*. New York: McGraw-Hill, 1987.
[18] O. J. Khen and D. Levy, "Software modeling for optimal field entry," in *Proc. Annu. Reliability Maintainability Symp.*, 1980, pp. 410-414.
[19] S. M. Ross, "Software reliability: The stopping rule problem," *IEEE Trans. Software Eng.*, vol. SE-11, pp. 1472-1476, 1985.
[20] A. Rockström, *An Introduction to the CCITT SDL*. Stockholm, Sweden: The Swedish Telecommunication Administration, 1985.

Adapting, Correcting, and Perfecting Software Estimates: A Maintenance Metaphor

Tarek K. Abdel-Hamid, Naval Postgraduate School

Continuous software estimation models are needed that can constantly evaluate costs and schedules. This article proposes a hybrid estimation model and demonstrates how to use it.

T he difficult problem of software cost and schedule estimation remains unresolved. While a number of estimation models have been developed in recent years, their utility has proven to be poor. Consequently, few software development organizations rely on them, and the organizations that do often use them only to check manual estimates.

The reason estimating software projects has been problematic is no mystery: Estimates of effort and cost must be done at a time when the *values* of many factors driving software development are unknown quantities. This applies both to product factors (such as product size and complexity) and to organization factors (such as staff skill and turnover rate).

As it progresses through the software development life cycle (SDLC), a product becomes better defined and uncertainties about the organizational parameters ease up. Software estimation researchers and practitioners have thus argued that estimating done at the beginning of a software project should not be considered unalterable.[1] Rather, estimation should be a *continuous* process enhanced through constant updates of feedback data collected from project monitoring and control activities. Londeix put it this way[2]:

> By comparing the actual data with the estimated data at each step, the accuracy of the next step-estimate can be improved. A large-scale project can often take a few years to complete, and during that time the development capability might change or an improved awareness of the initial conditions might be obtained. Thus, there is a great deal of scope for improving the estimate. At each step there is a need to be able to better predict future steps.

The continuous estimation "message" to the software project manager has been simple: "Just do it." Implicit in such a message is the premise that the current generation of models is well suited to support a continuous estimation process. In

Reprinted from *Computer*, Vol. 26 No. 3, Mar. 1993, pp. 20–29. Copyright © 1993 by The Institute of Electrical and Electronics Engineers, Inc. All rights reserved.

this article, I challenge that premise and propose a set of capabilities that genuinely continuous models need and most current models lack.

The maintenance metaphor

Let us characterize the continuous estimation process — the "it" in "just do it." Defining the meaning of a truly continuous estimation process is essential before we can address the issue of what types of models can support it and how. The prevalent characterization views the continuous estimation process as one of continuously *correcting* project estimates *during* the SDLC.[2]

This is a limiting characterization, reminiscent of early portrayals of software maintenance as an activity to correct lingering software errors. Gradually, software engineers realized that software maintenance comprises a richer set of activities for adapting, correcting, and perfecting the software system to keep it operational, responsive, and synchronized with an evolving user and operational environment.

Continuous estimation seeks to accomplish for initial project estimates what software maintenance seeks to accomplish for the software product. In maintenance, the *adaptive* activity often accommodates new system or user requirements or reflects new organizational realities (such as new government reporting requirements). Similarly, a software estimate often needs to be adapted to accommodate new organizational realities (for example, staffing constraints at any point in the SDLC or even at the project's initiation).
Corrective maintenance remedies an error detected in the software product. In software estimation, corrective action is often needed to correct initial assumptions that turn out to be faulty (for example, about product size).

Finally, *perfective* maintenance eliminates processing inefficiencies and enhances performance of the overall software system. For software estimation, poor initial estimation can lead to project inefficiencies (for example, in staffing). This creates a need for project postmortems to normalize (or perfect) project statistics and thus improve their utility as bases of future estimates.

Model capabilities to support continuous estimation

To support adaptive, corrective, and perfective estimation activities, genuinely continuous models must have certain capabilities.

Continuous-time modeling. According to Curtis,[3] one serious limitation of current models is their treatment of the software development process "as discrete rather than continuous in time." For example, when current models advise midstream corrections, most limit such corrections to *discrete* adjustments at the project's major SDLC milestones. The following quotes indicate the strategy:

- "The procedures are oriented around the collection of information and the updating of the software product's Cocomo (Constructive cost model) estimates at the project's major life-cycle milestones."[4]
- "At the end of each development phase or build, the manager should reestimate project size, effort, and schedule for inclusion in the software development/management plan."[5]
- "It is very important to continually reestimate effort and cost and to compare targets against actual expenditure at each major milestone."[6]

These examples reinforce the traditional view of software development as a discrete set of SDLC phases. In reality, the software artifact changes continuously — not in discrete jumps that are conveniently synchronized with the project's major milestones. Results of well-documented case studies at the Software Engineering Laboratory[5] clearly indicate a pattern of continuous, not discrete, changes over time. The organizational system's human intensive processes are never static. "Both the problems and the people are in constant flux . . . Even with a stable population, the people continually learn new skills and find different ways to solve problems."[7] Even management's major decisions on a project, which do appear as discrete events, are in fact continuous in nature. This has been accepted in the literature of organizational dynamics for 30 years.[8]

Capture management-system dynamics. The continuous estimation viewpoint rests on the premise that initial project plans do not necessarily constitute the best course of action to take during the project life cycle. Initial plans merely show what was considered best when the plan was formulated. Since actual events on a software project almost always differ from the assumed events the plans were designed to meet, project managers must react continuously to real-world events, not to those that might have occurred had the real world been kind enough to conform to the initial planning assumptions.

Research findings indicate that managerial interventions can affect project performance in significant ways.[7,9,10] The impact can be direct (for example, overlapping phases, eliminating requirements) or indirect (for example, adding staff, investing in new technology). Incorporating managerial decision-making dynamics into continuous estimation models should not only increase the fidelity of such models, but should also enable management to search for and test alternative interventions on a continuous basis. For example, if a schedule slippage occurs during the SDLC, the manager should be able to evaluate a range of options available (for instance, schedule extensions with no staffing changes, fixed schedules with additional staff, or a combination of the two). Organizational behavior researchers have long known that without such a facility, project feedback will only lead to frustration and perhaps defensive behavior as the manager confronts a poor-performance indicator with no idea how to correct it.

Computer-based simulation. "Not learning anything from a bad estimate is unforgivable," according to DeMarco.[11] Yet, software project managers do this all the time.

For example, it is nearly unheard of to conduct a software project postmortem. Except in the most successful projects, everyone scurries off at the end without even taking note of the actual total cost. Estimates for the next project are made as though the last project never happened, and no one benefits from past mistakes. If aircraft manufacturers were so cavalier about analysis of their failures (crashes), the public would be outraged. But in our field, ignoring the lessons of the past is the invariant rule. Of course, it ought not be that way; we ought to go poring over the wreckage of our failures, analyzing and looking for patterns in just the way that airplane investigators do.[11]

We need to exploit software project experiences to *perfect* software estimates, but dissecting a project experience to discern what worked and what didn't is not an easy task. The software project environment is a complex web of interrelated factors where cause and effect are often remote from each other in both time and space.

Over the past three decades, the work of Forrester and others in system dynamics has demonstrated both the feasibility and the utility of constructing computer-based simulation models to serve as diagnostic experimentation vehicles for management systems.

These simulation models have three benefits over analytical models. First,

Constructive cost model

Cocomo (an abbreviation for Constructive cost model) is one of the most widely accepted and applied models for software effort and schedule estimation. It was developed at TRW; Boehm explains it in full detail.[4]

Development effort in person-months (PM) and time for development (TDev) in months are modeled with power functions of the form

$$PM = a * (size)^b * E,$$
$$TDev = c * (PM)^d$$

where *a*, *b*, *c*, and *d* are constants that change with the level of the estimate desired. Cocomo provides a hierarchy of three increasingly detailed levels of project estimation: basic, intermediate, and detailed. Size is the principal factor that influences effort, but 15 other factors (called cost drivers) together determine the adjustment factor *E*. The cost drivers capture static attributes of the software product (for example, complexity), the hardware (for example, turnaround time), the personnel (for example, programmer capability), and the project environment (for example, use of modern programming practices).

their causal structure provides a superior explanatory power. By contrast, regression-based models might expose a statistical relationship between development factors and effort, but such models provide little understanding of why or under what conditions the relationship exists.

Second, the solution of analytical models usually specifies only the terminal or steady state that eventually results from changing the values of the controlled variables. Such models do not specify the intermediate transitional states. Computer-based simulation models expose the system's continuous transitions to the most rigorous study.

The third and perhaps most attractive benefit of simulation models is controlled experimentation. This was clearly stated by Forrester, the "father" of system dynamics:

> The effects of different assumptions and environmental factors can be tested. In the model system, unlike the real systems, the effect of changing one factor can be observed while all other factors are held unchanged. Such experimentation will yield new insights into the characteristics of the system that the model represents. By using a model of a complex system, more can be learned about internal interactions than would ever be possible through manipulation of the real system. Internally, the model provides complete control of the system's organizational structure, its policies, and its sensitivities to various events.[8]

Using continuous estimation models, the software manager, like the engineer, can simulate project behavior to get answers quickly and economically that would seldom be obtainable from an informal postmortem analysis.

Model implementation

The Naval Postgraduate School research group that I headed developed a model with the required capabilities to demonstrate the feasibility and utility of continuous estimation. It couples the system dynamics (SD) simulator of software development by Abdel-Hamid and Madnick[10] with a variety of algorithmic estimators. This article discusses an implementation using Boehm's Cocomo[4] (see the sidebar) and the SD simulator. Cocomo is programmed in C, while the SD simulator is implemented in Professional Dynamo Plus (PD+). The two models are interfaced through a C/PD+

DOS interface. Figure 1 shows this hybrid model.

The user engages the system through an interface that initiates the estimation process by eliciting a set of inputs. For Cocomo, these inputs include an estimate of project size and the values of the 15 cost drivers. The Cocomo module then calculates three estimates: effort, duration, and the project's productivity index (estimated project size in delivered source instructions divided by estimated effort).

In addition to the Cocomo drivers, the SD simulator requires two additional types of inputs: (1) parameters used to characterize the organizational system (for example, turnover rate and hiring delays), and (2) management policies (for example, for hiring and training). (Abdel-Hamid and Madnick explain the parameters in detail.[10])

For *initial* planning purposes, the hybrid model produces two types of estimates: (1) point predictions (such as cost and duration) and (2) continuous projections (such as staff loading over time). As the project progresses, all model variables can be adjusted in real time to reflect improved knowledge (such as about size and productivity). Additionally, implications of different managerial interventions can be evaluated. At project completion, the model can serve as an experimentation vehicle for postmortem analysis.

Model demonstration

Below, three examples demonstrate how the model can be used *before* the project starts to adapt the Cocomo estimates to organizational realities, *during* software development to correct initial assumptions about sizing, and *after* project completion to perfect model estimates.

Adapting initial estimates to organizational realities. The accurate projection of required staff levels is a critical function in software development:

> Improper staffing and schedules, often short of real needs, may lead to delays for customers, compromised methodology, volatile priorities, inadequate testing, poor product quality, and low project productivity. Projects that are correctly staffed and scheduled generally satisfy commitments to customers and favor increased productivity.[12]

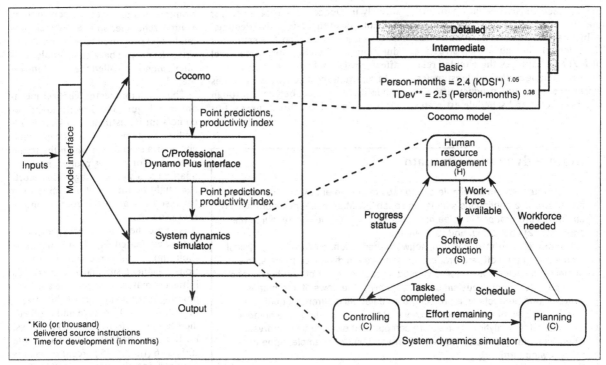

Figure 1. The hybrid model structure.

The project's average staffing level is calculated in Cocomo (as well as in most current-generation models) by dividing the estimated effort in person-months by the estimated duration in months. To develop a detailed month-by-month personnel plan, average estimates are calculated using Cocomo's SDLC phase distributions of effort and schedule.

Given these average personnel levels by phase and activity; given the PERT [Program evaluation and review technique] chart connecting phase, activity and calendar time; and given the initial WBS [work-breakdown structure] breakdown of activity by task, we can construct a detailed personnel plan indicating how many people will be needed for each task during each month of the project.[4]

This, of course, assumes that the estimated staff resources will be available when needed. Often, this is not the case. In fact, negotiating and obtaining staff resources is a major task for project managers.

The reality of staffing limitations is addressed only obliquely, if at all, in the estimation literature. For Cocomo, Boehm asserts that "Typically, the personnel plan will take three or four iterations to converge."[4] The iterations are, however, conducted without altering the Cocomo estimate for effort in person-months (and, hence, for productivity). That is, staffing needs are reconciled with staffing availability *outside* the estimation model (that is, while holding the effort and productivity estimates constant). Figure 2a shows this process.

This reconciliation process is, however, inconsistent with research findings indicating that workforce size determines communication and training overheads, which affect the team's productivity and ultimately the cost and schedule of the project.[9] Indeed, Jeffery's empirical results indicate that staff level affects productivity more than all other drivers except product size. This suggests that Figure 2a should be modified so that changes in resource constraints directly impact the initial estimation

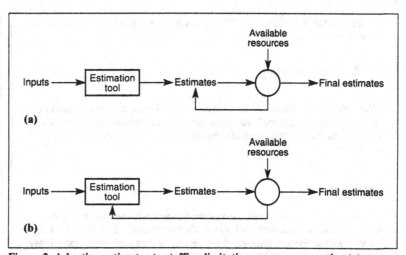

Figure 2. Adapting estimates to staffing limitations: common practice (a); proposed strategy (b).

process/mechanism, as shown in Figure 2b.

In the system dynamics simulator (see the sidebar), the causal loop structure of Figure 3 captures the circular relationships among cost/schedule estimates, workforce size, and productivity. On one hand, cost and schedule estimates directly influence workforce level (for example, desired staff size is calculated by dividing estimated cost by estimated duration), while the workforce level affects project schedule and cost.

In addition, cost/schedule estimates can influence project behavior through more subtle and less direct means. For example, if a project is perceived to be behind schedule, software developers might feel pressured to work harder to bring the project back on schedule. This phenomenon is called the "deadline effect."[4]

The simulator uses the feedback mechanism in Figure 3 to directly adapt Cocomo's initial estimates to staff availability. To demonstrate this capability, consider a scenario in which the initial estimates for a new project must be adapted to a staff shortage. This shortage might be the result of competition for resources among multiple concurrent projects.

Assume the new project (project N) has an estimated 64 KDSI (kilo — or thousand — delivered source instructions). Table 1 summarizes Cocomo's initial estimates. Next, assume a second ongoing project (project O) has a current staffing of 11 people and is scheduled to complete in 200 working days. Further, assume that the total available staff is 16 (that is, 75 percent of what is required for the two projects). With project O employing 11 people, project N is left with only five full-time staff in its startup phase.

One possible staffing plan for project N would be to start the project with the five available people and add additional people later in the SDLC when project O releases its staff. To compensate for the initial staff deficit and minimize schedule overrun, the plan would entail building project N's staff to a higher level than originally estimated. Figure 4a shows this adapted staffing plan. (As

---

System dynamics simulator

The system dynamics simulator captures management-system dynamics and provides a continuous simulation capability. Managerial decision-making structures are grouped in three major subsystems: (1) human resource management, (2) controlling, and (3) planning.

The model's fourth subsystem, software production, captures the physical production of the software product. Like all system dynamics models, this model's subsystems are interconnected through a series of *feedback* loops.

To provide a continuous simulation capability, the flows of information, resources, and products on a project are modeled as difference equations where variables of interest are functions of time. Calculations are numeric, as opposed to analytical. Values are computed at discrete time intervals where the intervals are very small. An integration, for example, appears in the following form:

$$WF_k = WF_j + (DT)(HR_{jk} - FR_{jk})$$

where WF equals workforce, k equals now, j equals immediate past, DT equals computation interval for the simulation, HR equals hiring rate, jk equals time interval from j to k, and FR equals firing rate.

Thus, the above equation states that the current value of the workforce (WF_k) is computed from its most recent past value (WF_j) plus changes from inflows and outflows that occurred in the intervening time ($HR_{jk} - FR_{jk}$). The simulation parameter DT represents a very small increment of time, defined as the length of simulated time between the previous computation (j) and the present (k). By rearranging the equation to read

$$\frac{WF_k - WF_j}{DT} = HR_{jk} - FR_{jk}$$

we see that for small values of DT, the equation is a discrete approximation of the differential equation

$$\frac{d(WF(t))}{dt} = HR(t) - FR(t)$$

Variables in the model are defined as arrays. This allows the model to be configured to simulate multiple concurrent projects. Abdel-Hamid and Madnick discuss the model's structure, mathematical formulation, and validation in detail.[10]

Further reading

For more information about the system dynamics technique, see J.W. Forrester, *Industrial Dynamics* (MIT Press, Cambridge, Mass., 1961) and E.F. Wolstenholme, *System Enquiry: A System Dynamics Approach* (John Wiley and Sons, New York, 1990).

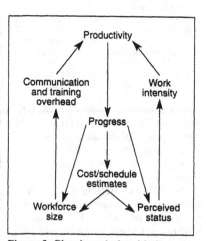

Figure 3. Circular relationship between estimates, workforce size, and productivity.

Table 1 Cocomo's initial estimates.

Project Characteristics	Values for Project N
Size (KDSI)	64.0
Effort (Person-days)	3,593.0
Development time (Days)	348.0
Staff level (People)	
Design	8.7
Programming	11.7
Integration and testing	8.7

Table 2. Comparison of the initial and adapted estimates.

Type of Estimate	Cost (Person-days)	Duration (Days)	Productivity (DSI Per Person-day)
Initial estimates	3,593	348	17.8
Adapted estimates	4,494	395	14.2

Table 3. Project N finishes on schedule (348 days) and regains most of its productivity.

Type of Estimate	Cost (Person-days)	Duration (Days)	Productivity (DSI* Per Person-day)
Initial estimates	3,593	348	17.8
Adapted estimates (1)	4,494	395	14.2
Adapted estimates (2)	3,660	348	17.5

the sidebar indicates, the hybrid model is capable of simulating multiple concurrent projects.)

As staff level changes and affects productivity, project N's cost and schedule change. Table 2 compares the initial and adapted estimates.

The drop in the overall productivity is caused by inefficiencies in the adapted staffing profile (which, in turn, was a response to the initial staffing constraint). This is a team-learning effect. As a project proceeds, team members learn more about the project and the development process. The more they learn, the more productive they become — up to a point. The earlier in the SDLC that all members become trained, the higher the overall project productivity. The delayed acquisition of the bulk of the project's staff in the adapted plan means fewer staff members will perform at their peak for less time over the SDLC.

Furthermore, in the adapted plan the project's staff builds to a significantly higher level than in the original plan. As the team size grows, the number of human intercommunication paths tends to increase to provide for proper coordination among program modules. Generally, individual productivity will tend to decrease and overall effort will tend to increase.

If projects N and O were two subsystems of a single project, management would have some added flexibility. For example, project O's scheduled completion date could be extended to approximately coincide with the completion date of project N. There would be no additional delay in the *total* project completion, and staffing would be more balanced. Figure 4b shows this adaptation. Note that project N finishes on schedule (in 348 days) and regains most of its productivity (see Table 3).

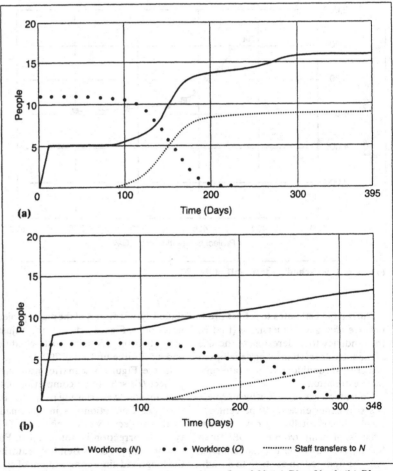

Figure 4. Adapting staffing plan for projects O and N: (a) Plan No. 1; (b) Plan No. 2.

121

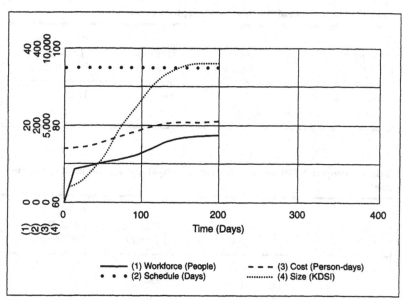

Figure 5. Adjustments to project variables up to day 200.

Legend:
- (1) Workforce (People)
- • • • (2) Schedule (Days)
- – – – (3) Cost (Person-days)
- ·········· (4) Size (KDSI)

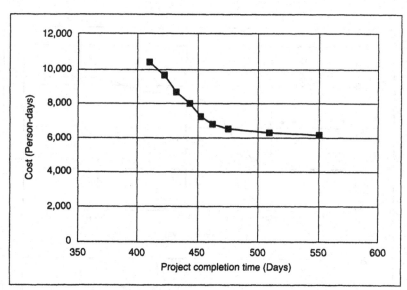

Figure 6. Cost/schedule trade-off at day 200.

Correcting estimates to reflect product-size changes. Undersizing (that is, the tendency to underestimate the size of the software system being developed) is a critical roadblock to accurate software estimation.

Consider a scenario in which project N's size experiences a 50 percent upward adjustment during development (that is, growing from 64 KDSI to 96 KDSI). As growth occurs, the estimates must be updated. In contrast to a traditional estimation tool, the hybrid model allows the estimates to be updated continuously, not merely at the major project milestones. Figure 5 depicts the adjustments to project N's size, cost, schedule, and workforce up to day 200.

In the Figure 5 scenario, note how project N's scheduled completion date remains stable even as the project's size increases. Corrections are, instead, made to the project's workforce level. This type of correction is not atypical. For example, at AT&T's Bell Laboratories the long-lead-time commitment of content and schedule on software projects severely constrains management's abil-

ity to alter the schedule early in the life cycle. "If it turns out that parts of the project were underestimated, it is difficult to alter schedules or product content," according to Taff, Borchering, and Hudgins.[1] "Management can only add resources to meet the commitment." DeMarco found political pressures cause similar behaviors in a number of organizations.[11]

Nevertheless, maintaining the project's initial schedule even as the project's size is adjusted upwards constitutes an *implicit* compression of project schedule. That, in turn, raises the questions: Is this implicit schedule compression feasible? If it is, is it economically justifiable? Without a continuous estimation capability, it is extremely difficult for software developers and their customers to find convincing answers to these questions.

According to Boehm, an important utility of estimation models is their ability to "support a family of estimates or a sensitivity analysis."[4] Using Cocomo, the project manager can, for example, conduct a cost/schedule trade-off analysis to assess the feasibility of schedule compressions and their impact on project cost. The limitation, however, is that such an analysis can only be done for the *initial* estimates and for the SDLC in toto. Cocomo's cost/schedule calculations "assume that the project manager knows about any required schedule acceleration or stretch-out in advance, and is able to plan and control the project in the most cost-effective way with respect to an off-nominal schedule."[4]

Cocomo's life-cycle cost/schedule relationships cannot be distributed across the SDLC (for example, using its SDLC phase distributions of effort and schedule) to conduct the analysis *during* the project for the individual phases. To understand why, assume that the opposite is true — that is, that Cocomo's life-cycle cost/schedule relationships can be distributed across the SDLC with values assigned to each individual phase. This would imply that, for example, the testing phase's schedule can always be compressed by X percent at an identical offsetting cost increase of some Y percent, irrespective of when the schedule compression decision is made. Thus, the decision could be made before the project starts as part of the initial plan, or just before the testing phase starts as a reaction to an unexpected delay in the programming phase — with the same results. However, empirical evidence indicates that not only will the cost be higher in the latter case, but that it might even be infeasible to compress the schedule at all so late in the life cycle.

The system dynamics simulator has been used to investigate the impact of late staff additions on project cost and schedule.[10] The results indicate that the net cumulative contribution of a newly acquired staff member could be positive or negative. Net contribution determines whether the project's schedule can be successfully compressed late in the life cycle. We must calculate the *net* contribution because an additional person's contribution to useful project work must be balanced against the staff resources that will be lost in training and communicating with the new staff member.

We must calculate the *cumulative* contribution. A new person's net contribution might be initially negative. But as training takes effect and the new person's productivity increases, the net contribution will become less negative and eventually (given enough training) the new person will start contributing positively. Only if the cumulative impact is negative will addition of the new staff member translate into a longer project completion time.

By providing a facility to conduct these calculations dynamically within a simulation, the hybrid model allows management to conduct cost/schedule trade-off analyses on a virtually continuous basis. Estimations can be obtained for any part of the SDLC. Figure 6 reflects the cost/schedule trade-off conducted at day 200. The results show that maintaining the original schedule of 348 is infeasible. The earliest possible completion time is 409 days at a cost of 10,450 person-days.

Perfecting estimation through postmortem experimentation. In a NASA postmortem, the dynamic behaviors of two concurrent software projects were studied in detail. The NASA-A and NASA-B projects (not actual names) involved the design, implementation, and testing of software systems for processing telemetry data and providing attitude determination and control for the NASA-A and NASA-B satellites, respectively. Because the two spacecraft were not identical (for example, they had different sensors, telemetry,

and orbits), two sets of requirements were produced for two separate software support systems. Table 4 shows initial estimates and actual project results.

Table 4. Initial estimates and actual project results.

Project	Initial Estimates	Actual Results
NASA-A		
Size (KDSI)	16.0	24.4
Cost (Person-days)	1,100	2,239
Schedule (Working days)	320	380
NASA-B		
Size (KDSI)	19.6	25.7
Cost (Person-days)	1,345	2,200
Schedule (Working days)	320	335

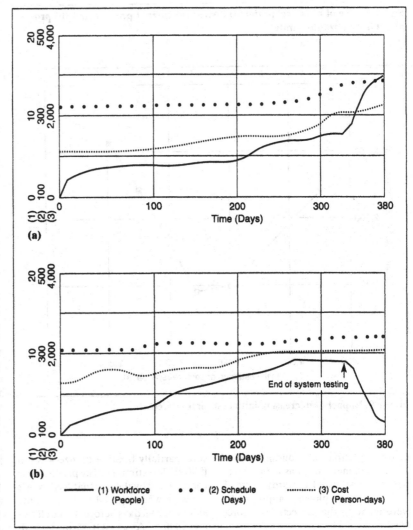

Figure 7. Project behavior: (a) NASA-A; (b) NASA-B.

Figure 7 illustrates how the staff, cost, and schedule variables for the two projects changed during their SDLCs. Note how management on both projects resisted adjusting the projects' sched-

123

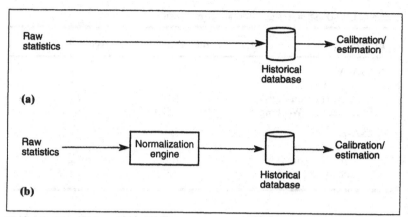

Figure 8. Use of historical project statistics: (a) current practice and (b) proposed normalization strategy.

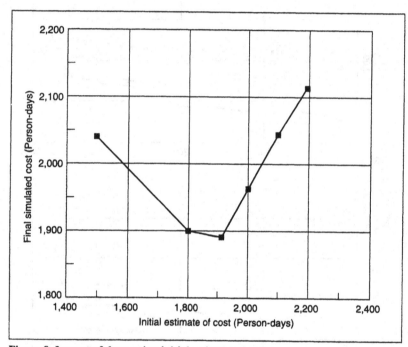

Figure 9. Impact of decreasing initial estimates on cost.

uled completion dates during most of the development, even as the projects' sizes were adjusted upwards. Instead, in the earlier phases, adjustments were made to the projects' workforce levels.

NASA-A's workforce pattern is atypical. Workforce buildups tend to follow a concave curve that rises, peaks, and then drops back to lower levels as a project proceeds toward the system-testing phase. Two factors explain NASA-A's workforce pattern. First, the project was under serious schedule pres-

sure, partially because its size was initially underestimated. The problem was complicated by the fact that NASA-A's software was required to be accepted and frozen 90 days before the satellite's launch date. As a result, serious schedule slippages were not tolerated. As the launch date approached, pressures developed that overrode normal workforce stability considerations. That is, management became willing to "pay any price" to avoid overshooting the pre-launch target. As Figure 7 indicates, this translated into a management that

was increasingly willing to add more people.

Serendipitously, the NASA-B project was winding down, hence its staff was available for quick transfer to NASA-A. This explains why the NASA-A project staff increase was so dramatic.

As standard procedure at this NASA flight center, a postmortem was conducted to evaluate the project experience and document the lessons learned. In addition, the project results were incorporated into the center's database of historical project statistics. This database supports the development, calibration, and fine-tuning of the center's software estimation models (see Figure 8a). The underlying assumption here is that such project results constitute the most preferred and reliable benchmarks for future estimation purposes since they are *actual* values.

However, considering NASA-A's project history, the project's final cost of 2,200 person-days might not be a desirable benchmark for future estimates. The value reflects staffing inefficiencies incurred as a result of initial undersizing. The next time a project similar in size (24.4 KDSI) to NASA-A is undertaken, a more effective staffing plan could be devised that avoids a last-minute staff explosion. As a result, the new project should require less than 2,200 person-days to accomplish.

Note that I used the word *should* rather than *would*. If NASA-A's (inflated) 2,200 person-days value was adopted as the benchmark for estimating the new 24.4 KDSI project, the organization might not realize any savings. The reason: The self-fulfilling prophecy of Parkinson's law, which says work on a software project can expand in many different forms to fill the available time.

Work expansion could take the form of goldplating (that is, adding features to the software product that make the job bigger and more expensive but which provide little or no utility in practice), or it could take the form of an increase in nonproductive slack-time activities.[4]

What is needed is a strategy that capitalizes on NASA-A's (learning) experience by wringing out the cost excesses caused by the initial undersizing and that derives a posterior set of *normalized* cost and schedule estimation benchmarks (see Figure 8b).

The hybrid model developed for this study is an appropriate tool for this task. By using it as a "laboratory" for

124

conducting controlled experimentation, the effect of changing one factor can be observed while all other factors are held unchanged.

Specifically, the strategy involves re-simulation of the NASA-A project with no undersizing. In multiple simulation runs, the initial schedule estimate was held constant at 380 days, while the initial cost estimate was gradually decreased from the actual value of 2,200 person-days (see Figure 9). The x axis depicts the different initial cost (person-day) estimates, while the y axis depicts the project's final (simulated) cost in person-days.

The results indicate that using NASA-A's (inflated) raw experience value of 2,200 person-days would indeed be wasteful. As the initial person-day estimate for the project is gradually lowered, savings are achieved as wasteful project practices decrease. This continues until an initial cost estimate of about 1,900 person-days is reached.

Lowering the project's initial cost estimate below this point becomes counterproductive because the project not only sheds all its excess but begins to suffer the effects of underestimation. Initial underestimation is costly because it leads to an initial understaffing, followed by a costly staff buildup later in the life cycle. (This is exactly what happened with NASA-A.)

This indicates that the widely held notion that *raw* historical project results are a preferred benchmark for future estimation is flawed. In the NASA-A case, a 1,900 person-day value is clearly a more preferred benchmark (for inclusion in the normalized database of historical project results) over NASA-A's raw 2,200 person-day cost. The simulations indicate that the normalized cost estimate and its associated staffing plan would reduce NASA's cost on the new project by about 10 percent.

According to Boehm, "Good software cost estimation is not an end in itself, but rather a means toward more effective software life-cycle management."[4] Indeed, without a reliable software estimation capability, effective project planning and control is next to impossible. Software estimates provide the basis for planning what resources to commit to a project and, in retrospect, for judging how well these resources were used.

The hybrid model I discussed is the focus of two ongoing research efforts. In the first, the model is deployed on a two-year project to develop a two-subsystem space application at NASA's Jet Propulsion Laboratory. The objective of this research exercise is to assess the impact of continuous estimation using the hybrid model on managerial decision-making and in turn, on software project performance. The model is being used to support the design and coding phases of subsystem 1, while subsystem 2, being developed in parallel, will be managed using traditional models.

The objective of the second research effort is to investigate possible enhancements to the model's continuous estimation-correcting capabilities. For example, a statistical analysis of historical project profiles is being conducted to quantify effort and schedule relationships between the different phases of the SDLC (for example, correlations between design effort and coding effort). In addition, the JPL staff is investigating possible structures to synthesize managerial judgement with statistical methods to make mid-project corrections.

All real-life estimation requires exercising some judgement. One major research issue in this effort is the *extent* to which managerial judgement should be used at the different phases of the SDLC. Another is *how* the interaction of judgement with statistical methods should be structured. ∎

References

1. L. Taff, J. Borchering, and W. Hudgins, "Estimeetings: Development Estimates and a Front-End Process for a Large Project," *IEEE Trans. Software Eng.*, Vol. 17, No. 8, Aug. 1991, pp. 839-849.

2. B. Londeix, *Cost Estimation for Software Development*, Addison-Wesley, Wokingham, England, 1987.

3. B. Curtis, "Three Problems Overcome with Behavioral Models of the Software Development Process," *Proc. 11th Int'l Conf. Software Eng.*, IEEE CS Press, Los Alamitos, Calif., Order No. 1941 (microfiche only), 1989.

4. B.W. Bochm, *Software Eng. Economics*, Prentice Hall, Englewood Cliffs, N.J., 1981.

5. *Manager's Handbook for Software Development*, Software Engineering Laboratory series, Goddard Space Flight Center, Greenbelt, Md., Nov. 1990.

6. A. von Mayrhauser, *Software Eng.: Methods and Management*, Academic Press, Boston, 1990, pp. 723-725.

7. W. Humphrey, *Managing the Software Process*, Addison-Wesley, Reading, Mass. 1989.

8. J.W. Forrester, *Industrial Dynamics*, MIT Press, Cambridge, Mass., 1961.

9. D. Jeffery, "The Relationship Between Team Size, Experience, and Attitudes and Software Development Productivity." *Compsac 87, 11th Int'l Computer Software and Applications Conf.*, IEEE CS Press, Los Alamitos, Calif., Order No. 806 (microfiche only), 1987, pp. 2-8.

10. T.K. Abdel-Hamid and S.E. Madnick, *Software Project Dynamics: An Integrated Approach*, Prentice Hall, Englewood Cliffs, N.J, 1991.

11. T. DeMarco, *Controlling Software Projects*, Yourdon Press, N.Y., 1982.

12. W. Lehder, P. Smith, and W. Yu," Software Estimation Technology." *AT&T Technical J.*, July/Aug. 1988, pp. 10-18.

Readers can contact Abdel-Hamid at the Naval Postgraduate School, Department of Administrative Sciences, Code AS/AH, Monterey, CA 93943. His e-mail address is 3991p@vml.cc.nps.navy. mil.

Enhanced Availability of Transaction Oriented Systems using Failure Tests *

Erol Gelenbe   Marisela Hernández[†]

EHEI. Université René Descartes
45, Rue des Saints Pères
Paris. 75006. FRANCE

Abstract

For a transaction oriented system this paper proposes that in addition to the conventional recovery techniques, such as dumps and roll-back recovery, system availability be enhanced by the introduction of "failure tests". We present a model to analyze the effect of the failure rate, the failure tests, and the periodic dumps, on global system availability. We then compute the optimum value of the interval between dumps, and also the best time interval between failure tests for this system. Numerical examples are presented for various failure models.

keywords: *software reliability, performance evaluation of fault-tolerant systems.*

1 Introduction

All large software systems have to be protected from catastrophic failures, in case portions of the system architecture which support them fail. This is particularly true for large database systems in which several layers of recovery procedures are usually built into the software [HR83]. In such systems, variants of the checkpoint and roll-back recovery mechanism are used in order to enhance overall system reliability [SG86, Bou79].

The problem also arises in other systems which have a transaction-like behaviour. For instance, in a large software development project in which modifications are carried out progressively and then validated periodically, very much as in a transaction oriented system in which updates are made and then validated, it may be necessary to introduce failure recovery mechanisms which protect the development activity from losses of information which may occur when there are system or sub-system failures.

Any such failure recovery mechanism is bound to induce additional costs and overhead, both during normal operation and during failure recovery. This is why much attention has been devoted to the performance of failure recovery mechanisms.

The earliest work in this area is that of [You74] who has attempted to optimize the time between check-

points in a database so as to obtain a satisfactory compromise between the time it takes to create a checkpoint, and the time it takes to recover from a failure. Indeed, the cost of checkpointing is high if checkpoints are frequent, but the advantage is then that in case of failure the recovery time will be shorter [CBDU75]. Other authors have analyzed the transaction queue length, or maximized system availability [GD78, Gel79], or considered response time as a primary measure of system performance [Bac81], or examined the creation of checkpoints as a function of the number of transactions which occur between successive checkpoints [NK83]. These results have been extended to distributed systems [Bou79, GFT86, KT87], and to time dependent failure rates [GH90]. The relationship of these models to queueing systems with service time interruptions has also been considered [Nic86].

The purpose of this paper is to propose a new technique which we call "failure tests" for enhancing system availability. It is assumed that the system operates with a dumping and roll-back recovery strategy for secondary memory failures. However, in addition, we imagine that certain database "failures" are in fact due to the introduction into the system of inconsistent or erroneous data, which at a later time may lead to the detection of a failure.

Thus we propose that in addition to the conventional recovery technique, the system availability be enhanced by the introduction of "failure tests", which would be implemented as a set of procedures which examine the data and/or the log of transactions which have been executed, in order to detect potential sources of failures or of inconsistencies.

After each failure test, one or more errors may or may not be detected in the system or data. If at least an error is detected, we assume that the system treats it as a failure; the system then goes through a recovery procedure just as if there had been a failure. Otherwise transaction processing proceeds normally.

As a result of these "failure tests" we expect the global system failure rate to behave in saw-tooth fashion as a function of time. Just after a failure test, possibly followed by a recovery procedure, the system failure rate drops to a low value because some failures could have been detected in the failure test. It then

---

*Research supported in part by Programme C3-CNRS, Pôle Algorithmique Distribuée.

[†]On leave from Universidad de Los Andes, Venezuela.

increases as transaction processing proceeds and as we move away from the failure test. Thus these checks can be viewed as a form of preventive maintenance carried out on the system's data and past transactions.

The purpose of this new procedure is to improve system availability. Therefore in the next section we shall present a model of the system in order to analyze the effect of the failure rate, the failure tests, and the periodic dumps, on global system availability. We then compute the optimum value of the interval between dumps, and also the best time interval between failure tests for this system. The primary performance measure considered is the availability of the system for useful transaction processing.

The computation of the optimum dump interval is presented in Section 3, while Section 4 is devoted to the computation of the number of failure tests between dumps.

In section 5 an algorithm is proposed to obtain the optimal dump interval and the number of failure tests between dumps, computational problems associated with the model, and numerical examples, are discussed as well.

The work presented in this paper can be viewed as a logical consequence of [Gel79], where a roll-back recovery mechanism was analyzed and the problem of choosing an optimum checkpoint interval was formulated and solved, as well as of [GH90] where the mathematical tools for handling time-dependent failure rates in such models have been developed.

The results of the present paper are obtained as a function of certain parameters, such as the cost of creating dumps, the cost of making a failure test, the failure rate with the saw-tooth behaviour described above or with constant or other time-dependent behaviour. These parameters can be chosen arbitrarily and introduced into the model.

2   The model

Let X_t be the state of the system at time t. X_t is given by:

$$X_t = \begin{cases} 0, & \text{the system is in normal operation} \\ 1, & \text{it is recovering from a failure} \\ 2, & \text{it is making a dump} \\ 3, & \text{it is making a failure test} \end{cases}$$

We assume that at time 0 the system is initialized in normal operation, i.e. X_t for $t \geq 0$ is constructed as follows.

1. Let the variable Y_t (age) be the total time spent by the system in state 0 since the most recent dump preceding t:

$$Y_t = \int_{t'}^{t} 1(X_u = 0) du$$

where $t' = \sup\{v : v < t \quad \text{and} \quad X_v = 2\}$

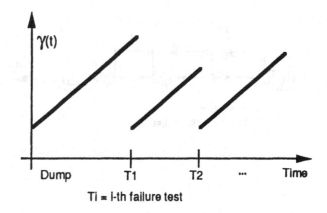

Figure 1: The behaviour of the failure rate $\gamma(t)$

A transition from state 0 to state 1 occurs at some instant t due to the occurrence of a failure. Then the recovery time i.e. the time spent in state 1 before the return to state 0, is given by a function $h(Y_t)$ which depends linearly on the age Y_t, where

$$h(Y_t) = \alpha Y_t + \beta$$

and α, $\beta > 0$ are constants. This formula can be justified as follows. After a failure, all the work done during time Y_t must be done again; this takes a time αY_t. β will be the fixed time necessary to restart and reload the system.

2. It can be assumed, with no loss of generality, that failures do not occur during dumping (state 2), during the failure test (state 3) or during recovery (state 1).

3. The system enters state 3 if a failure test is being made, and the time for making a failure test is a random variable of general distribution function and with finite expected value ECC. At the end of the check with probability p an error is detected and the system enters state 1 for recovery, otherwise, it returns to state 0. The recovery function $h'(Y_t)$ in this case will differ from $h(Y_t)$ in the fixed cost.

$$h'(Y_t) = \alpha Y_t + \beta'$$

4. We denote by z_i the total time spent in state 0 (normal operation time) between the $(i-1)-th$ and $i-th$ failure tests, the 0th failure test is considered to be the time in normal operation between the most recent dump and the first failure test.

5. The instants of failure constitute a time-dependent Poisson process of parameter $\gamma(Y_t)$. The failure tests have an effect on the time dependent failure rate as shown in Figure 1. A

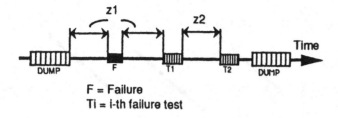

F = Failure
T_i = i-th failure test

Figure 2: The interval between dumps

failure at time t will force X_t to go from state 0 to state 1.

6. When the process enters state 2 it remains there for a random period independent of its past history, i.e. the time necessary for creating a dump, of general distribution function and with finite expected value EC. At the end of this time it returns to state 0.

7. The availability of the system is simply the proportion of time spent by the system in state 0. In steady-state, it is the probability that the system is in state 0.

8. It is assumed that the workload after a period of unavailability remains the same as before the interruption (dump, failure or failure test).

3 The interval between dumps

We begin the analysis of the system by considering an interval between two successive dumps, during which failure tests are made and failures may occur. In Fig.2 we represent one such typical interval.

The average length of such an interval will be the sum of the total expected times spent in normal operation, in failure recovery, in carrying out the failure tests and creating the dumps. We shall examine each component of this duration, and compute its average value.

Let us first consider the total expected time spent in failure recovery between successive dumps. Clearly, it will be the expected time for recovery from failure test errors plus the expected recovery time for the time dependent Poisson failures. We first compute the latter.

Assuming that there are n failures between the $(i-1)-th$ and $i-th$ failure tests, i.e. during z_i time units in normal operation, let $x_1 < \ldots < x_n$ be the failure instants. As a consequence of the age-dependent Poisson assumption about failure instants, it is known (e.g. [CM65] p.153) that for small enough

interval of time δ_j, the conditional probability that failure j will occur in the small interval $[m_j, m_j + \delta_j]$ is given by

$$P[m_j \leq x_j < m_j + \delta_j, 1 \leq j \leq n \mid$$

n failures during z_i time units in normal operation]

$$= \prod_{j=1}^{n} \left(\frac{\gamma(m_j)}{\Gamma(z_i)} \right) \delta_j$$

where

$$\Gamma(y) = \int_0^y \gamma(u) du$$

The recovery time from the n failures occurred in the ith failure test interval, will then be

$$\int_{z_{i-1}}^{z_{i-1}+z_i} dm_1 ... dm_n \int_{z_{i-1}}^{z_{i-1}+z_i}$$

$$\prod_{j=1}^{n} \left(\frac{\gamma(m_j)}{\Gamma(z_i)} \right) h(z_1 + \cdots z_{i-1} + m_j)$$

$$= n \int_{z_{i-1}}^{z_{i-1}+z_i} \frac{\gamma(u)}{\Gamma(z_i)} h(z_1 + \cdots z_{i-1} + u) du$$

because the cost function for recovery $h(.)$ implies that all transactions which were processed by the system since the most recent dump have to be processed again.

Taking the expected value with respect to the number of failures we obtain the following expression for the average recovery cost from random failures during z_i units of normal operation:

$$\sum_{n=0}^{\infty} n \frac{e^{-\Gamma(z_i)} \Gamma(z_i)^n}{n!} \frac{1}{\Gamma(z_i)} \int_{z_{i-1}}^{z_{i-1}+z_i} \gamma(u) h(z_1 + \cdots z_{i-1} + u) du$$

$$= \int_{z_{i-1}}^{z_{i-1}+z_i} \gamma(u) h(z_1 + \cdots z_{i-1} + u) du$$

If we assume that there are k failure tests in the dump interval, we have the following expression for the total expected time for recovery in between two successive dumps:

$$Q_k(z_1, \ldots, z_k) = p \sum_{i=1}^{k} \int_0^{z_1 + \cdots z_i} h'(u) du$$

$$+ \sum_{i=1}^{k+1} \int_{z_{i-1}}^{z_{i-1}+z_i} \gamma(u) h(z_1 + \cdots z_{i-1} + u) du$$

128

and the total expected length of the interval between dumps, which we denote by $EI(k)$ is:

$$EI(k) = EC + kECC + \sum_{j=1}^{k+1} z_j + p\sum_{i=1}^{k} \int_0^{z_1 + \cdots z_i} h'(u)du$$

$$+ \sum_{i=1}^{k+1} \int_{z_{i-1}}^{z_{i-1}+z_i} \gamma(u)h(z_1 + \cdots z_{i-1} + u)du$$

or

$$EI(k) = EC + kECC + \sum_{j=1}^{k+1} z_j + Q_k(z_1, \ldots, z_k)$$

This expectation allows us to compute the stationary probabilities (Π_j) of the process $\{X_t, t \geq 0\}$, applying the regenerative property [Çin75] to the interval between dumps $EI(k)$:

$$\Pi_j \triangleq \lim_{t \to \infty} P[X_t = j] \quad j = 0, 1, 2, 3$$

and to compute them as follows:

$$\Pi_0 = \frac{\sum_{j=1}^{k+1} z_j}{EI(k)}$$

$$\Pi_1 = \frac{Q_k(z_1, \ldots, z_k)}{EI(k)}$$

$$\Pi_2 = \frac{EC}{EI(k)}$$

$$\Pi_3 = \frac{kECC}{EI(k)}$$

Obviously, we have the normalizing constraint:

$$\Pi_0 + \Pi_1 + \Pi_2 + \Pi_3 = 1$$

Indeed, it can be seen that $\{X_t, t \geq 0\}$ is a Markov renewal process, where the instants before or after each dump are the regeneration points of the process, and these formulae are a simple consequence of this fact.

3.1 Computation of the failure test intervals

In the previous section we computed the total average time between successive dumps, assuming that the length of each of the intervals between failure tests was given. In this section we turn our attention to the appropriate choice of the z_i.

We shall make the following assumption which is based on a physical motivation: the total expected cost of each failure test in the same interval between dumps is kept constant. The "common sense" motivation behind this assumption is that during system operation, we would like that the availability of the

system to normal transaction processing remain constant. Indeed, it would be rather annoying to a user that the quality of service received is very different depending on when the system is being accessed.

As a consequence of this assumption, we shall see that as we move away in time from the most recent dump, the successive failure tests must be carried out more frequently. Indeed, the expected cost of a failure test (which includes the cost of carrying out failure recovery) obviously increases as we move away from the most recent dump. This effect will be more or less important depending on the value of the probability of discovering an error during a failure test.

This assumption translates into the following general expression which relates the expected cost of the first failure test, to that of the $i - th$:

$$\int_0^{z_1} \gamma(u)h(u)du + p\int_0^{z_1} h'(u)du =$$

$$\alpha(z_1 + \cdots + z_{i-1})\int_{z_{i-1}}^{z_{i-1}+z_i} \gamma(u)du$$

$$+ p\int_0^{z_1 + \cdots + z_i} h'(u)du + \int_{z_{i-1}}^{z_{i-1}+z_i} \gamma(u)h(u)du$$

$$\forall \; i = 2, \ldots, k \qquad (1)$$

In order to simplify the notation we write:

$$\Gamma H(z_i) = \int_{z_{i-1}}^{z_{i-1}+z_i} \gamma(u)h(u)du$$

$$\Gamma(z_i) = \int_0^{z_i} \gamma(u)du$$

$$H'(z_i) = \int_0^{z_i} h'(u)du = \int_0^{z_i} (\alpha u + \beta')du$$

and (1) becomes:

$$\Gamma H(z_1) + pH'(z_1) = \alpha(z_1 + \cdots z_{i-1})\Gamma(z_i)$$
$$+ pH'(z_1 + \cdots z_i) + \Gamma H(z_i)$$
$$\forall \; i = 2, \ldots, k \qquad (2)$$

which allows us to compute the different z_i as a function of z_1 with the constraint that each z_i must be positive.

Thus we have now reduced the problem of computing the z_i to that of computing z_1. This will be carried out algorithmically in Section 5, and Section 5.1 .

3.1.1 An example of a time-dependent failure rate

An often used time-dependent failure rate is the Weibull density [Ros83] given by :

$$\gamma(u) = \gamma\theta u^{\theta-1} + \gamma_0$$

where $u \geq 0$ represents the time parameter and γ, $\gamma_0 \geq 0$ and $\theta > 0$ are constants. Notice that this is a slight generalization of the usual Weibull failure rate [Tri82] often used in reliability theory. When $\theta = 1$, we merely have a time independent failure rate $\gamma + \gamma_0$ corresponding to a Poisson failure process. When $\theta = 2$ we have a linearly increasing failure rate; in general, the failure rate increases when $\theta > 1$. This failure process is thus a convenient representation of increasing, decreasing, or constant failure rates.

Substituting in (2) we obtain the following equation for z_i, the length of the $i-th$ interval between failure tests, which can be obtained numerically from:

$$\alpha S_1^{i-1}\left(\gamma(z_{i-1}+z_i)^\theta + \gamma_0 z_i - \gamma z_{i-1}^\theta\right)$$
$$+\frac{p\alpha}{2}(S2_1^i) + p\beta'(S_1^i) + \frac{\gamma\alpha\theta}{\theta+1}(z_{i-1}+z_i)^{\theta+1}$$
$$+\frac{\gamma_0\alpha}{2}(2z_{i-1}z_i + z_i^2) + \gamma\beta(z_{i-1}+z_i)^\theta$$
$$+\gamma_0\beta z_i - \frac{\gamma\alpha\theta}{\theta+1}(z_{i-1})^{\theta+1}$$
$$-\gamma\beta(z_{i-1})^\theta - \frac{\gamma\alpha\theta}{\theta+1}z_1^{\theta+1}$$
$$-\frac{p\alpha}{2}z_1^2 - \beta' z_1 = 0$$

$$(3)$$

where:

$$S_1^{i-1} = \sum_{m=1}^{i-1} z_m$$

$$S2_1^i = \sum_{m=1}^{i} z_m^2$$

$$P_1^{i-1} = \sum_{m=1}^{i-1}\sum_{n=1}^{m-1} z_n z_m$$

3.1.2 An example with the saw-tooth failure rate

In this case, $\gamma(u)$ has the behaviour described in the following equations, which can be seen in Fig. 1.

$$\gamma(t) = \gamma_0 + \gamma t \qquad\qquad 0 \leq t < z_1$$
$$\gamma(t) = \gamma_0 + \gamma(t - z_1) \qquad z_1 \leq t < z_1 + z_2$$
$$\gamma(t) = \gamma_0 + \gamma(t - \sum_{j=1}^{i-1} z_j) \quad \sum_{j=1}^{i-1} z_j \leq t < \sum_{j=1}^{i} z_j$$

Clearly,

$$\Gamma(z_i) = \gamma\frac{z_i^2}{2} + \gamma_0 z_i$$

$$\Gamma H(z_i) = \gamma\alpha\frac{z_i^3}{3} + (\gamma_0\alpha + \gamma\beta)\frac{z_i^2}{2} + \gamma_0\beta z_i$$

Substituting in (2) we obtain the following equation for the interval z_i as a function of the $i-1$ preceding intervals:

$$\frac{z_i^3}{3}\gamma\alpha + \frac{z_i^2}{2}\gamma(\alpha S_1^{i-1} + \beta) + z_i^2\frac{\alpha}{2}(p + \gamma_0)$$
$$+z_i(\alpha\gamma_0 S_1^{i-1} + p\beta' + \gamma_0\beta + p\alpha S_1^{i-1})$$
$$+\frac{p\alpha}{2}(S2_2^{i-1}) + p\alpha P_1^{i-1} + \beta'(S_1^{i-1} - z_1) - \frac{z_1^3}{3}\gamma\alpha$$
$$-\gamma\beta\frac{z_i^2}{2} - \gamma_0\alpha\frac{z_1^2}{2} - z_1\gamma_0\beta = 0$$

$$(4)$$

4 The number of failure tests

In the previous sections we have:

* obtained the system availability assuming that the z_i are known and that the number of failure tests k is fixed,

* derived a relationship between the successive z_i, assuming that z_1 is given.

Thus we now have to develop a method to compute both k and z_1 in order to have a complete analysis of the system. These will be computed with the objective of maximizing system availability.

Let us turn to the problem of choosing k. We formulate it as follows:

* After the $(i-1)-th$ failure test, a dump is carried out if the total expected cost associated with a new failure test is greater than the cost of making a dump.

More formally let k be the number of failure tests made in the interval between two successive dumps; we then choose :

$$k = \inf\{i : Q_i(z_1, \cdots, z_i) \geq EC\} \qquad (5)$$

k will be determined numerically from the above expression, and will lead to the system availability Π_0 as a function of z_1 :

$$\Pi_0 = \frac{\sum_{j=1}^{k+1} z_j}{EC + kECC + \sum_{j=1}^{k+1} z_j + Q_k(z_1, \ldots, z_k)} \qquad (6)$$

Finally, z_1 will be chosen so as to maximize Π_0 as shown in the next section.

5 Numerical implementation

We now turn to the numerical implementation of the above results.

The first problem we have to face is the computation of the first interval between the last dump and the first failure test (z_1), which then leads to the computation of the remaining z_i.

The second problem to be solved is the computation of the number (k) of failure tests in the interval between dumps satisfying (5).

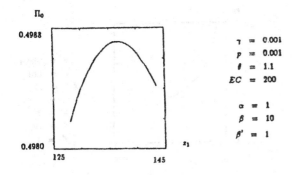

Figure 3: Behaviour of Π_0 as a function of z_1

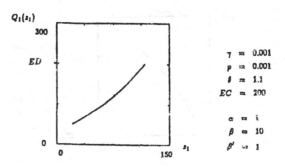

Figure 4: Behaviour of $Q_1(z_1)$ as a function of z_1

Both of these computational problems will be solved using the algorithm given below:

We first choose an arbitrary z_1 and read the parameters of the model α, β, γ, p, θ, EC, ECC where:

α = proportion of transactions to be reprocessed if a failure has been detected
β = fixed reloading cost of recovery
β' = fixed cost of recovery
γ = parameter of the failure rate
p = probability of finding a failure test error
θ = parameter of the Weibull failure rate
EC = expected time for making a dump
ECC = expected time for making a failure test

We have a formula to compute z_i as a function of $z_1, \ldots, z_{i-1}$ (see equation 3 or 4 depending on the shape of the failure rate). In other words, we can compute z_2 if we know z_1, z_3 using the values of z_1 and the computed z_2 and so on. This sequence of computations should be stopped as soon as the expected cost for reprocessing transactions is larger than or equal the expected time EC for making a dump as indicated in (5).

Since the availability depends on a given value of z_1, let us call it $\Pi_0(z_1)$. We then determine numerically the value of z_1 maximizing Π_0, and call this optimal value z_1^*.

On Figure 3, we present a numerical example of the dependence of $\Pi_0(z_1)$ on z_1.

Clearly $Q_1(z_1)$ is an increasing function with values in $[0, EC]$. Then, z_1^* will be bound by the condition

$$Q_1(z_1) \leq EC$$

See Fig. 4 for some examples of $Q_1(z_1)$.

z_1^*, is found by carrying out a binary search in the interval:

$[L_I, L_S]$ where:

$$L_I = 0 \quad \text{and} \quad L_S = \min\{x : Q_1(x) = EC\}$$

where the lower bound of z_1^* is clearly 0, while its upper bound is determined so that the expected total cost $Q_1(z_1)$ of the first failure test interval does not exceed EC.

5.1 The algorithm

In the following we detail the procedure Pi-0(z_1) which computes Π_0 for a given z_1, and the procedure search-z_1^* for the binary search of z_1^*. Note that in the case of a general Weibull rate we compute z_i using equation 3 and in the case of a saw-tooth failure rate we use equation 4.

procedure Pi-0(z_1)

```
    Take  z_1
    Read  the parameters α, β, γ, p, θ, EC, ECC
    i=1
    repeat
        i = i + 1
        compute z_i using eq.(3)
    until  Q_i(z_1, ···, z_i) ≥ EC (eq. (5))
    k=i-1
    compute Π_0(z_1)  (eq. (6))
    Send  Π_0(z_1)
```

search-z_1^*

```
    ε ← small
    L_I ← 0
    Find L_S = min x : Q_1(x) = EC
    compute Π_0(L_I) ; compute Π_0(L_S)
    repeat
        If  Π_0(L_I) ≤ Π_0(L_S)
            then begin
                L_I = (L_I+L_S)/2 ;
                compute Π_0(L_I)
            end

            else  begin
```

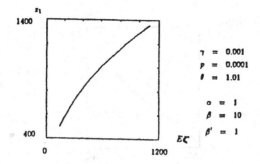

Figure 5: z_1 as a function of EC (Weibull)

$$L_S = \frac{L_I + L_S}{2} \, ;$$
compute $\Pi_0(L_S)$
end
until $\Pi_0(L_I) = \Pi_0(L_S) + \epsilon$
Send $z_1^* = L_I$

5.2 Numerical results for Weibull failure rates

The results are presented for the Weibull failure rate wich has been widely used in reliability models. We first present some numerical examples concerning z_1^* the total time in normal operation between the last dump and the first failure test. Then we turn to various numerical examples showing how system parameters affect system availability when z_1^* and k are chosen so as to maximize it.

With regard to z_1^* we notice the following effects:

- If the cost EC for making a dump increases then the interval z_1^* also increases. (see Fig. 5)

- If the parameter γ of the failure rate increases (for the three cases constant, linear and Weibull) clearly the failure rate also increases and the first failure test has to be made earlier. Indeed, if the risk of failure is larger, it would be better to make a failure test earlier than if this risk is smaller (see Fig. 6)

- Similarly, if the probability p of discovering an error during a failure test is greater, then the interval z_1^* should be smaller (see Fig. 7)

Let us now turn to some results concerning system availability:

- If the probability p of finding a failure test error decreases then the availability will increase (see Fig. 8)

- If the cost EC of a dump increases, then the availability will obviously decrease (see Fig. 9)

The results were also verified for a saw-tooth failure rate.

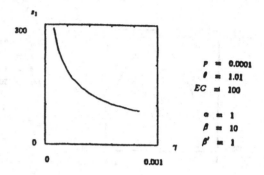

Figure 6: z_1 as a function of γ (Weibull)

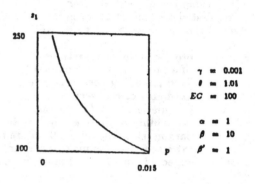

Figure 7: z_1 as a function of p (Weibull)

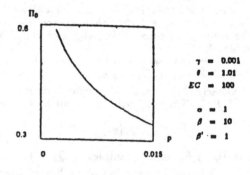

Figure 8: Π_0 as a function of p (Weibull)

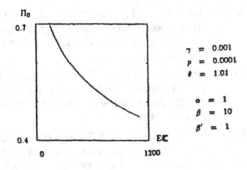

Figure 9: Π_0 as a function of EC (Weibull)

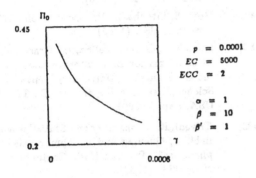

Figure 10: Π_0 as a function of γ_0 (Saw-tooth)

5.3 Numerical results for a saw-tooth failure rate

In Figure 10 we consider the behaviour of the availability Π_0 for a sawtooth-type time-dependent failure rate discussed in Section 3.1.2 . This corresponds to the case where during a failure test, errors are detected with a certain probability p and a recovery procedure is carried out. Then the system failure rate drops to a low value as soon as the system begins its operation, but increases as time goes by and the system is used until a new failure test is carried out.

Π_0 is plotted against γ_0 for the saw-tooth failure rate. We observe that as γ_0 (the rate of increase of the failure rate) increases, the availability Π_0 decreases, as one may expect. Keeping the same model parameters ($\alpha=1$, $\beta=10$, $\beta'=1$, $p=0.0001$, $EC=5000$, $ECC=2$) as in Figure 10, we show the variation of Π_0 versus γ for the case of a linear Weibull failure rate (i.e. without the sawtooth behaviour) in Figure 11. We see that the availability is appreciably greater in the saw-tooth case, showing that the failure tests are having

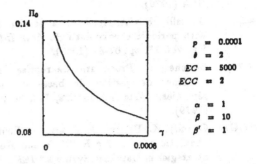

Figure 11: Π_0 as a function of γ (Weibull)

the desired effect of improving system availability.

6 Conclusions

In this paper we propose the use of "failure tests" in order to enhance the reliability and availability of a transaction oriented software system.

The basic idea is to carry out software tests and verifications at regular intervals concerning the data the system contains, and/or the transactions it has executed, in order to detect possible errors or inconsistencies. The purpose is to reduce the consequence such errors may have on system crashes, or to eliminate errors which would be detected later during normal system operation.

We discuss the appropriate choice of the number of failure tests and of the time between successive checks, assuming that the system is prone to failures. We expect that the system will also be equipped with a "roll-back recovery" type mechanism in order to handle failures; this mechanism will be used for failure recovery both after a failure test and for random failures which occur during system operation. The basic time structure of system operation is established by the sequence of dumps, and failure tests are carried between successive dumps.

A model is constructed in order to compute the best possible choice of intervals between dumps and failure test intervals so as to maximize system availability. This model is based on techniques initially developed in [Gel79] for computing optimal checkpoint intervals, and in a recent paper [GH90] which is devoted to time-dependent failure mechanisms and their analysis.

Numerical procedures for handling our model are developed and described, and examples are presented to illustrate the results we obtain.

It is hoped that this paper will contribute to the theory and practice of software systems having enhanced reliability properties.

References

[Çin75]   Çinlar, E. "Introduction to Stochastic Processes". Prentice-Hall. Englewood Cliffs, N.J.,

USA (1975).

[Bac81] Baccelli, F. "Analysis of a service facility with periodic checkpointing". *Acta Informatica, Vol. 15*, pp. 67-81 (1981).

[Bou79] Bouchet, P. "Procédures de reprise dans les systèmes de gestion de bases de données réparties." *Acta Informatica, Vol. 11*, 305-340 (1979).

[CBDU75] Chandy, K., Browne, J., Dissly, C., Uhring, W. "Analytic Models for Rollback and Recovery Strategies in Database Systems." *IEEE. Trans. Software Eng. SE-1*, No. 1, 100-110 (March 1975).

[CM65] Cox, D., Miller. "The Theory of Stochastic Processes." Methuen and Co Ltd., London and Colchester (1965).

[Gel79] Gelenbe, E. "On the Optimum Checkpoint Interval". *Journal ACM, Vol. 26, No. 2*, pp. 259-270 (April 1979).

[GD78] Gelenbe, E., Derochette, D. "Performance of Rollback Recovery Systems Under Intermittent Failures." *Communications ACM, Vol. 21, No. 6*, 493-499 (June 1978).

[GFT86] Gelenbe, E., Finkel, D., Tripathi, S. "Availability of a Distributed Computer System with Failures." *Acta Informatica, Vol. 23*, 643-655 (1986).

[GH90] Gelenbe, E., Hernández, M. "Optimum Checkpoints with Age Dependent Failures". *Acta Informatica, Vol. 27*, 519-531, (1990).

[HR83] Haerder, T., Reuter, A. "Principles of Transaction-Oriented Database Recovery." *Computing Surveys Vol. 1, No.4*, 287-317 (December 1983).

[KT87] Koo, R., Toueg, S. "Checkpointing and Rollback-Recovery for Distributed Systems." *IEEE. Trans. Software Eng. Vol. SE-13, No.1* (January 1987).

[NK83] Nicola, V., Kilstra, F. "A Model of Checkpointing and Recovery with a Specified Number of Transactions Between Checkpoints." *Performance'83*, Agrawala, Tripathi, eds., Elsevier Science Publishers, North-Holland, 83-99, New York, (1983).

[Nic86] Nicola, V. "A Single Server Queue with Mixed Types of Interruptions." *Acta Informatica, Vol. 23*, 6465-486 (1986).

[Ros83] Ross, S. "Stochastic Processes." John Wiley & sons Inc., USA (1983).

[SG86] Salem, K., Garcia-Molina, H. "Crash Recovery Mechanisms for Main Storage Database Systems." Princeton University, Dept. Computer Science, Research Report No. CS-TR-034-86, USA, (April 1986).

[Tri82] Trivedi, K. "Probability and Statistics with Reliability, Queuing and Computer Science Applications". Prentice-Hall. Englewood Cliffs, N.J., USA. (1982).

[You74] Young, J. "A First Order Approximation to the Checkpoint Interval." *Communications ACM, Vol. 17, No.9*, 530-531, (1974).

ABOUT THE AUTHOR

Hoang Pham received his BS in mathematics and his BS in computer science, both with high honors, from Northeastern Illinois University. He received his MS in statistics from the University of Illinois at Urbana-Champaign, and his MS and PhD in industrial engineering from the State University of New York at Buffalo. He is on the faculty of the Department of Industrial Engineering at Rutgers University. From March 1989 to July 1990, he was a senior specialist engineer with the Boeing Company in Seattle. Since then, he worked as a senior engineering specialist with the Idaho National Engineering Laboratory until August 1993. His research interests include reliability and availability modeling, software reliability, applied probability and optimization, reliability theory, and fault-tolerant computing. He is the (co)editor of six volumes and the author of over 70 research papers.

He is founder and editor-in-chief of the *International Journal of Reliability, Quality and Safety Engineering*. He is editor of Van Nostrand Reinhold's series of books on Quality and Reliability. He is also an associate technical editor of *IEEE Communications Magazine*, an associate editor of the *International Journal of Modelling and Simulation*, and an editorial board member of the *Journal of Computer and Software Engineering*. He has been a guest editor for *IEEE Transactions on Reliability, Journal of Systems Engineering, IEEE Communications Journal*, and *Journal of Systems and Software*.

Dr. Pham was conference program chairman and the organizing committee chairman of the Second International Conference on Reliability and Quality in Design. He was general chairman of the IASTED Pacific-Rim International Conference on Reliability Engineering and Its Applications, conference program chairman of the Third International Conference on Reliability, Quality Control, and Risk Assessment, and conference program chairman and the organizing committee chairman of the First International Conference on Reliability and Quality in Design. Dr. Pham was also conference program vice chairman of the IEEE 1994 Annual Reliability and Maintainability Symposium and conference program chairman of the International Conference on Reliability, Quality Control, and Risk Assessment in 1992 and 1993. He has served on technical committees for many major national and international conferences. He is a senior member of the IEEE.